Praise for Karen Valby's

The Swans of Harlem

"Utterly absorbing, flawlessly researched. . . . Vibrant, propulsive, and inspiring. . . . A richly drawn portrait of five courageous women whose contributions have been silenced for too long!" —Tia Williams,
New York Times bestselling author of *Seven Days in June*

"These five original DTH ballerinas fell in love with an art form that most of America believed was white and should remain so. . . . Valby weaves their stories together as a choreographer would. . . . It's thrilling to watch as they join forces at last and claim their unique place in American ballet's past, present, and future." —Margo Jefferson,
author of *Constructing a Nervous System*

"Vibrant, lovingly researched." —*Chicago Tribune*

"Valby gracefully recounts the dance careers and personal lives of these five trailblazing ballerinas. . . . What results is a book suffused with rich character studies and memorable details . . . that will captivate dance experts and novices alike." —Oprah Daily

"A loving tribute." —*Smithsonian*

"Insightful. . . . Valby tells the stories of Lydia Abarca, Gayle McKinney-Griffith, Sheila Rohan, Karlya Shelton, and Marcia Sells, celebrating the contributions they made to their art form and giving them the recognition they so greatly deserve." —*Town & Country*

"Riveting. . . . A fascinating look into what was momentous and nearly lost to time. . . . Now history has found them again."
—*New York Journal of Books*

"Valby's group biography of five Black ballerinas who forever transformed the art form at the height of the civil rights movement uncovers the rich and hidden history of Black ballet, spotlighting the trailblazers who paved the way for the Misty Copelands of the world."
—*The Millions*

"Extraordinary. . . . Valby structure[s] a wide-ranging, complex narrative that's both engaging and emotional. . . . This story needed to be told, and Valby and the Swans have collectively created something marvelous by telling it."
—*PopMatters*

"A marvel of history."
—Broadway Direct

"Remarkable. . . . Spirited. . . . Valby's extensive interviews with the dancers lend an intimacy to the narrative, the details of their lives elevated and their perspectives clearly observed. The women of the 152nd Street Black Ballet Legacy Council are determined to bring their story out of obscurity. In *The Swans of Harlem*, they become unforgettable."
—*BookPage*

"A remarkable underdog story. . . . This feels, rightly, like the beginning of a larger conversation. . . . There are so many stories still to tell; these efforts might help the next Black ballerina to find her wings."
—*The Sunday Telegraph*

"With vivid character development and detailed storytelling, Valby has crafted an engaging and informative account of five Black ballerinas, fifty years of sisterhood, and a passionate reclamation of a truly groundbreaking history. . . . I found myself completely immersed. . . . *The Swans of Harlem* is an ideal read for Black History Month but a vital read for every month of the year."
—The Independent Critic

"A vibrant and captivating look at five trailblazing women."
—*Arlington* magazine

"Incredible."
—*Dance Teacher*

"For those who love *Hidden Figures* and are interested in dance and culture. . . . Captivating, rich in vivid detail and character, and steeped in the glamour and grit of professional ballet, *The Swans of Harlem* is a riveting account of five extraordinarily accomplished women, a celebration of their historic careers, and a window into the robust history of Black ballet, hidden for too long." —*Texas Lifestyle Magazine*

"A skilled storyteller with an eye for significant details and thematic complexity. . . . Dynamic, tumultuous, and inspiring. . . . Deeply researched and full of heart. A rich, detailed, and complex history of Harlem's first prima ballerinas." —*Kirkus Reviews*

"Engaging and insightful. . . . A powerful narrative of professional triumphs and personal challenges that celebrates Black excellence in ballet. Anyone who appreciates dance will be enriched and inspired by the stories of these five intrepid dancers." —*Booklist*

"There is joy in the way the women discuss their decades-long friendships and trailblazing performances in this book. Valby gives each dancer space for their stories to naturally flow, writing them as fully realized individuals with their own hopes and dreams. . . . Heartwarming."
—*Library Journal*

"Vibrant. . . . A captivating corrective to an often-whitewashed history."
—*Publishers Weekly* (starred review)

"A story that you'll be glad you know now, one you'll be satisfied to've read. So find *The Swans of Harlem*. You want it, so don't waste a minute."
—New Jersey Urban News

Karen Valby

The Swans of Harlem

Karen Valby is a writer living in Austin, Texas. She is a contributing editor at *Vanity Fair*, and her work has appeared in *The New York Times*; *O, The Oprah Magazine*; *Glamour*; *Fast Company*; and *Entertainment Weekly*, where she spent fifteen years writing about culture.

ALSO BY KAREN VALBY

Welcome to Utopia

The Swans of Harlem

The
Swans
of
Harlem

Five Black Ballerinas,
Fifty Years of Sisterhood,
and Their Reclamation of
a Groundbreaking History

KAREN VALBY

VINTAGE BOOKS
A Division of Penguin Random House LLC
New York

Published in the United States by Vintage Books, a division of Penguin Random House LLC, New York, and distributed in Canada by Penguin Random House Canada Limited, Toronto. Originally published in hardcover in the United States by Pantheon Books, a division of Penguin Random House LLC, New York, in 2024.

Vintage and colophon are registered trademarks of Penguin Random House LLC.

The Library of Congress has cataloged the Pantheon Books edition as follows:
Name: Valby, Karen, author.
Title: The swans of Harlem : five Black ballerinas, fifty years of sisterhood, and their reclamation of a groundbreaking history / Karen Valby.
Description: First edition. | New York : Pantheon Books, 2024. |
Includes bibliographical references and index.
Identifiers: LCCN 2023028575 (print) | LCCN 2023028576 (ebook)
Subjects: LCSH: Abarca, Lydia. | McKinney, Gayle. | Rohan, Sheila. | Sells, Marcia Lynn. | Shelton, Karlya. | Dance Theatre of Harlem—History. | African American ballerinas—Biography. | Ballet—United States—History.
Classification: LCC GV1785.A1 V34 2024 (print) | LCC GV1785.A1 (ebook) |
DDC 792.809747/1—dc23
LC record available at https://lccn.loc.gov/2023028575
LC ebook record available at https://lccn.loc.gov/2023028576

Vintage Books Trade Paperback ISBN: 978-0-593-46966-8
eBook ISBN: 978-0-593-31753-2

Author photograph © Anna Krachey
Book design by Cassandra J. Pappas

vintagebooks.com

Printed in the United States of America
10 9 8 7 6 5 4 3 2 1

For Ava and Zinnia, always

The Swans of Harlem

Prologue

A t the height of the civil rights movement, Lydia Abarca was a prima ballerina for a major international company, starring in iconic works like George Balanchine's *Agon* and *Swan Lake,* Jerome Robbins's *Afternoon of a Faun,* and William Dollar's *Le Combat.* Critics described her as "the dreaming soul of dance," and "a living ode to beauty, incapable of an ugly gesture or a false movement." She was the first Black company ballerina ever to grace the cover of *Dance Magazine.* She performed for queens and kings, in the movie production of *The Wiz,* and for Bob Fosse on Broadway. She was one of Revlon's original Charlie models. An *Essence* cover star. The object of affection for everyone from Mick Jagger to David Bowie. Roses collected at her feet around the globe.

Half a century later, during Black History Month, Abarca's thirty-two-year-old daughter Daniella wanted to brag about her mother to their friends and family. She went looking for evidence of all Abarca had done—all the barriers she had broken, all the history she had made—but in researching the history of Black ballet, she could find only stories about one young woman, Misty Copeland. Misty Copeland, Misty Copeland, Misty Copeland. The first Black ballerina, insisted the internet. And indeed, in 2015, Copeland became the first African American woman to be promoted to principal dancer at American Ballet Theatre (ABT), breaking the company's seventy-five-year record of whiteness. Thank God for Copeland's talent and her perseverance, for the breaking of poisonous runs. But why, Daniella cried, had her own mother been so thoroughly disappeared from the telling of Copeland's accomplishments?

Just days later Abarca's only grandchild, Hannah, came home from preschool in the suburbs of Atlanta, her head flooded with stories about the singularity of Misty Copeland. Four girls in her class had chosen the ubiquitous ballerina as the subject of their Famous Black Americans project. Hannah had sat confused on the class rug, listening to how Copeland had been the first to kick down doors so that children like her could live more comfortably in their dreams.

"But what about Grandma?" Hannah blurted out at the dinner table that night.

Daniella was furious, unsure where even to direct her anger. "Where's your name?" she cried to her forgotten mother. "Where's your name?"

GEORGE BALANCHINE, long considered the father of American ballet, and the co-founder and artistic director of New York City Ballet, was famously said to prefer his ballerinas "the color of a peeled apple." (His apologists insist he was talking only about Suzanne Farrell, one of his most iconic muses.) To this day, City Ballet has yet to anoint a Black principal ballerina.

But it was also Balanchine, along with his City Ballet co-founder Lincoln Kirstein, who recognized greatness in Harlem's own Arthur Mitchell and encouraged his rise to become the company's first Black principal dancer. Kirstein had been in the audience for Mitchell's high school graduation exercise at the School of the Performing Arts, when he performed a solo entitled *Wail,* choreographed to Béla Bartók's music. Mitchell had lacked formal dance training when he'd been accepted into the school, relying instead on his exuberant sense of showmanship, auditioning in a rented white top hat and tails with a tap dance routine to Fred Astaire's "Steppin' Out with My Baby," taught to him by a vaudevillian performer he'd looked up in the phone book. Throughout his time there, Mitchell withstood pressure from the school's administration, which pushed him toward modern dance. They said "it was better for 'primitive peoples,'" he explained to a *People* reporter in 1975. "I said to hell with that; I wasn't raised speaking Swahili or doing native dances. Why not classical ballet?"

Upon Mitchell's graduation, Kirstein offered him a scholarship to the School of American Ballet, the preparatory school for the New York City Ballet, telling the young dancer what so many successful Black people know to be true. "Lincoln put it to me with brutal frankness," Mitchell said. "He told me I would have to work twice as hard as anyone in my class."

Mitchell entered the company in 1955, the same year an exhausted Rosa Parks was told to give up her seat on a Montgomery, Alabama, bus. Some critics reduced a Black man in City Ballet to a "casting novelty" on Balanchine's part. Some said worse. In his debut performance, Mitchell appeared on stage with Balanchine's then-wife Tanaquil Le Clercq in *Western Symphony.* At the sight of him, an old white man seated behind the conductor exclaimed, "My god, they've got a n***** in the company!" Commercial television would hold out for years before it aired a performance of Mitchell partnering a white woman, but in 1968 he and Suzanne Farrell danced a pas de deux from Balanchine's *Slaughter on Tenth Avenue* on *The Johnny Carson Show.* "And in living color, darling!" he cheekily told a reporter afterward.

Balanchine helped launch Mitchell into stardom by setting his 1957 abstract masterpiece, the central pas de deux in *Agon,* on his lone Black danseur and the white Southern ballerina Diana Adams. "My skin color against hers, it became part of the choreography," said Mitchell. His athleticism and technique were put to the highest test in a dance that was as sensual as it was intricate and austere. When a stagehand in the South balked at training the spotlight on a Black man, Balanchine told Mitchell to call upon the reserves of his own internal glow. Fellow City Ballet principal danseur Jacques d'Amboise remembered hearing Balanchine tell Mitchell, "You know, just make light brighter and don't worry."

Mitchell turned the lights up in every room he ever entered. On stage and off, the force of his beauty and charisma hit like a wave. The man had key hooks for cheekbones and flashbulbs for teeth. He didn't smile; he shone. He didn't dance; he set a stage aflame. His herculean work ethic and his preternatural gifts as a performer, coupled with Balanchine's favor, earned him groundbreaking agency over his career. He became the first Black premier danseur in history, a beloved international star who performed on classical stages around the world, on Broadway, in the movies. Everywhere he went, critics hailed him as the exception to the rule that Black people had no place in ballet. But where some might have rested, fat on individual achievement, Mitchell only looked outside himself, wanting to do more.

In 1968, his career at City Ballet still going strong, Mitchell was under commission to form the National Ballet Company of Brazil in Rio de Janeiro when news of Dr. Martin Luther King, Jr.'s, assassination shook the world. The trauma ignited within him a sense of spiritual purpose. He was needed at home. He would build a ballet school in Harlem, the neighborhood that had raised him up. And because children deserve role models who show them what is possible, he would simultaneously establish the first permanent Black professional ballet company.

Art is activism. Let the gorgeous lines of his dancers' bodies serve as fists in the air.

WHEN MITCHELL'S CLASSES first started, in a church basement that doubled as a basketball gym, Lydia Abarca was a teenager living in the projects in Harlem with her parents and six younger siblings. She'd never had a Black dance teacher before. She'd performed only once in her life, as a fourth grader at St. Joseph's Catholic School, to a nun's choreography of "Waltz of the Flowers" from *The Nutcracker*. But as soon as she descended those basement stairs, Mitchell grabbed hold of her long, elegant feet and swept her into his tornado.

Abarca was a girl who loved to dance, who wanted to be a star, who fantasized about making enough money to buy her devoted parents a house and finally move them out of the projects. She wanted to be like her childhood heroes Ginger Rogers and Natalie Wood, emerging from limousines onto red carpets to snapping bulbs, the plot of her life playing out like one of the feel-good *Million Dollar Movie* films she loved to watch on her family's black-and-white television. And for a flash of time, a decade of her youth, she had a taste of all that, as Mitchell's muse and Dance Theatre of Harlem's first prima ballerina.

But by the time her granddaughter came home confused and upset during Black History Month, all that was left of Abarca's legend were a few dusty plastic bins in the basement full of yellowing photographs, stacks of old programs, and an invitation for Abarca to perform for the queen. There were profiles from *People* and *The Washington Post* that delighted in the star power of Mitchell's young ballerina. Her face beamed from magazine covers, reviews marveled over her beauty and talent. Her exquisite profile and flower stem neck had been etched into a Revlon perfume box. Whatever remained of her spotlight years now lived in a couple of click-top bins and a shaky eleven-minute VHS recording of her breathtaking pas de deux in Balanchine's *Bugaku*.

Daniella knew the bones of her mother's past. But what she experienced in the day-to-day was a modest woman who took her administrative work in a doctor's office seriously, who'd taught ballet classes in Daniella's elementary school cafeteria, and later helped her high school step team with their routines. She knew that her mother kept her figure to a strict size eight and that she booked extra work on local movie productions to make some cash on the side. And she also knew that in the evenings her mother drank too much rum, to the point that Daniella kept Hannah away from her, to spare her child from seeing her beloved grandmother slur or stumble. Daniella, a pastor and a single mother, had found the empty bottles hidden in her mother's trunk, behind her hair products under the bathroom sink. She understood that Abarca was lost or unhappy in ways her mother didn't yet have the language to express.

The gaslighting of one's own history can mess with a person's head. Abarca was doubting the facts of her own life. The past and present had to converge if she was going to find any real way forward. She'd need the women who had been with her at the beginning of it all alongside her again. And they, it turned out, needed her too.

AT THE START of the Covid-19 pandemic, divorced from the normal rhythms and routines of their lives, five founding and first-generation Dance Theatre of Harlem ballerinas formed the 152nd Street Black Ballet Legacy Council, named for the street they helped make famous. Lydia Abarca-Mitchell (no relation to Arthur), Gayle McKinney-Griffith, Sheila Rohan, Marcia Sells, and Karlya Shelton-Benjamin had held each other up half a century earlier, and they would do so again through the dysregulating trudge of Covid. They all had been knocked off balance by the anointing of Misty Copeland, by what felt like a deliberate scrubbing of their groundbreaking history. They would make peace with quarantine by gathering online every Tuesday afternoon, to throw out an anchor to one another from their scattered perches across the country. They would take advantage of this unexpected time to right a grievous wrong—they would take control of their own history. However daunting that task might have seemed, no matter. They had accomplished the impossible before.

These five intrepid girls had previously joined forces and made one of the most iconic childhood fantasies come true. Originally strangers, in so many ways the five had nothing in common, despite their being reduced in some early press reports to "black slum youngsters" and "high school drop-outs." These young dancers were all unique human beings who came from specifically loving homes. Lydia Abarca was raised by working-class parents and had been bound for Fordham University on a partial academic scholarship when she first met Arthur Mitchell. Gayle McKinney-Griffith's father was a draftsman at a submarine engineer firm, and she was raised in a two-story colonial house on acres of land in Connecticut. Sheila Rohan's father died when she was a baby, and her immigrant West Indian mother cleaned houses in Staten Island to put food on the table for her eight daughters. Marcia Sells grew up on a Cincinnati cul-de-sac with a father who had his Ph.D. and a mother who went back to school for her master's in her forties. And Karlya Shelton grew up in Denver in a working-class family that belonged to the local A.M.E. church and took elaborately planned road trips every summer to national landmarks in their Chevrolet station wagon.

What they shared, and what would forever bind them to each other, was a calling to the classical stage.

IT'S A RITE OF PASSAGE for so many children to spend some portion of Saturday dressed in leotard and bunching tights, standing in buckling row of other knock-kneed ducks. Casting fantasies while twirling in front of a mirror. The future is like a snow globe, where a young girl imagines herself as the star, fairy dust floating down upon her growing limbs. There is perhaps no more traditional, and traditionally white, feminine ideal than the ballerina—immune to gravity, the embodiment of an aesthetic too pure and fabulous for the grounding of our tedious world. Now imagine a little Black girl twirling in front of her bedroom mirror in a country that had yet to pass the Civil Rights Act or the Voting Rights Act. The innocence and audacity of that child's dream.

Karlya Shelton was seventeen years old when she became the first Black American ballerina chosen to represent the United States at the prestigious international Prix de Lausanne competition in Switzerland. "The thing is, I never thought of ballet as a white art form," she says, "because I could do it. So how could it not belong to me too?" She and the other women missed out on meandering childhoods of slumber parties and pep rallies and school dances. They trained in pointe shoes that felt like cement blocks on their feet, practicing until their toes bled and their nails peeled off in surrender. They obsessed over their every line and angle and gesture. And they gave of themselves gratefully. All that discipline, all that grind, they undertook as acts of love. They worked to master their technique so they might experience the ecstasy of breaking free of their self-conscious mind on stage. They quested for perfection while living with the knowledge that a ballerina will dance a flawless performance just a handful of times in her entire career. Says Shelton, "But when you get it right, when everything works, there is magic. You become the music, and you let it carry you, and you ride on it like waves."

McKinney-Griffith describes ballet as her "choice of expression." Before every performance she'd knock three times on the wooden stage for luck, then hope to cross over from the mortal to the divine. "It's like there's an energy curtain," she says of that last steadying breath in the wings, exhaling the calamity of expectation. "And then you break through. It's so powerful because that's when you break free of your stress. No more training. No more pressure. You show your gift."

"Yes, that's exactly it, Gayle!" says Shelton. "This was our gift. This is what we were given. To deny ourselves, or anyone else, of our gift? No, that just wouldn't do. We danced because we loved to dance, and we loved dancing with each other. We felt beautiful on stage together. There was a love between us that was tangible."

Now, years later, when the Legacy Council is able to gather in person, their bodies curve together in a circle. As they speak, they reach for one another's hands or lean to touch shoulders, their proximity bolstering, providing cushion.

"These are my sisters," McKinney-Griffith says. "We first came together at a very special time in our lives. Then we'd all gone off and had our own journeys. And now here we are coming together again in our old age. We're still a nucleus. We're able to tell each other all that we've been through. We laugh, and laughter is healing. And we can cry too, because we've taken all our burdens and thrown them out."

"These were women of great courage," says Tania León, Pulitzer Prize–winning composer and Dance Theatre of Harlem's first musical director. "There was something in them that believed in themselves, and nothing was going to stop them. That is something Arthur had a good eye for—that commitment. I remember when Sheila Rohan danced *Concerto Barocco* the first time. She was literally crying because her feet were in so much pain."

At eighty-one years old, a great-grandmother seven times over, Rohan is the oldest of the five women. She was a twenty-seven-year-old mother of three when she first joined the company, keeping quiet about her age and about her children back home so as not to jeopardize her acceptance. "You know how they talk about planting seeds?" she says. "Arthur Mitchell planted a seed in me, and these women helped to nurture that seed and make it grow. It was like a rebirth for me. I felt strong. I felt confident. I started to know myself. Coming from Staten Island, I was a country girl from the projects. My first time on a plane was to go to Europe to dance on stages in theaters that looked like museums. I thanked God every day for the experience. But you put things behind you. You move on. Coming together again, I remember how much it all meant to me. I didn't have to be a star ballerina. It was enough that I was there. I was there. I was there."

I was there. I was there. I was there.

That repeated statement of fact knocked something loose in Abarca. "When I'm with you all, I remember that I used to feel important back then," she says, her face crumpling. Shelton tears up at her friend's distress, covering her own trembling mouth with her hand until she's able to speak. "I know just what Lydia means," she says. "I find myself questioning my own past. Was I really a principal dancer?" Yes, her sisters assure her, you were. We know because we were there too.

And there were so many others, the corps de Black ballet that upended and elevated an art form so stubbornly snagged in the past. For over fifty years, Dance Theatre of Harlem has been a home for those who'd been made to feel wrong in their muscles and curves. Who'd been told their feet were too genetically flat for a proper relevé. Who'd been denied auditions or pushed into modern classes because their teachers couldn't imagine them in the historically white roles of classic ballets. Who'd been told there was no room for a Black swan in a corps de ballet because her color would break the line. "We must remember those who are no longer with us," says Marcia Sells, the baby of the group at sixty-three. "Before we too are gone."

How Arthur Mitchell gave of himself when he rose like a lighthouse for generations of dancers. He inspired them, molded them, demanded of them, broke a few of them. And what of the dancers themselves? "I always say when the curtain came up, it wasn't him on stage," says Abarca. "We were." The women spent their slim professional window being told they could be replaced at whim if they fell out of Mitchell's favor. They too gave and they gave and they gave.

When the Tony Award–winning choreographer and designer Geoffrey Holder was setting his Caribbean-inspired ballet *Dougla* on Dance Theatre of Harlem in 1974, he liked to remind the company of what life was like for the tokenized Black artist beyond its sacred doors. "There can only be one," he warned about the tragic narrowness of our cultural lens when it comes to Black excellence.

By Holder's logic, it makes dreary sense that the story of Misty Copeland's triumph was pitched as a singular achievement. The press, the ballet world, and the brands and institutions profiting from her success all painted the young ballerina as if she'd sprung from an ocean of whiteness. But Copeland, as she herself ardently insists, stands on the shoulders of all the early Dance Theatre of Harlem ballerinas, who in turn owe a debt to pioneers like Delores Browne, Janet Collins, Katherine Dunham, Sandra Fortune, Claire Haywood, Thelma Hill, Judith Jamison, Doris Jones, Carmen de Lavallade, Joan Myers Brown, Betty Nichols, Maria Tallchief, and Raven Wilkinson, and to women like Lauren Anderson, Aesha Ash, Debra Austin, and Cynthia Lochard who carried the torch forward. Black excellence is not a one-off but a spectacular ongoing fact. The narrative of the successful Black woman as a lonely outlier, rather than part of a collective force, persists because we let it. No longer, the Legacy Council decided. No longer would they allow themselves to be written out of history, nor the women who came before and after them.

Our history books, our cultural awareness, and our children's imaginations should reflect the truth of the world. And part of that truth is that fifty years after Dance Theatre of Harlem showed that it should and could be otherwise, Black ballet dancers continue to endure a tradition sick with racism and bias. Near the beginning of my time with the Legacy Council, *The New York Times* ran a story about Chloé Lopes Gomes, the only Black female dancer at the Staatsballett Berlin. Before she danced in *Swan Lake,* the young woman was told by her ballet mistress to apply whitening makeup to blunt the fact of her Blackness on stage.

I STARTED JOINING the ballerinas on Tuesdays during the fall of 2020, the tape of George Floyd's murder playing on our screens in a loop. I wrote about the Legacy Council for *The New York Times*'s "Arts and Leisure" section, in a piece that mourned their erased legacies but barely scratched the surface of the rich narrative they'd begun to weave for me. I'm a white woman with two Black daughters who are dancers themselves. It is because of those founding Dance Theatre of Harlem ballerinas that today my girls and other young women of color can buy shoes and tights that match their skin tones. I think the Legacy Council's investment in my girls is part of the reason the women have allowed me so completely into their lives to tell their fuller story.

Over the last three years, as the five women invited me into their homes and families and communities, they've shared stories about the enormity of their childhood dreams, the fight to make them real, the sustaining gifts of Mitchell's energy and vision as well as the cost of his ego and temper. They had decades-old wounds that needed airing and healing, and a present day that demanded processing. The world goes hard on us all, even mythical creatures like ballerinas. Their lives have been set to thunderous applause and the damp hush of obscurity. They once soared under the brightest of spotlights but have struggled since to find contentment and in some cases equilibrium and financial security. They drifted apart during their second acts, living in different countries, subsumed by the demands of motherhood and bills and illness and divorce and aging parents. But now they've embarked together on a third act of their own urgent making. Their highest power has always been in company with each other.

SOME THIRD ACTS begin in tragedy. Not long after that miserable February when Daniella went looking in vain for proof of her mother's past, Abarca hit her emotional and physical bottom. After surviving her darkest night, she received a four-page handwritten letter from her daughter, urging her to trust in the path ahead. "There's many chapters in life and this one you're experiencing now is called 'BREAKTHROUGH,'" Daniella wrote. She included in the letter a prayer she hoped her mother would get in the habit of reading aloud. Every night since, Abarca has recited the prayer, the power and vibration of her daughter's words allowing her whole body to relax. Toward the end is a line that feels particularly resonant as five forgotten ballerinas risk entering the spotlight again.

"I bind love to me. I bind joy to me. I bind up negative thoughts and loose the peace of God in my life."

May this book be a literal binding of the 152nd Street Black Ballet Legacy Council's lives as artists and pioneers and wives and mothers and friends. May it acknowledge their intrinsic value as women as much as it celebrates their achievements as ballerinas. May it free them of plaguing thoughts so that they can release themselves of grievance and shame. May they find peace in the telling of their stories, and in the fact of our finally paying attention.

Act One

1

Harlem kids lived in a world of their own making. Not on the busy avenues like Broadway or Amsterdam, but on the quieter side streets, where there was more freedom. They played double Dutch and jacks and stickball. They hit the local playground, the Battlegrounds, for the monkey bars and swings, and for hoops on the cracked courts if they could hold their own. They played street games, like the tag game Ringolevio or Hot Peas and Butter, where the leader hid a belt behind a stoop or a trash can and then yelled out to the others, "Hot Peas and Butter, come and get your supper!"

They were kids with parents who expected them back inside when the streetlights came on and neighbors who looked down from open windows with chins in hands, ready to pull them out of trouble by their ears. Kids who knew when someone's older brother or cousin had started sniffing glue or trying heroin and would learn to avoid them when they got to acting like strangers. Kids who'd lived through six days of rioting in their neighborhoods in 1964, as people took to the streets to protest the murder of a fifteen-year-old Black boy who had been gunned down by a white police officer in front of his friends and a dozen witnesses. And kids who lived too through the awful spring of 1968, when Reverend Dr. Martin Luther King, Jr., was murdered on the balcony of a second-floor Memphis motel room, just a few days before he was set to join a march on behalf of striking sanitation workers.

When news of King's death rained down upon Harlem, Lydia Abarca was seventeen. She remembers her mother, Josephine, crying at their kitchen table. "What are we going to do now?" her mother said. "They killed this one hope."

Folks in Harlem were used to being abandoned to deal with their grief and struggle. They certainly didn't look to government leaders to take seriously their housing crisis or the breakdown of their public schools or the trash that collected in heaps on their street corners. Now a man who'd been fighting on their behalf was gone. So they'd go on getting by on grit and stubbornness, if not hope.

But two months after Dr. King's murder, one of Abarca's five sisters came home from her violin classes with ground-shifting news: "Lydia, they've got a Black man up there. He's going to be teaching ballet." Sandra, seven years Lydia's junior, had seen a flyer at the Harlem School of the Arts, which was run out of the basement of the St. James Presbyterian Church on 141st Street and St. Nicholas. Somebody named Arthur Mitchell was starting a ballet program for kids in the neighborhood, and he wanted grown dancers too.

Lydia Abarca had let ballet go when she was fifteen, tired of giving her whole self over to something that never seemed to love her back. When she heard about Arthur Mitchell's new school, she'd just graduated high school and was headed on a partial scholarship to Fordham University in the fall. She was going to be the first Abarca to go to college—Josephine liked to think her baby could be a doctor—and in the meantime, she needed to make a little money working a summer job as a secretary in the lobby at a bank down the street from their projects. Monday through Friday, she'd rotate through her same three outfits—twelve years in a Catholic school uniform doesn't build an impressive wardrobe—for a paycheck doing work she hated and wasn't especially good at. The trash can by her desk at the bank was filled with balled-up evidence of her struggle, the Wite-Out on her typos like a crime scene covered in glue. When her sister told her about this Black man looking for dancers, she couldn't get the thought out of her head. "I'd never had a Black ballet teacher before," she says. "Maybe he would put a little soul in the steps to make them come alive."

THE HARLEM SCHOOL OF THE ARTS was the creation of Dorothy Maynor, the international concert soprano and the first Black American to perform at a presidential inauguration (for President Truman in 1945, and then President Eisenhower in 1953). Maynor believed that all children, no matter their zip code, deserved world-class training in the arts. In 1963 she launched her arts education program out of St. James Church, where her husband was the pastor, beginning with piano classes for a dozen students. As her ideals took root, so did her courting of Arthur Mitchell. She wanted him to lend his pedigree to the start of a dance program. It would take the assassination of Reverend Dr. Martin Luther King, Jr., for him to answer her call.

The night of the assassination, as grief hung over Harlem like a shroud, Mitchell summoned two of his dearest friends, the celebrated actors Cicely Tyson and Brock Peters, from their beds at one-thirty in the morning, inviting them to his West 78th Street apartment. He was expected in Rio de Janeiro that week, to continue with his launch of the National Company of Brazil. But this was not a time, he realized, for leaving. The three sat on the floor of Mitchell's apartment helping him hash out his response to this national moment of helplessness and heartbreak. By sunrise, he had a plan.

Mitchell would bring ballet home to the neighborhood that had raised him or, rather, that had witnessed his raising of himself. When he was twelve years old, Mitchell's alcoholic father went to jail after confessing to the murder of a numbers racketeer. "I called the family together and said, 'I will take care of everybody, don't you worry,' " Mitchell said in a 2016 recording with The HistoryMakers, a digital archive of filmed oral histories from prominent African Americans. He assumed responsibility for his mother, who worked coat check at the "21" Club, and his four younger siblings. He took on his father's superintendent duties in their apartment building, got a paper route, worked for a butcher, and ran errands for the hookers who lived across the street in a bordello. After he spent a year of studying tap and modern at the School of the Performing Arts, Mitchell's teachers told him he would never be a dancer, not with his bad feet and tight muscles. Determined to prove them wrong, he threw himself so headlong into his training that he promptly ripped his stomach muscles apart. His work ethic was his superpower. He'd expect everyone else to match his zealousness of character for the rest of his life.

And so Mitchell accepted Maynor's offer to lead the dance division of her arts center. He vowed to build an internationally renowned school that would once and for all prove that a person's skin color was irrelevant to their right or relationship to classical dance. His guiding ethos was as simple as it was revolutionary: Ballet belongs to everyone. Ballet benefits everyone. The discipline it demands, and the beauty it gives back, can transform lives. As he put it more bluntly, "You're not going to stick a needle in your arm when your instrument is your body."

He turned to his friend and financial adviser Charles De Rose for help. A street kid like Mitchell, De Rose was an Italian boy who grew up thirty blocks north in Washington Heights before climbing the ranks to become a partner in a Wall Street investing firm. At the height of Mitchell's City Ballet career, he had asked De Rose to put some of his money away so he wouldn't blow it. "Now he's calling me saying 'I need my savings. I want to build a school. I need to buy the kids toe shoes and build a special floor,'" says De Rose. "I said, 'Arthur, you're coming to the end of your earned income life as a dancer. You can't lift the girls anymore because your back is killing you.'"

But Mitchell felt divinely called to his mission and wasn't going to let any practical concerns cloud his vision. "We were offered to be a part of Lincoln Center," De Rose recalls, "to come under their umbrella, where they would do the fundraising for us. Arthur said 'Why do people of color always have to go downtown? Why can't people start coming uptown?' He told me, 'Charles, what I want is for the Dance Theatre of Harlem to be like a little diamond on the beach. When people are walking by, they'll see something sparkling, and we'll make them come over and see what it is.' This was the burn-the-boats mentality he had. How do you not fight alongside somebody like that?"

THAT SUMMER Mitchell juggled his early-morning swims at the Y, daily classes at City Ballet, and rehearsals for the Broadway musical revue *Noël*

Coward's Sweet Potato, in which he acted, sang, and danced, all while getting his Harlem operation off the ground. In his first month at the school, a reporter captured him instructing sixteen little Black girls at the barre. "Now I don't want to see spaghetti," he warned the children, who loved their boisterous new teacher but also complained to their mothers that he was mean. "I want to see straight knees. Keep that knee straight, Fatso!"

When Lydia Abarca first stepped into Mitchell's studio, that windowless basement of St. James, she saw a couple of lamps casting a dirty yellow glow on the floor of the gym where the church's AAU team practiced. The only source of light in the room was Mitchell himself, a man with movie star good looks, wearing flared trousers and a tight jersey shirt that appeared painted onto his lithe muscles. His style of speech was fast and clipped, every elongated vowel and sharp consonant potent with urgency.

"Kick off your shoes, let me see your feet!" Mitchell barked at Abarca by way of greeting. She slid out of her street shoes and angled her stockinged feet for him, extending and arching them into the shape of perfect cashews. A dance critic would later praise "those feet, so curved and strong one can imagine her picking up the stage with them." Mitchell took in her willowy figure, her flute of a neck. His mind whirled with possibilities for this shy sundae of girl, standing before him in leg warmers she'd knit for herself on her living room couch. He told her to join the dancers he'd summoned to audition for the company the following day.

Abarca did as she was told. She returned to the studio the next day for the audition, looking upon the tiny group in awe. There was Walter Raines, who had trained at the School of American Ballet. He had performed with the Stuttgart Ballet in Germany before the grind of trying to convince white companies of his talent led him to quit dancing. And Llanchie Stevenson (who would change her name to Aminah Ahmad after converting to Islam and retiring from dance in the early seventies), who had graduated from the School of American Ballet only to be told that Balanchine wasn't ready for a Black ballerina to break the color line of his corps de ballet. "When I came up, I did not blend in," says Ahmad. "Raven Wilkinson could blend in when she was at the Ballet Russe de Monte Carlo. Janet Collins too at the Metropolitan Opera. I was darker." But Stevenson was able to find work as the first Black female dancer in Frederic Franklin's National Ballet of Washington. In 1968, she'd already been touring with the company throughout the United States for a year, resigned to the fact that in some Southern cities she'd be told during rehearsal that she'd have to sit out the evening's performance for safety reasons.

Mitchell spoke to his gathered dancers with the passion of a preacher. He asked them all to consider the magnitude of his vision—a permanent Black company that would show all the institutions that had denied, tokenized, or marginalized their talents how much bigger and grander ballet could be. Mitchell had already enlisted Karel Shook, an early mentor whom he convinced to leave his post as ballet master at the Dutch National Ballet for Harlem. Under their guidance, the dancers would be groundbreakers, ambassadors, and most of all artists, whose destiny would be determined solely by their ability, their work ethic, and their commitment to excellence. "We're going to show people that Black people can do ballet," he told the dancers, still breathing hard from the exertion of his class. "We're going to shock the world!"

As Abarca packed her bag at the end of the audition, her head spinning from the fervor of Mitchell's speech, he appeared at her side, tapping his wooden counting stick on the floor. When he told her to come back the following day at the same time, she explained that she was expected at the bank in the morning. Mitchell brushed off her concerns. He offered Abarca $150 a week to quit her job and let him transform her into a ballerina. "All I heard was $150, and I said, 'I'm here, I'm yours.'"

Her mother was apprehensive. Giving up a good job for another man's dream? She worried that her beautiful daughter was naïve, ready to follow anyone down the yellow brick road. "My mother would always say of Lydia, 'She has these big eyes,'" remembers Abarca's sister Celia, the second oldest of the family. "They took up her whole face. She would always talk about how they scared her a little when Lydia was a baby because my mother had never seen eyes that big."

But when Josephine told Lydia's father that their daughter was quitting the bank to dance, he didn't interfere. Francisco, or Tito as he was known in the neighborhood, worked as a custodial engineer—Josephine hated anyone ever referring to him as a janitor—at Brooklyn College and Macy's. With a seventh-grade education, Francisco wasn't a reader and talked even less. He relied on Josephine, a part-time telephone operator who worked two nights a week, to read him the want ads and fill out his job applications. He was a father who'd grown up without a father, so he left the emotional work of parenting to Josephine. After they retired, Francisco and Josephine would visit Lydia and her family in Georgia, and Francisco would spend most of the time sitting out on the back patio by himself, smoking his cigar in silence. One afternoon Lydia asked her father, who had a view of an auto repair shop back home, how he liked her big yard. "This is boring," he snapped. "There's nothing but trees back here."

Born and raised in Puerto Rico, Francisco demanded that English be spoken in his house, which perhaps explained his lack of conversation skills. The only time he ever slipped into his native tongue was to bark orders at the kids. *Cállate la boca! Siéntate! No toques eso!* No reading at the table. No walking around in bare feet. When he got home from work, Francisco liked to disappear into his room to watch his science fiction shows on TV. His days were long, and he wanted the house quiet at night. "Face the wall, go to sleep!" he'd shout if he heard any of his seven kids playing past their strict seven-thirty bedtime.

Lydia shared a room with her brother Julio, the only boy of the family. (When Francisco finally got his son after five girls, he banged on every door in the apartment building to share his triumph.) While Julio slept, Lydia would stay up late reading library books—Nancy Drew, Greek mythology—under the covers with a flashlight, eager for a portal into worlds free from the sour smell of government cheese and powdered milk.

The family lived in a first-floor apartment in the Grant Houses, a public housing project on 125th Street and Broadway, with bars over three layers of windowpane that had always made Lydia worry as a girl about how Santa Claus would get to them on Christmas morning. In the summertime, they roasted from the heat with only a box fan for a breeze. Lydia was the ringleader of her six younger siblings, directing them in little dance routines and games of make-believe. They'd play on the concrete playground out front, hiding in the cement barrels or hanging on the monkey bars, but whenever it rained, four of the siblings inevitably started coughing and wheezing until their faces turned blue. Josephine would pile the asthmatics into a cab, and they'd rush over to Columbia

Presbyterian, where she had given birth to all seven babies. One night, triaged in a booth with an emergency room doctor, Lydia and her mother were presented with the newly invented rescue inhaler that would save her again and again, no matter the weather.

The children were a tight-knit unit; Josephine discouraged them from looking outside the family for friendship. See how the other girls in the building took offense at Lydia's loose Puerto Rican curls, she pointed out. See how they'd look at her with curled lip. *You think you're cute 'cause you got that good hair?* they'd sneer at her. "They're jealous of you," Josephine warned. "You can't trust them."

Lydia spent hours sitting cross-legged in front of their black-and-white television watching frothy RKO musicals like *Top Hat* and *The Gay Divorcee*. Watching those movies on repeat made her fall in love with dancing. "I was a shy, quiet kid," she says. "You could say boo to me, and I'd jump. I was so skinny my knees looked at each other. But those movies lit up something in me. Dance was Hollywood and the gowns and the limousines and the big bands playing behind you. I didn't see any of that in my neighborhood, but I saw it in all those movies with their happy endings. And I wanted that for myself."

A family who lived on the other side of the elevator bank from their apartment had a record player. Josephine would let Lydia cross the lobby and dance along with them to the latest songs by Martha and the Vandellas and the Marvelettes. Celia would sometimes look at her sister, struck by the invisible string that seemed to keep Lydia hovering aloft from everyone else. "It was almost like Lydia was born to be a dancer," says Celia, who took a free dance class at PS 125 as a little girl. When the teacher pointed out that her leotard was on backward, she was so embarrassed that she never danced again. "My parents would always tell me as a child, 'Sit up straight!'" says Celia. "Nobody ever had to tell that to Lydia."

Every Sunday the family went to St. Joseph's Catholic Church, two blocks from their apartment on Morningside, where their daddy would nod off during the Latin mass, making his children giggle. Josephine found a way to send four of her seven kids to St. Joseph's Catholic School, where Lydia met her class for a half-hour mass every morning before school. It was a nun at St. Joseph's who first saw the ballerina inside Lydia, after choreographing a brief number from *The Nutcracker Suite*'s "Waltz of the Flowers" for her fourth graders to perform at a school recital. The sounds of Tchaikovsky on the fuzzy speaker, and the thrill of finding both freedom and order in a simple routine, released something vital in the girl. "I was in heaven. Whatever the nun gave us, she got 150 percent of Lydia doing it. And when we did the performance, and the steps matched the music, and there was a big crescendo in the music, it was all just so fabulous. At nine years old, I was fulfilled." Afterward the nun pulled Josephine aside and begged her to get her daughter into some formal training.

Resourceful to her core, Josephine discovered that Juilliard, at the time located just two blocks down from their projects on Broadway, was hosting auditions for dance classes. "You're going to go, and it's going to be a lot of white people sitting at a table," Josephine told her daughter beforehand. "I don't want you to be nervous, but you're going to have to perform for them." The little experience Lydia had of white people in Harlem—nuns, police, the dentist—had made her wary. But on the big day, she walked head held high into a room with a glittering chandelier, mirrors on the walls, and a grand piano in the corner. The row of white people holding pencils to paper vanished as the girl disappeared into melody. Lydia could sense when the pianist was wrapping up and decided to pull out her split for a grand finale, waggling her hands over her head as the judges peered down at her. She was awarded a full scholarship for Saturday ballet classes.

But oh, how that first class let her down! A stern white man told Lydia to go stand facing the wall. She grabbed hold of a barre with the rest of the girls, their feet already planted in tight *V*'s. Bend your knees, straighten your knees, over and over. "Ma, I thought this was going to be a dance class," she fussed to Josephine once she was safely back in their apartment. "When do we dance?" Josephine waved her off, telling her, "Just do what they tell you to do."

Every Saturday for four years, Lydia stood at the barre, bending, straightening, wondering when they'd finally start dancing. She kept going because she understood the cachet of being a Juilliard student. One day when she was swinging on the monkey bars at Riverside Park, a white couple walked by and noticed her pointed feet. "You have ballerina feet. You should try dancing!" the woman told her. Lydia loved calling back, "I go to Juilliard!" That meant something to the outside world, even if it didn't mean much to her. And the white girls in class were nice enough. She got friendly with one of them, who invited her to spend the weekend with her family. "But I almost felt like a little show-and-tell in their big old house," says Lydia. "So I just went the one time." She had her mother in her ear when it came to girlfriends. "Don't need 'em, don't trust 'em."

As the oldest, Lydia had always been tasked with the bulk of baby-sitting and housework. By the time she'd turned ten, though, she'd just wanted to float away into her movies and her novels. So one afternoon, resentful of her load of responsibilities, she ran away to Grandma Goldie's apartment, twenty blocks uptown. Goldie took sympathy on the crying girl and as a treat suggested they spend the afternoon with her cousin Iris. (Iris and her husband, Dwight Raiford, would go on to form the Harlem Little League in 1989 so that their eight-year-old son and the other boys in the neighborhood would have access to America's pastime.) The girls were told they could go either to the Coliseum or to Radio City Music Hall. Lydia voted for the Coliseum because it sounded like the one in Rome she had seen in books, and what was so great about a radio station anyway? But Iris wanted Radio City Music Hall. Their grandma cast the deciding vote. The three headed downtown for an afternoon showing of the new Jerome Robbins movie, *West Side Story*.

Of course, this was no radio station. First the Rockettes performed, and Lydia felt like she was watching the cast of one of her *Million Dollar Movie* films kick free from the television. And that was just the windup to the main event. When the lights darkened, the brilliant curtain opened onto a world of operatic tension and high romance, with Puerto Ricans and their working-class white rivals dancing and singing for their lives in a neighborhood that looked just like hers. Lydia was a goner. *I want to do that, I want to do that,* she remembers thinking. *The movie was dancing, and it told a story, and it's in Harlem, and it's about Spanish people!* Soon she had her siblings calling themselves the 550 Jets, in honor of their address, 550 West 125th Street. When her godfather gave the family a record player, she wore out the grooves on the movie's soundtrack.

By thirteen, Lydia was already poring over issues of *Variety* and *Back-stage*, hungry for her big break. When she saw an open casting call for the musical *Hair*, she recruited an older friend from her building to escort her down to the theater district. After checking in at the second-floor waiting room, she noticed that all the other hopefuls were holding copies of sheet music. Panicked, she ran downstairs to Colony Records looking for any song she recognized before grabbing a copy of American Breed's "Bend Me, Shape Me." In her audition, the pianist asked Abarca what key she wanted him to play. Cluelessly, she blurted out "F?" Afterward her friend yelled at her on the sidewalk, "Are you crazy? What the hell was that?" as Lydia cried to him, "I thought they were going to ask me to dance!"

In high school, she was granted a scholarship to Harkness Ballet's professional training program, which was run out of a four-story brick mansion on East 75th Street, just off Fifth Avenue. "I would get off the bus and be in another world completely," she says. "Doormen opening doors for you, taxicabs everywhere." After school and all day Saturdays, she diligently took her pointe classes, and adagio classes, and Russian character classes, enduring the stiffness of all that training without her teachers ever paying her proper mind, let alone giving her a reason for all her hard work. A dancer trains for the stage, yet never once in all those years was Abarca given an opportunity to perform. Sometimes she'd linger outside company rehearsals, only to find herself shooed back to class. "Move on," they'd scold the curious Black girl. "Don't stand in the doorway."

Harkness soon shifted its scholarship program to the June Taylor studios on the Upper West Side. One afternoon, Abarca heard live drumming and music coming from across the hall. She sneaked out of her ballet class and discovered Jaime Rogers, the diminutive Puerto Rican actor who'd played Loco in her beloved *West Side Story*, leading a spirited jazz class. Now here was some dancing. Abarca started sneaking into his workshop, desperate for some of that pulse and joy. But when school officials caught wind that Rogers had a stowaway, they marched Abarca back to her ballet class. Listening to their reprimand, she realized with cold certainty that she was finished pretending she was ever going to be a ballerina. Why train and train without the promise ever of a stage? "I'd become convinced that for a girl like me, ballet was an impossible climb straight to a dead end."

Lydia Abarca was fifteen when she quit dancing. She focused on her grades. She took a year of Latin. She joined the drum corps in her school band. She got into college and picked her first-semester courses—economics, theology, Spanish, and philosophy. She fell in love with her first boyfriend and tried to keep him a secret from her father.

But now Arthur Mitchell was telling her that ballet was meant to be shared with audiences, that he was going to give her a stage. She hadn't realized the history of aspiring dancers being turned away from companies because of the color of their skin. Listening to Mitchell, she realized for the first time that ballet could represent something larger than a series of technical exercises to be silently endured. "Wait a minute, you're telling me I can make a living from this?" she remembers feeling. "You're telling me that we can prove to the world how incredible we are, despite and because of our skin color?"

She begged her mother to understand that this wasn't just Arthur Mitchell's dream now but hers as well. "I've got to do this, Ma. This is my one shot."

Abarca would go on to drop out of Fordham after one semester. She'd fail two of her classes, after missing so many because of Mitchell's rehearsal schedule. "To hell with you guys," she thought to herself, after saying a final goodbye to the Bronx campus. "I'm on my way to something huge." Her brokenhearted mother ate the cost of the tuition not covered by scholarship. Abarca vowed to herself that when Dance Theatre of Harlem really made it big, she'd repay her parents with a house, moving them out of the projects once and for all.

A MONTH LATER four of Mitchell's new dancers—Lydia Abarca, Llanchie Stevenson, Walter Raines, and Gerald Banks—made the three-hour bus ride to Rensselaerville, New York, to perform in front of a library audience. Mitchell was busy in rehearsals for his Broadway show, so Karel Shook accompanied the dancers to their first lecture-demonstration.

In their makeshift dressing room, Abarca applied some simple lipstick and mascara. When she looked over at Stevenson, who had laid a towel on top of a dresser and neatly unpacked her entire makeup kit, her stomach dropped. Rows of lipstick and eye shadow. Trays of false eyelashes, which Abarca had never even seen before. Stevenson had come up as the first Black ballerina to perform with Radio City Music Hall, where she'd been expected to wear a full face of stage makeup that would last through the day's four shows. When she toured with the National Ballet of Washington, she'd traveled with her personal makeup case, knowing she was on her own in a white company. "Nobody else had the base that I needed," remembers Stevenson. "My color was 11N. Nobody else had 11N. They used to kid me about that. 'We can't lend you this 2W because you're 11N.'"

In Rensselaerville, Abarca studied Stevenson's trays of false eyelashes on the dresser top and knew she was in trouble. (Mitchell eventually realized he'd have to spring for a company makeup class, in which a flamboyant older woman with ostrich plumes for eyelashes schooled the dancers. "There should be no line of demarcation," she'd shout about the art of applying base. "No line!") Raines, who was so skilled with makeup he could contour a cleft onto his chin, took pity on Abarca's naked face. "Walter told me, 'The audience has to be able to see your eyes and your mouth!' I'm telling you, he beat my face. I'm looking in the mirror as he works, going, 'Oh, my God, I look beautiful. I've never seen myself look this good before!'"

When it was time for the performance to begin, Shook introduced the small audience of cultural elites who'd gathered in the library to Arthur Mitchell's four new dancers. The program started at the barre and then proceeded to center work, where the dancers progressed into more dynamic, full-body movements. Stevenson and Raines danced a pas de deux from Mitchell's *Holberg Suite,* still a work-in-progress then. And Abarca and Banks performed the pas de deux from what later would become the first movement of Mitchell's *Tones.* It was her first time ever dancing on pointe in front of an audience.

"By no stretch of the imagination could one have called this a good performance," Raines would tell Jacqueline Moore Latham for her 1973 Ph.D. dissertation on Arthur Mitchell. "The four of us could hardly stand up, let alone dance. Llanchie and I had danced more than Lydia and Gerry, but that made little difference as we were literally falling all over the place." But Raines quickly realized he'd underestimated the emotional power of their raw artistry. "It was the reaction of the people after we had finished that struck me. It was the look on their faces—expressing that they had just witnessed one of the most beautiful things that they had ever seen in their lives."

Sitting among the audience that day was Abarca's grandmother Goldie, the only family member who could take the day to make the journey upstate. After the show, Goldie hugged her granddaughter tight. "You looked a little shaky up there," she told Abarca, her voice thick with pride. "But honey, I can tell you're going to be really good."

2

That same summer Sheila Rohan traveled by bus, ferry, and two different subway lines to get from Staten Island to Harlem. Her sister Nanette had sent her looking for a man named Arthur Mitchell, who was putting together what she understood to be a little theater group for Black people. When Sheila arrived, weary from the commute, having arranged with family beforehand to watch her three young children, she was taken aback by the scene at the church. *Oh my God, they're real ballerinas,* she remembers thinking.

There was Lydia Abarca, stretching her endless legs at the barre. And Virginia Johnson, who'd spent her childhood in Washington, D.C., training at the Washington School of Ballet, only to be told by her teacher when she graduated that she would never have a career in ballet. Now she was a student at New York University, looking to avoid being shunted off on the modern dance department. There was regal Patsy Ricketts, who came up in Jamaica's National Dance Theatre Company and then trained at the Martha Graham School of Contemporary Dance. Meanwhile Sheila Rohan was a twenty-seven-year-old wife and mother who'd long since tucked away her pointe shoes and resigned ballet to a chapter of her youth. She had a part-time job selling insurance to help make her family's monthly rent of sixty-seven dollars. But when Mitchell saw her on the steps, he told her to go on already and find a place at the barre.

. . .

SHEILA'S MOTHER, Marie Elizabeth, born on July 4, 1900, left the French side of Saint Martin alone by boat as a young girl. Eliza landed on Ellis Island, then in quarantine, and finally with relatives in New Brighton, a West Indian enclave on Staten Island. Sheila's father, Frederick, who'd grown up with Eliza, would later immigrate to America and settle in New Brighton too. Reunited in a community so thick with relatives and immigrants it felt in its own way like their island village, Eliza and Frederick married. She would go on to give birth to eight daughters, one every two years for nearly two decades.

Frederick found work as a tailor, at a dry cleaner, and on the docks. Eliza—whose family and friends called her "Za," or sometimes when praising her, "The Great Za!"—was a domestic worker. She cleaned the houses and helped raise the children of prominent Jewish and Italian doctors and businessmen in Staten Island's wealthy Todt Hill neighborhood. The family lived in a second-floor apartment, with floorboards so thin the sisters could spy through the holes at the congregation caterwauling below in the storefront Pentecostal church. On Saturdays, the girls went to a neighbor and got their hair pressed. On Sundays, they went to the Bethel A.M.E. Church; Eliza was as devoted to the Sunday service as she was to the traditional full-course meal she prepared for her daughters afterward.

Shortly after Sheila turned one, Frederick died of a stroke. He was in his early forties. His body lay in an open casket in their tiny living room for the weekend, as family and neighbors gathered to comfort and weep. Eliza slept with the baby in bed with her, while the other seven sisters piled on top of each other like kittens in the second bedroom. They were never alone in their grief. Eliza's sister lived next door, and there were cousins and aunties all up and down the street who sustained them in their time of loss.

As a single mother, Eliza had to be strict, strong, and unsentimental. "You'd better do it right when she said it" was how one of Rohan's sisters, Delores, described her parenting style. No rolling your eyes and putting your hands on your hips, or you'd get smacked with whatever she happened to be holding in her hand. Eliza had eight girls to raise and no time for foolishness. Even with all that responsibility on her shoulders, Eliza still made room for joy. In the summers, she would pack sack lunches and pile her daughters onto the train for day trips to Rye Beach or Bear Mountain. There were birthday parties at the apartment and New Year's Eve gatherings that could go on for days. Twice a year she'd have all the girls dress up, and they'd make the trek into the city for the big West Indian dances at the Harlem Renaissance Ballroom, where they'd reunite with cousins from other neighborhoods.

Eliza was a large woman, in both force and girth, a fixture in the church pews and on her religiously swept front stoop. She pored over the newspaper every day, though Sheila would later wonder if her mother had just been looking at the pictures and hadn't really known how to read. Eliza wasn't formally educated, but she was smart, and she was tough. If she had to work two jobs to keep the lights on, so be it. She raised her girls with a firm dictum in all their ears: *Do good in school, don't surprise me, learn how to be self-sufficient.* "That's all she wanted," says Sheila. "For us to know that we didn't need a man to take care of us."

Everybody babied Sheila, and not just because she was the baby. She had asthma and was prone to bouts of pneumonia; every winter cold knocked her flat. She was the only one of Eliza's girls who fell victim to the polio epidemic that blew through Staten Island in the late 1940s. Seven years old, a bird of a child with legs suddenly caged in thick braces, Sheila had to miss an entire year of school. A nurse came by the house three times a week to exercise her limbs on the living room sofa. Delores remembers the time as awash in worry: a mother who couldn't skip work, and seven sisters trading off care. Someone was always telling the baby in the family goodbye, promising to play paper dolls later or read together that night. Somehow Sheila held on to faith that this too would pass. "I just kept thinking I'm going to get up and get over this," she says. "I always believed I would walk again." When she finally emerged back into the brightness of childhood, her legs were diminished but throbbed once more with feeling. The family doctor prescribed exercise. Movement was the only thing that would bring this child's body fully back to life.

Sheila's second-oldest sister, Nanette, had an idea for how to help. A lover of art and design, Nanette was a student at the Fashion Institute of Technology when she signed with the Harlem-based Ophelia DeVore modeling agency. She became one of the first African American models to book print commercial work, in advertisements for brands like Lysol and Jaguar. At a fashion show, Nanette met Romare Bearden, the collagist and painter, who a preeminent Manhattan gallery owner once referred to as "the pictorial historian of the Black world." In 1954, she married Bearden in her Staten Island church, then celebrated with a modest reception at Eliza's house. Nanette would go on to give a pragmatic thrust to her husband's career.

But beginning as a young woman, Nanette loved the world of dance and studied with teachers Thelma Hill, James Truitte, and Phil Black. Her talent as a dancer was outmatched by her love of dancers themselves, though. In 1968 she'd go on to launch the Chamber Dance Group, which evolved into the Nanette Bearden Contemporary Dance Theatre, a non-profit dance company that nurtured countless careers of dancers and choreographers of color until it shuttered after her death in 1996.

But Nanette's patronage of dancers began at home. Told of the doctor's orders for Sheila's recovery, she found and paid for weekly tap and ballet classes at a storefront studio in Staten Island's Stapleton district. She bought Sheila her first leotard, tights, and ballet shoes. "I don't see how my mother could have afforded it otherwise," says Sheila. "Even if classes were only ten dollars. In those days, ten dollars was groceries."

Blessed by Nanette's generosity, Sheila developed a new Saturday routine. Each week she and Delores would set off on the three-mile walk over the hill from their home to the George Sturgis dance studio. Delores would linger in the cluttered space watching her sister, the only Black girl in the class, form her body in ways precise and new. At the spring recital, the whole family, which felt like half the neighborhood really, came to watch Sheila's first performance. "I never wanted to dance," says Delores, who as a child chose the softball field over the dance studio. "But when Sheila was on stage, I could imagine myself up there. That's what she did when she danced. She let me be in my imagination for a bit."

It wasn't long before gentle Mr. Sturgis would pull Nanette aside, humble with the knowledge that he'd taken her talented sister as far as his skill set allowed. Nanette convinced their mother that Sheila, by now around thirteen, was old enough to ride the ferry into Manhattan. Nanette would meet her on the Manhattan side and escort her to private lessons she'd arranged in Midtown with the stern Italian instructor Vincenzo Celli, a former principal dancer and choreographer at La Scala Opera House. She paid for the classes, the car services, more leotards and tights, and the first pair of pointe shoes, which felt like rocks on Sheila's feet. Nanette took Sheila to museums and concerts and plays and to Lincoln Center to see *The Nutcracker.*

Years later Nanette would similarly broaden the horizons of Sheila's three children. "I would spend summers and breaks at Nanette and Romare's Canal Street loft," says Sheila's middle child, Charlene. "That's how I got immersed in the arts. My cousins and I went to museums, backstage of all the Black shows that were hitting Broadway at the time—*Ma Rainey's Black Bottom, Your Arms Too Short to Box with God, Ain't Misbehavin',* and *The Wiz* with Stephanie Mills. We would traipse all over the city, never worried about money. Aunt Nanette would tell us, 'Go tell Uncle Romy goodbye, we're going for the day.' And he'd say, 'Okay, here you go darling, here you go darling,' and give us each five dollars that we'd put in our little purses."

Nanette had a talent for recognizing the spark of artistry in a person and blowing it aflame. Sheila took lessons in ballet, tap, modern, and African, always learning from the back row because of her shyness. The precision of ballet, the demands it placed on her muscles and line—it called to her, even if her ambitions were modest. She knew that Black girls weren't welcome in classical institutions like the School of American Ballet or Juilliard. That they couldn't even hope for an audition at the American Ballet Theatre. She'd read stories about her hero Raven Wilkinson, who'd spent five years dancing with the Ballet Russe de Monte Carlo, facing ugly rejections from segregated hotels and narrow escapes from the Ku Klux Klan on tours through the South. One night in Montgomery, Alabama, Wilkinson was forbidden from performing on stage, warned by the company manager to stay in her hotel and not open the door for anyone. While the Ballet Russe de Monte Carlo enchanted the audience with their gift, Wilkinson watched a cross burn outside her hotel room window. After being told it was too dangerous for her to continue traveling with the company through the South, she left the company and eventually found work with the Dutch National Ballet. Wilkinson was never again hired by an American ballet company.

Sheila had no interest in leaving her life on Staten Island to try and join some white company abroad. "I was dancing for the love of this wonderful art, not to be on stage," she says. "I danced for my own self-expression and to help me come to a greater understanding of life." She was also the child of a deeply practical mother. Rohan was raised to graduate from high school with honors, then go on to college to study and become a teacher. That was the plan, and Eliza expected her daughter to stick to it.

BUT THEN SHEILA met Ellsworth. She was sixteen, at a friend's house for a backyard barbecue. She stepped out the back door wearing a pink dress. The glow of her under the porch light nearly struck dumb a handsome and charming boy from the next neighborhood over. "My goodness," Ellsworth said to his friend. "That girl's the one for me."

When she got pregnant at eighteen, Sheila knew to expect Eliza's rage. "But then the worst thing was, she cried. And you can imagine how awful that was because Mama was not the type to cry." Ellsworth had already graduated from high school and left for a stint in the army, working as a cook on kitchen patrol duty. Sheila's sisters sent him a registered post that hit him like a fist. "You better get your ass back home and take care of this damn child!" says Ellsworth, paraphrasing the contents of their letter. He rushed to Eliza's house, pledging to do right by mother and child. As one of thirteen children, family was the most important thing in Ellsworth's life too.

Eliza wasn't so easily placated. "I remember when Ellsworth came over, Mama got after him with a knife, she was so mad," says Rohan. "And she was the kind who would cut your throat too." She laughs with a wince. "The Great Za!" The young couple married at Borough Hall, and Eliza would forever refer to her son-in-law as "the little bastard" or "that line cook."

Sheila brought her firstborn, a son named Gary, home from the hospital to Eliza's house. After Ellsworth got out of the service, they moved into a small apartment in nearby West Brighton. Charlene was born two years later, and Little Sheila arrived in 1965. Sometimes Sheila would practice ballet exercises in her kitchen while the children napped, but she assumed her days of classical dance were behind her. Nanette would call her up every now and then, telling her it was time to go on back to class. "Three kids!" says Rohan. "I'm in the kitchen washing dishes, and she'd be calling trying to pull me back. I think she wanted me to have the life because she wanted to be a dancer."

After Ellsworth had saved enough money, the family moved into the nearby Markham Homes projects. They lived in a one-story brick row house with a tiny front yard and a tiny back yard, and train tracks across the street. Sheila's best friend Sajda Musawwir Ladner lived directly behind them, the families so close that Ladner's daughter was known to let herself in their back door and make herself a sandwich from Sheila's refrigerator. Neighbors were family, or friends who felt like family, like Papa Grimm and his wife, Ma Pearl, an old Southern woman who did the neighborhood kids' hair on her front stoop. Children played stickball and hopscotch and double Dutch in the playground; neighbors gathered for kung fu movies in the community center. A DJ spun records in the local park on the Fourth of July. On the weekends, Sheila took her kids and their cousins to Ladner's storefront dress shop down on Richmond Avenue. The children took a sewing class from Ladner, then a pottery class at the studio next door, and then she would give them a ballet lesson on the second floor above the dress shop. Afterward the kids would all go next door to the bakery that sold chocolate chip cookies the size of your head for a nickel.

Sheila and her Staten Island friends Sajda, Rosita, Loria, and Nubia left the term *hippies* to the white people they saw on TV and in magazines, but they were experiencing their own awakening. "We were opening up, becoming cultured," says Rohan. "That was our whole thing: to educate ourselves and become better human beings. We were all searching for the art spirit." Her cousin Fred, named after Rohan's father, invited her to join his new ensemble called the Brothers and Sisters United; they performed music, dance, and theater around the city. Inspired by the Black Is Beautiful movement and a growing desire to return to their roots, they started wearing daishikis and their hair in afros. "My mother hated it," Rohan says of her natural hair. "That's the whole culture: Caribbean, colonialism. They want you to have what they call 'good hair,' light skin. 'Don't date that man because he's too dark, and then your kids are going to be dark.' When people started wearing their hair in afros, she hated it. She'd say 'Don't come in this house! You look like a jigaboo. I didn't raise you like that!'"

They were young people breaking free from the strictures of generations above, moved by the righteous demands of the Black Power movement. Ellsworth worked as a custodian at the local marine hospital, but he devoted his after hours to community organizing, working on political campaigns for Black candidates and the local Manpower job-finding agency. Rohan worked in the Student Nonviolent Coordinating Committee (SNCC) office in Manhattan and for Manpower on Staten Island. She marched in only one rally; Charlene remembers her mother worrying that she'd catch a cold, so they abandoned the line of protesters to warm up in a friend's unlocked car.

In 1967 the young couple, along with friends like Ladner, visual artist Andrea Phillips and her artist husband, Maurice Phillips, founded an arts community called the Universal Temple of the Arts. Six decades later the nonprofit's mission endures: "To quicken the creative spirit in the individual and community and foster brotherly love." In those heady early years, Sheila and Ellsworth and their friends staged plays like Lorraine Hansberry's *A Raisin in the Sun*, poetry readings, concerts, and community youth outreach events celebrating Black culture. Sheila's best friend Ladner would go on to start the popular Staten Island Jazz Festival in 1988 and lead the Universal Temple of the Arts until her death in 2021. Charlene remembers her mother as always dancing—in the house, in the park with Sajda and Andrea as their drummer friends kept the beat, even on the Staten Island Ferry, where they'd spontaneously perform for the commuters. Sometimes Sheila and Ellsworth would perform at a community event together, while she danced along to the sound of his beautiful baritone.

Theirs was a full life on Staten Island, and it was a world unto itself. But then came the summer of 1968, when Nanette saw an advertisement in *The New York Times*:

"Arthur Mitchell, of the New York City Ballet, will hold auditions for Negro dancers next Monday at the Harlem School of the Arts, St. Nicholas Avenue and 141st Street, for a company being formed at the school. Both modern and classically trained dancers are invited, girls at noon and boys at 2 p.m."

She immediately called Sheila with the news. "There's a Black man in Harlem," said a breathless Nanette. "He's going to start a dance group. You got to go up there." She rushed out the bones of Mitchell's résumé—Balanchine, City Ballet, *Agon*. But none of that was what moved Sheila to leave the dishes in the sink and drop her children at her sister's house. It was the notion of dancing once more in pointe shoes, but this time with her people.

In the church basement, Mitchell promised to transform their lives. "His energy is what I remember," says Rohan. " 'I'm going to build a company and it's going to be a great company and you're all going to be ballerinas and principal dancers!' That's when I realized this wasn't some little community organization." When Mitchell asked Rohan about herself after class, she lied and told him that she was twenty. She said nothing of her husband and children waiting for her back home. "When he said he was going to transform us into ballerinas, I had to make a conscious choice," she explains. "I wanted to stay there with everyone, and I knew that in those days, after a certain age it was considered impossible to dance let alone have a child, and I had three!"

That night she told Ellsworth she was going to quit her part-time job at the insurance company for one that would barely cover the cost of her new commute into the city. Mitchell had taken her on as an apprentice. She started commuting into the city several times a week, leaving meals in covered dishes for Ellsworth and the children in the refrigerator. Her feet screamed in pointe shoes, she was so unused to the torture of them. "Because she wasn't as experienced, the pain that Sheila went through was extraordinary," says Stevenson, who coached Rohan to wear her pointe shoes everywhere to acclimate her feet. "It was torture, but it went with the job," says Rohan. "We were working hours after hours, and Mr. Mitchell wanted us in pointe shoes all the time. It's not like he would let us mark the dance in our slippers and dance full-out later. My legs and my technique needed to get stronger."

No amount of pain was going to stand in her way. She had until recently resigned herself to an ordinary life, clocking into a desk job for hourly wages. Now she took her place among dancers a decade younger on an unfinished platform stage, which had been designed by Balanchine—the completion of the stage would have to wait until Mitchell could raise more funds. The dancers would sweep away the rubble to make room for company class and rehearse for hours. Long after the sun had set, Rohan would take the trains, then the ferry home, where she'd soak her aching feet in a bucket of ice so she could do it all over again in the morning.

3

~

Every dancer that followed Arthur Mitchell to Harlem entered his studio with the same sense of urgency. The man who had broken all the rules by rising to the top of the ballet world thought he could do the same for them. After being hailed as the first at City Ballet back in 1955, nobody had come up behind him since, and he hated the idea of being held up as some outlier to his race. "As a grownup, I've met people who'd never before spoken to a Negro," he told a reporter in 1968. "'You,' they say, 'are an exception.' No, I'm not. They haven't learned that people are individuals, no matter what color. But I do believe the arts, especially the dance, where you don't have to verbalize, can and will cut through the barriers. My only thought is and has always been: Let's train the kids to dance. Someone's got to be prepared when the doors open, if they open, and they'd better open."

Mitchell needed his young dancers to see that ballet was a *performing* art. The fact that Abarca, his most exciting discovery, had spent most of her childhood at the barre, and no one had ever thought to give the girl a stage, was unacceptable. Not long after they'd begun working together, he told her to meet him at the stage door of Lincoln Center, where he was performing with the New York City Ballet. He'd have a ticket waiting for her there.

Before the performance, Lydia Abarca sat alone in the balcony, quietly soaking in the glamour of the evening. She was one stop on the express train and an entire universe from the Grant Houses. Let her siblings argue over who got to watch what on the television that night. She'd been invited here by one of the stars that this fancy audience had paid good money to see. A man who believed he could get her on a stage as grand as this one day.

The well-heeled crowd buzzed and hushed into their seats, a collective sigh of anticipation wafting over the room. Members of the live orchestra busied into position in the pit. Abarca was so engrossed in what lay ahead that she didn't notice the young woman peeking over at her from the end of their row.

GAYLE MCKINNEY-GRIFFITH HAD rushed into the balcony, eager to find her seat before the lights in the theater dimmed. As a rising third-year Juilliard student, attending cultural events was a part of her curriculum. Once she was settled into her seat, she was surprised to see a light-skinned Black girl with a long neck and limbs folded delicately into her chair down the row. Could it be that this girl was a bunhead like her? And if so, had she also started to wilt under the pressure of a doubting world?

McKinney-Griffith was too shy to introduce herself. Too tender to risk another rejection. "I dared not," she tells Abarca with a laugh as the two older women reminisce over the evening. "Suppose you'd said 'Who are you? Mind your business!' I would've been devastated." It was enough to share space for the evening, to rise together to their feet and give Arthur Mitchell the standing ovation he deserved. He had performed his iconic role of Puck from *A Midsummer Night's Dream*, which Balanchine first choreographed for him in 1962 and that would later be captured in a 1967 film adaptation. Mitchell's Puck was like a lightning storm on stage. His lithe five-foot-nine frame, painted up in a sheen of glitter, shimmered as he raced about, causing mischief and havoc with Puck's plucked flower. "I've often threatened to attach a pedometer to my waist just to see how many miles I run per performance," he said. "It must be at least ten miles. But I love every minute of it." That night he left the audience in a swoon, no one more so than the two young dancers up in balcony seats.

"All those other people on the stage, and he was the shining star," says

Abarca. "His dancing was down to earth, it was personable, it was clean, it was sharp. Oh my God! You can be real in ballet? It's okay to have Motown in your bones and do Balanchine at the same time? His character wasn't just this ethereal thing anymore. He was Puck, but then he'd drop the whole facade and go a little street. It all just clicked for me. This is what he wants me working toward."

That night Mitchell showed Abarca how much bigger and bolder ballet could be than she'd imagined. He freed the art form from the prison of the barre, a series of repetitive movements without pride or personality. He wasn't a Black man who dared to dance ballet. He was a dancer who dared ballet to see and celebrate his Blackness.

Mitchell's dancing left McKinney-Griffith similarly inspired. "The feeling of pride I felt was enormous," she says, her gentle voice still full of gratitude. "He was representing us. He was showing the audience that we could be ballet dancers too."

SOME OF MCKINNEY-GRIFFITH'S fondest memories as a child were watching her parents get dressed up for nights out at the Savoy, the Lenox Avenue ballroom that the poet Langston Hughes once called "the heartbeat of Harlem." Gayle's sister, Maxine, fourteen years her senior, remembers her parents taking her there as a child to see the "President of Jazz," saxophonist Lester Young, and the thrill of entering such a sophisticated world of cool. But however happy Maxine's childhood was, it grew tenfold more so when her parents brought her baby sister, Gayle, home from the hospital to their courtyard apartment on 111th Street and Lenox. From then on, wherever Maxine went, she took her sister with her in a stroller, though her parents drew the line when she tried to bring the baby to the Wednesday-night dances at Central Park's Park Palace.

When Gayle was five, her father, Harold, got a mechanical design engineering job offer in Connecticut that he couldn't turn down. With his deep, resounding baritone, Harold interviewed for the position over the phone. He believed that the company thought it had hired a white man and didn't know how to turn him away when he reported for his first day of work. For most of his illustrious career, he was the only Black draftsman in his division.

In Connecticut, he bought a colonial-style house, to which McKinney-Griffith would eventually return after her father's death to care for her mother, Millicent, until her death in 2019 at the age of 101. Maxine deferred her acceptance to Fordham University to watch over Gayle in Connecticut, while Millicent stayed behind in Harlem for a year, waiting for the telephone company where she worked to transfer her job. She finally was transferred, but she was also demoted to long-distance operator, which she attributed to the color of her skin. Without complaint, she worked the night shift, eventually marching her way back up the ladder to supervisor. "She surpassed all of the people that didn't want her to move forward," says McKinney-Griffith.

Harold and Millicent adjusted to life outside Harlem by pouring themselves into their new home. Millicent developed a green thumb, spending her precious free time in her gardens, planting lilacs, wisteria, roses, and a hill of daffodils on the far side of the lawn. Harold filled their house with beautiful furniture he designed and made himself. He refinished the stately wooden balustrade on the stairs leading up to the second floor that his children and their friends would keep forever smooth by sliding down. Years later he would build Gayle's daughter Khadija a dollhouse that was a replica of their house on a hill, down to its white wraparound porch. And outside his engineering work, he was a volunteer fireman, eventually serving as both treasurer and secretary for the local fire-police association. He loved the pomp of his uniform and the sense of brotherhood that went along with it, the satisfaction of riding atop a float in his small town's Fourth of July parade.

It was Gayle who pined for Harlem. Her parents hoped dance might be a balm for their homesick daughter, who'd been taking dance classes at Carnegie Hall before they moved. They found a local studio run by an old Russian couple, Maximillian and Olga Froman, who had once performed with the Bolshoi. All the white girls in the new studio carried round, pink dance bags to match their pink tights and shoes. Harold bought his daughter a rectangular black patent leather dance bag and painted her name on it in his artful script. Every time she entered the studio, he wanted her to know that she was precious and deserving.

Connecticut wasn't Harlem, but the Fromans helped Gayle feel at home. Maximillian played the piano, and Olga taught classes. It was under their tender care that she fell forever in love with a room with a barre and mirrors. "There's some feeling of magic that comes over me when I walk into a dance studio," she says. "Maybe it's the smell of the wood, the cedar. But there's an atmosphere that surrounds you. My heart starts beating faster in my chest every time I get close to one." Olga took exquisite care of her new student's training, invested in every degree of her port de bras, and provided a safe space where her talent could bloom. Hearing of this woman's care with her friend, Sheila Rohan remarks, "Your teacher was a true dance artist. She wasn't seeing this little Black girl at the barre. She saw a dancer." By the time she was ten, Gayle began her transition onto pointe, funneled into an advanced group of demi-soloists. She was chosen to perform the "Four Swans" variation in *Swan Lake*.

There is a gracefulness to Gayle McKinney-Griffith's spirit that softens whatever space she enters. Throughout her childhood, people gravitated to her gentle and competent energy. She was elected secretary of her high school class, then president of the Waterford High Dance Club, and she received a scholarship to attend the annual American Dance Festival hosted by Connecticut College. There she took classes from the likes of the formidable Martha Graham, the mother of modern dance. She remembers Graham wielding her training stick like a weapon against mediocrity in the studio. "She would just hit you on the back yelling, 'Contract! Contract!'"

In the evenings at home, it was showtime. While Millicent went in for the night shift at the phone company, Gayle made Harold and her niece, Victoria, seven years her junior—whom Maxine and her husband had sent to live with her grandparents for the better public school system—her captive audience. She would perform elaborate concerts and plays for them. One night she paired a sequin minidress she'd constructed in her home economics class with earrings she'd fashioned out of Styrofoam balls and sequins and treated them to a rousing performance of Tina Turner's "Proud Mary."

Knowing her parents expected her to go to college, Gayle set her sights on Juilliard. The audition process was a three-day blur of anxiety. On the first day, she found herself assigned to the modern dancers, despite her extensive ballet résumé. After letting her talent speak for itself, she was allowed, grudgingly, she felt, to join the pool of prospective ballet dancers. She was the only dancer of color in the group, an exhausting fact for which she'd long since developed coping skills. "When you live in this skin, you grow up knowing you have a special position in the world that you must protect," she says. "I don't think that we're even aware of when we're doing it. But we're always protecting ourselves—in school, in different communities. You have to wear blinders and focus. When you walk into a room and you're the only Black person there, you right away develop this persona that is protective but also standing strong. You're used to thinking two things at once: *Yes, I'm the only Black person here* and *Yes, let's do this.*"

Gayle was accepted into Juilliard and moved into Maxine's family's three-bedroom apartment in Morningside Heights, sleeping on the pullout sofa in their den. Her dancing garnered immediate notice in her new school. The Uruguayan teacher and dancer Alfredo Corvino personally requested her in his ballet class, despite the administration grumbling about the extra course expense on top of her regular load. Antony Tudor, choreographer emeritus for American Ballet Theatre at the time of his death in 1987, likewise asked for her to take his class, believing he could push her pointe work even further. Grateful for his encouragement, she tried her best to ignore the way her white male classmates flinched when they were told to partner her.

But no matter the potential these giants of ballet saw in her, Juilliard's administration wouldn't budge when it came time for McKinney-Griffith to declare a major. In a private conference, she was pressed to let go of her dreams of ballet. They told her she'd never get hired by a professional company. There likely wouldn't even be opportunities to audition. The fact of her talent, which seemed devastatingly beside the point, was never mentioned. It was time for her to be practical and move into the modern dance department. It wasn't what she wanted, and it also didn't make sense. Her friends in the modern department were lifetimes ahead of her in terms of their training and passion for the form. She was a ballerina, not a modern dancer. She grasped for examples of women of color who had proved themselves exceptions. What about Maria Tallchief? Or Mary Hinkson? Or Kathleen Stanford Grant?

McKinney-Griffith left the office holding back her tears and sank to the floor of the hallway in defeat. "My God, this is not working," she remembers crying to herself. "Why am I even here?" One of her friends from the modern dance department happened upon her that way, and after learning the cause of her distress, she pulled McKinney-Griffith to her feet with life-changing news. "Arthur Mitchell is auditioning today. For an all-Black ballet company. Stop your whining and go!"

As McKinney-Griffith emerged from the subway station onto familiar streets, she fell in lockstep with a graceful Black woman, who walked in the familiar slue-footed style of a ballerina, her toes turned out like a duck. Virginia Johnson, another founding ballerina of Dance Theatre of Harlem, whom Mitchell would personally tap to revive the company as its artistic director in 2009, entered the church basement right alongside her. The ramshackle space was a far cry from Juilliard's gleaming studios. But the sight of all these brown and Black dancers, the kitchens on the backs of the women's necks pinned up like hers, allowed her to unclench. She could dance here without the weight of her armor.

"I don't know how to describe the feeling of looking around that room other than magical," says McKinney-Griffith. "The sheer numbers of us! I had never seen such handsome, sculpted men in my life. And then the women! All so statuesque and elegant. Everybody doing the same thing that I've loved all my life."

Karel Shook was leading the class with his trademark Kent cigarette hanging from his mouth, as he did for much of his tenure at Dance Theatre of Harlem, until he died of throat cancer in 1985. He was an intellectual man with melancholy eyes, whose wryness was a welcome counterpart to Mitchell's brio. He liked to lean in close to the dancers' ears and whisper a joke to test their focus. When he was feeling cheeky, he'd hold his lit cigarette underneath a dancer's leg as motivation for her to continue holding her arabesque longer than she'd ever thought herself able.

After class, Mitchell burst into the room, harried from another fundraising meeting. Shook introduced the promising new girl from Juilliard to him. "Hmm. Hmmm, put your pointe shoes on," said Mitchell. "Let me see you turn." Satisfied by the grace of her pirouettes, Mitchell handed her a piece of paper. "Go learn this dance. We're rehearsing the first movement of *Tones* tomorrow, so be here first thing in the morning." Then he marched off in his high-heeled boots to his next order of business. He didn't wait for her to tell him that she had class in the morning or to wonder if those few minutes before him counted as her official audition. The only thing she knew for sure was that she had to find a way to stay in this room, where for the first time in her life as a dancer, she was one of many.

MCKINNEY-GRIFFITH SHOWED UP the next morning, just as she'd been told to, to learn one of Dance Theatre of Harlem's first ballets. *Tones* was the first ballet music composed by Mitchell's twenty-four-year-old accompanist Tania León. A Cuban refugee new to the country on a scholarship to NYU, she'd aligned with Mitchell by chance. She'd been filling in for a sick friend as a substitute piano teacher at the Harlem School of the Arts on the day Mitchell was taking stock of possible studio space. She was noodling around on the baby grand piano during breaks between students, playing her own melodies, when Mitchell happened to pass by the open door, then passed by a second time to get a closer listen. She noticed the startlingly attractive man hovering outside. When he finally stepped forward to introduce himself, León could only hold up her hands and say, "No English." Mitchell made the motions of a telephone with his hands and got the phone number to the Bronx apartment where she was camping out with friends. Two weeks later he called her up and asked León in a garble of Spanish and Italian to come play for him again.

When León returned to Harlem School of the Arts, she joined Mitchell and four dancers who were waiting at a barre set up in the middle of the basketball court. Mitchell balked when León pulled out some of her friend's music books, asking her instead to pay attention to the movement and the sound of his voice. As Mitchell walked around the dancers tapping his stick and calling out "One, two, three, four!" she began improvising at the upright piano. "The four ballerinas were Lydia, Sheila, Virginia Johnson, and Patsy Ricketts," she says. "I still have a little Kodak picture of these four young women standing at the barre. He told me to follow his counts based on watching the movements, and I just started creating all these pieces."

After class, Mitchell talked to León about his mission, the opportunity he was trying to provide for Black classical dancers, and offered her a job as his full-time accompanist. "When I found out that the whole project was to demonstrate that people of color could dance ballet, I got immediately hooked," says León. As a child in Cuba, her beloved grandmother had wanted her to learn ballet. But when she took her granddaughter to the dance school for classes, they turned León away because of the color of her skin.

As he did everyone else, Mitchell threw León onto his wild seesaw of approval. If León's playing was too slow for his liking, he would scream at her, "You're killing the dancers!" Other times he cried out with sunny approval: "Yes! Yes! Just like that, remember that. That's perfect!" But no matter his shifting mood, he recognized greatness in her. He called her Taniacita, and she became one of the founding partners of Dance Theatre of Harlem.

"After that Arthur made me do everything," says León. "I was the pianist. I was the music director. I was the head of the school. I was like an octopus person. Arthur said, 'Compose a piece for me!' Now I was a composer. 'You want to conduct the orchestra? You know all the ballets, you know everything, you can do it.' Now I was a conductor. It's like he could see into the future." León would go on to be awarded a Pulitzer Prize for her orchestral work *Stride,* and in 2022 she was a Kennedy Center honoree for her tremendous contribution to American culture, but to this day, when she steps in front of an audience, she hears Mitchell's voice in her ears: *"Always walk on stage like you are somebody!"*

FOR A FEW EXHAUSTING WEEKS, Gayle McKinney-Griffith tied herself in knots juggling a full course load at Juilliard with Mitchell's six-hour-plus daily rehearsals. Finally, fed up with her racing into the studio late and always leaving in a rush back to school, Shook and Mitchell cornered her at the end of a long afternoon session. Mitchell asked how much longer she was going to keep dragging her butt back and forth to Juilliard. She stammered over her idea of hanging on to both college and the company. "Well, I'm giving you an ultimatum," Mitchell said, cutting her off. "You're either going to dance here or you're going to dance at Juilliard. Now you have to make up your mind." Shook, sensing her torment, patted her softly on the back, but Mitchell barked, "Ding ding ding ding!" before turning on his heel.

That night she flopped onto her sister's sofa in misery. She couldn't bear disappointing their parents and wasting all that money that they'd spent on her tuition. And yet something vital had been restored in her under Mitchell's eye.

Gayle called her parents with the news that she was dropping out of college. She told them about Mitchell, his exquisite vision, about Abarca and Rohan and Johnson and the rest of the artists who would dance that vision into existence. Her voice dripped with so much passion that all her parents could do was sigh quietly and tell her that they believed in her too.

Just two years after that phone call, Dance Theatre of Harlem would travel to Connecticut and perform at the college not far from the family's house on the hill. A widowed Madame Froman would sit in the audience with tears in her eyes. "Look at what you did!" McKinney-Griffith wanted to call out to her teacher during the company bows.

BY THE END of that first summer, student enrollment in Mitchell's dance program mushroomed to 250 kids. On warm days, he threw the bay doors open to sidewalk traffic for the breeze. He added live drummers to the mix of León's piano as a lure to anyone turned off by classical music. When neighborhood kids lingered outside the garage, mesmerized by the scene of beautiful young women in tights, Mitchell was able to entice them inside, assuring the boys they could wear their street clothes if that was their hang-up. "What's your sport?" he'd call out. "Basketball? What if I could teach you to jump two feet higher than anyone else on your team? All you need to learn is something called the plié." McKinney-Griffith remembers having to lead the occasionally unruly youth class. "They'd be chewing gum in their dungarees," she says. " 'Whatcha mean, don't lean on the barre!' "

Meanwhile Mitchell was feverishly developing choreography for his rapidly improving company's repertoire. He finished the first movement of *Tones,* a neoclassical ballet of angles and form set to León's atonal score. His *Holberg Suite* was a romantic confection also choreographed in Balanchine's neoclassical style. He revived *Rhythmetron,* a ballet he'd first choreographed during his time in Brazil, set to Marlos Nobre's thirty-three-percussive-instrument score. The ballet fused classical technique with African ritual and would quickly emerge as the company's signature piece. Finally, he created *Biosfera,* a pas de deux also set to the Brazilian Nobre's music. He cast Abarca in the female lead, with Rohan as her understudy.

Llanchie Stevenson, though, had begun to second-guess her decision to follow Mitchell to Harlem. For starters, Mitchell had taken a clear shine to the younger Abarca. "Because Walter Raines and I had the background, we were supposed to be the establishment of the company and push it forward," she says. "But in my opinion, Arthur quickly decided, 'Forget about it. I got Lydia.'" She worked up the nerve to tell Mitchell that she missed National Ballet's established repertory and the smooth-running engine of its day-to-day operations. Despite his angry protestations that she was abandoning ship, she returned to Washington, D.C. But there she remained relegated to the corps until the company started preparing for its annual run of *The Nutcracker.* During casting for the show, a white ballet dancer suggested to the director Frederic Franklin that instead of painting her in Black face to play the role of the Arabian, he just use Stevenson. And so after a year of Mitchell calling her on the phone, telling her it was time to return to New York where she belonged, Stevenson rejoined Dance Theatre of Harlem. "I wanted to be in a company of dancers who grew up like me, felt like me, and looked like me," she says. "I wanted to have the opportunity to be partnered with a premier danseur, which I wouldn't ever have anywhere else."

Mitchell told his dancers, and the world repeated the fact over and over, that there was nowhere else for them to go to realize their full potential. In a June 2021 interview for *The New York Times* about the Legacy Council, Virginia Johnson described the feverish time. "There was so much on the line! I think one of the beautiful things about those early years of Dance Theatre of Harlem was every single one of us had been told, 'No, you can't do this.' And then Arthur Mitchell gave us a place to do it and gave us a way to achieve a high level of excellence. So yes, there was opportunity, but it was about grit. It was a fight. People had told us we couldn't do it and we had to show them we could. Remember, this was the middle of the Black Power movement. There were plenty of Black people who did not think that we should be trying to succeed in 'the white man's art form.' And there were plenty of white people who didn't think we should be either."

"We all understood this to be a higher calling," says McKinney-Griffith. "Suddenly that step on pointe made a difference. We were a group of brown people, of all different shades from different cities and countries. For those of us who'd felt for so long adrift and like a lonely standard bearer—to look around and feel the power of numbers was just extraordinary. We were en masse, so we were protected. Can you imagine the energy that freed up? The freedom to just focus on our craft. We never had to justify to each other our right to ballet."

4

"My Best Day—We went to the Dance Theater of Harlem. I would like to be a ballet dancer. They used their feet and legs. Sometimes the music went low and high."

—John, P.S. 161, 499 West 133rd Street

"I did not like it for a while, then it was great. At first, I thought it was going to be different, but it turned out to be wonderful."

—Wendy, P.S. 161

"The performance you gave to us on Monday was terrific. The dancers were all great. Someday, maybe, I will be with your dance group."

—Eric, P.S. 161

Dance Theatre of Harlem was formally incorporated in 1969, with Arthur Mitchell assembling a powerhouse board that included, among others, Cicely Tyson and Brock Peters, as well as George Balanchine, Lincoln Kirstein, and Charles De Rose, who'd taken on what was basically a second full-time job as the company's first treasurer.

Shortly thereafter Mitchell's relationship with Dorothy Maynor devolved into a clash of egos, and suddenly the dancers were out of a home. They relocated to another church basement, at the Church of the Master across the street from Morningside Park on 122nd Street, where as a child he'd once attended a free camp. Mitchell described their new neighborhood as "the worst dope area in Harlem." But he liked to brag that because of his alliance with a local gang leader who respected his hustle, vandals skipped over Dance Theatre of Harlem, and the dope dealers left the dancers and the kids alone.

The new space was beaten down to say the least. Leaking pipes overhead had left the floor badly buckled. The dancers had to pitch in their change to meet the costs of getting a new floor laid so they wouldn't injure themselves. The girls' dressing room consisted of costume and lighting crates for benches and a Chinese screen for privacy. But still, the basement blessed them with a large studio space with a raised deck that could accommodate up to sixty spectators. Soon after the move, Mitchell began opening their Wednesday rehearsals to an audience, as a shrewd method of community outreach.

Folks in the neighborhood came to recognize and look forward to seeing the dancers on their way to and from the studio. The women gave themselves away with their high buns slicked back in Murray's pomade, hurrying down the sidewalk on their orchid-stem legs, their feet turned out like ducks. Each morning on her walk to work, Lydia Abarca passed the same drowsy clump of testosterone on a building stoop, sitting around listening to music and smoking cigarettes. "Hey baby!" they'd catcall for her attention. "Hey, I'm talkin' to you! You too stuck up to talk to a brotha?" Tired of their baiting, she'd eventually reclaim control of the situation with one graceful swivel. "Hi, my name is Lydia, and I don't usually talk to strangers," she said, looking each of her antagonists in the eye. "I have to walk through here to get to work every day, and now that you know my name, I'll make sure to say hello." From then on, she found herself greeted with a respectful chorus of "Good morning, Lydia!"

Dance Theatre of Harlem quickly became an important symbol of possibility in the community. Says De Rose, "What Arthur did was raise people's pride. He said, 'This is what people said Blacks couldn't do. They never said we couldn't play basketball. They never said we couldn't box. They never said we couldn't tap-dance. But classical dance was a no-no.' And Arthur Mitchell said, 'Bullshit! Any child given the same opportunity is going to have the same results.'"

Mitchell had dumped the remainder of his savings into keeping his new school and company afloat, taking on personal loans so as not to default on his dancers' modest salaries or his students' scholarship stipends. Within two months of their move into the Church of the Master, the rent jumped from $170 to $600 per month. Ballet companies live on three sources of income. The first was box office (of which Dance Theatre of Harlem had none). The second was school tuition (fifty cents per child per class, which clearly wasn't going to pay the bills). So that meant that from the beginning their budget relied unhealthily on the third, unearned income, or donations. Mitchell and De Rose had to learn the art of hustling for money on the fly. "I would always ask Arthur, 'What happens when your money runs out?'" says De Rose. "He said to me something I never forgot. 'When your motives are pure, an invisible hand will always come out to help you.'"

They were making the right ask at the right time. The country was reeling from Dr. King's assassination. Foundations and folks with fat wallets were eager to support a Black cause to feel like they were somehow part of a solution instead of the problem. "We were going to Capezio, to the New York Mets, to Diane von Furstenberg for funds," says De Rose. "Six out of ten times I got a check back." The payoff of having ballet giants like Balanchine and Kirstein on the board was immediate. Because of their influence, Mitchell's proposal to the Ford Foundation was signed as soon as it hit the top brass's desk. Dance Theatre of Harlem was blessed with a gift of $315,000, contingent upon them bringing in $151,000 of earned income.

AS HE HIT the fundraising circuit in earnest, Mitchell enlisted Abarca to serve as a kind of billboard for his new company. With her model good looks and youthful, leggy figure cut straight from the Balanchinean mold, she was perfect for the role. "Lydia, have you ever been to a Broadway show?" he would ask her, knowing full well the answer. "I'm going to take you. Let's go."

Now in the evenings, when Francisco Abarca would bark at her siblings to shut up and get in bed, Lydia would be leaving the apartment in a flutter, dressed as well as her modest wardrobe would allow, to catch a cab downtown. She'd promise, as she flew out the door, that she'd get to the sink full of dishes upon her return.

With every outing, Mitchell was showing her by his own lived example how to dress, how to walk into a room with confidence, how to behave in exclusive spaces, and how to be such a galvanizing source of energy once she was in them that the lights seemed to dim upon her exit. He became a father figure to her, though one who couldn't be more diametrically opposed in temperament to that of her stoic, faithful daddy. "It was refreshing to be with someone so eloquent and charismatic," says Abarca. "Anytime I went to my father, it was like, 'Hey Daddy, how are you doing?' 'Uh, okay, let me get your mother.'"

Mitchell took her to see Melba Moore in *Purlie,* choreographed by the great Louis Johnson, who he'd trained with at the School of American Ballet. They saw Brock Peters in the play *Lost in the Stars,* based on Alan Paton's apartheid novel *Cry, the Beloved Country.* Abarca remembers struggling backstage for words. "I was beating my brains trying to think of something nice to say to Mr. Peters," says Abarca. "But I thought the play was so boring. No dancing! All I could come up with was 'How do you remember all those words?' And he smiled at me and said, 'How do you remember all those steps?'"

When Abarca would worry about embarrassing herself in front of Mitchell's muckety-muck friends, she turned to Hutaff Lennon, Celia's best friend's brother, who she'd helped get a job in the costuming department by lying to Mitchell and saying that he was her cousin. Lennon was the first gay man she had known and loved. He sewed his own clothes and painted his apartment walls in brilliant shades of red and yellow. Abarca never told the other girls in the company about her evening's plans with Mitchell, out of fear they'd be jealous or think something untoward was going on between the two, but she felt safe telling Lennon. The costuming assistant, who would eventually move to Hollywood and work with Luther Vandross and do the wardrobe on movies like *B.A.P.S.,* always reminded Abarca of her only real assignment when she was out with the boss: "Just look pretty. Don't say anything."

One night she accompanied Mitchell and De Rose to a party at Nelson Rockefeller's sprawling Pocantico Hills estate. "He fawned all over us, even taking us down to see his private art collection," says De Rose. "His attention wasn't because of me, I can assure you that. He was so taken with Lydia."

When asked what made Abarca the perfect plus-one for these types of events, De Rose doesn't mince words. "Oh, because she was light-skinned," he says. "She represented the cross between the African American and the Caucasian. She was not what others expected. Light-skinned, long, dainty, elegant, soft-spoken. She was our star."

Abarca was still just a teenager, too busy trying to survive the gauntlet of these glamorous evenings to question what made her the chosen one. She was desperately shy and out of her comfort zone, terrified whenever Mitchell left her side to work the room. She'd find a quiet place to sit, with her back ramrod straight and her long legs crossed at her ankles, testing the weight of the crystal ashtray on Rockefeller's side table that likely cost more than her father made in year. She longed for the comfort of money, even if antiques weren't her favorite—something about the smell of old furniture always reminded her of her grandfather's thrift store.

Eventually Mitchell would round her up and show her off to the slick-lipped partygoers as one of his dancers, his star who was going to disprove ballet's Black fallacy once and for all. "I felt so privileged that he'd chosen me to represent his ballerinas," she says. "But I was just glorified wall-paper. I had no interest in sharing who Lydia Abarca was with all those rich people. 'Oh hi, I have six sisters and a brother, and we live in the projects.' No! I didn't want anyone looking at me like *Oh, you poor thing.*"

As Mitchell's guest at a gala for the New York City Ballet, she paired a cheap shiny lavender minidress with modest heels and fake pearl drop earrings, her hair styled in a low ballerina bun. "Everyone's walking around in these fur coats and ball gowns," she says, "and here I am with Mr. Mitchell. 'This is Lydia Abarca, one of my ballerinas.' I didn't have any kind of personality for a room like that. I was a mouse." The company did a performance of *Allegro Brillante* that evening that felt to Abarca like a gauntlet thrown. "The ballet was all quick steps, smiles, and intricate choreography that I was beginning to understand were typical of Balanchine. I remember watching those white women up on stage, knowing they've studied ballet since they were two years old, thinking here I am at eighteen still thinking I'm accomplishing something when I do a split! That's when I understood that I had to learn how to be a lead ballerina. I didn't have a role model. I didn't have somebody I could look up to and say 'I want to be just like that.' But I wasn't frightened or intimidated. I couldn't wait."

It wasn't long after that, at a cocktail party on Fifth Avenue, that Abarca came to resist her role as "glorified wallpaper." She was nursing the one glass of wine she allowed herself, mute and sublime at Mitchell's side. As the booze flowed, the host turned on some popular music and formed a circle around the evening's two Black guests of honor. "Come on Arthur and Lydia!" she remembers the room cheering. "Get up and dance for us! Come on." All the froth of the evening hardened at the well-heeled crowd's aggressive prodding. "I felt like an organ grinder monkey," says Abarca. "I wanted to tell them, 'Go to a theater and watch us perform. I'm not going to dance for you here.'"

But Mitchell was willing to play the game when it came to charming potential donors into opening their wallets. "I learned to be a beggar," he once told a crowd of students at Radcliffe. "That was probably the hardest thing I've ever had to do in my life." Abarca remembers him plastering on a smile, taking her hand, and leading her out onto the impromptu dance floor where she swayed uncomfortably to an R&B song as the party cheered. On the sidewalk outside afterward, the two walked in uncomfortable silence as he put her in a cab.

WHILE MITCHELL TURNED ON the charm with potential donors, it was not how he led his studio. Shook was less bombastic as a teacher, but his technical standards in the daily company class were just as high. For Mitchell, every gesture, every tilt of the head, every step had to have a purpose, and it needed to be perfect. Rehearsals would be scheduled for an hour and last for five. If he wasn't tired, the dancers better not be either. "In the beginning, Dance Theatre wasn't mediocre, it was good," says De Rose. "But it wasn't up to world-class standards. Arthur was unrelenting. 'Your leg has to be higher; you have to be better; you have to be straighter, you have to walk better, your hands, your feet. You either hit the high C or you don't. Do it again! And this time, do it right! No, do it again! Again!' Arthur was no teddy bear, but he brought more out of you than you ever knew you had to give. And he did it by example. He was the first one into the studio, and the last one to leave at night."

After rehearsals, the dancers would freeze in a line, bracing for Mitchell's corrections. Nobody dared slouch or sigh or sneeze, lest they make themselves the target of his fusillade of judgment. "We got in trouble for everything," says Abarca. "If you didn't hold your passé, if you didn't hold your little toe by your knee, if you didn't hold your knee up, if your foot was sickled. Every little detail. You could never be good enough for him. But you also understood he was our third eye. If we could please him, we would please the audience." Mitchell would often echo the warning Kirstein had given him as teenager. "Everything you see them do," he'd say, referencing the top ballet companies, "you have to be ten times better."

The poison of his tongue would thicken depending on his stress level. "Sometimes he could just be goofing around with you," says Gayle McKinney-Griffith. "He had this big, wonderful boisterous laugh, so if he was laughing, everyone was laughing." But inevitably, he'd turn on you. He'd arrive at the studio after what he thought was a lucrative fundraising meeting, only to discover that the promise of money at lunch had evaporated during his commute uptown—his temper would hit like a fire hose. Remembers Sheila Rohan: "If your leg wasn't high that day, or your back was weak, Mr. Mitchell would pick on you. He would call you out by name. 'You, you with the butt! You with the thighs! You with the attitude!' I mean, he could absolutely destroy a person."

"I've been called an ogre, a taskmaster, and you better believe it's true," Mitchell once said. "Just ask the kids. Hey, I'm not running a party here. This is something very important to me, to Harlem, to Black people everywhere. No one's going to hand anything to us."

His philosophy was: better he be the one to grind a dancer's ego to dust than someone outside the family, of which he'd immediately cast himself in the role of formidable patriarch. He began boasting to reporters of teaching his dancers how to dress, where to buy their clothes, how he'd paid for some of them to get their teeth fixed. If a dancer ever showed up to class in raggedy leg warmers or tights, he'd make them go home and change. He wanted smooth ballet buns on every woman, forbidding them to wear their hair in cornrows or beads (though somehow Rohan, who had come into the company with a short afro, was spared his disapproval). He'd insist upon meeting his dancers' boyfriends and girlfriends, telling them to dump suitors whom he found lacking. When reporters would ask Mitchell if he had any intention of marrying, his grin slid like an ocean liner across his face. "No, but I have thirty-one children," he'd respond, referring to his company of dancers and his support staff, who made up the scaffolding of his lean operation. Mitchell's most familiar refrain to his dancers was that they represented something larger than their individual selves. So they'd better get right with shouldering the pressures and responsibilities that came with being an ambassador.

The studio's observation deck had begun hosting crowds that could in one afternoon rehearsal include children from the neighborhood Head Start program, high society dowagers, and celebrities like Cicely Tyson, Lena Horne, and the modern dance pioneer Ted Shawn. The actress Butterfly McQueen, who'd played Prissy in *Gone with the Wind,* and famously was unable to attend the movie's premiere because it was held in a whites-only theater, was one of several celebrities who dropped in for a class. "She came in full tutu," says McKinney-Griffith. "I mean, ballerina-decked—a tiny tiara, scarves, ballet slippers that weren't tied very well." The dancers knew to mask their excitement over the increasingly high-profile audiences who'd begun flocking to their cramped studio. If they messed up and embarrassed Mitchell in front of his fancy friends, he'd kill them.

BECAUSE OF the earned income expectation in the grant that he'd received from the Ford Foundation, Mitchell had to throw his young company out on the road immediately. Students typically train for a decade in classical academies before moving to the professional stage. Mitchell had his dancers performing in ten weeks. In its first year alone, the company presented ninety-eight lecture-demonstrations in public schools throughout the state of New York and beyond, as well as one-night performances in front of college audiences, charity associations, and arts councils. He even arranged for a few company appearances at Riker's Island for the male inmates. "In the beginning the crowd was catcalling us and laughing," says McKinney-Griffith. "They quieted down because Mr. Mitchell was talking a mile a minute. We were anxious to get out of there, but we knew Mr. Mitchell was never going to let anything bad happen to us."

In those early years, the only crew at the lecture-demonstrations were the dancers themselves. They'd haul the lights, costumes, wires, and booms onto the buses before every show, then unload them at the venue and lug everything inside. They'd attach the barres on the stage themselves. "There was an esprit de corps at Dance Theatre of Harlem like I had never seen," says De Rose. "When trucks would get to a certain venue, like Syracuse, New York, when it was snowing and cold, the kids would unload the trucks themselves and form a conga line and pass the different sets and costumes down. Everybody had skin in the game."

Before showtime, they'd shake up cans of Coca-Cola and spray them onto the waxed gymnasium floors, using rags to spread the liquid around evenly in hopes of giving their pointe shoes some protective stick. Abarca remembers one engagement at a public school where the women had to drape sheets over a clothesline to give the ballerinas a separate changing area from the men. When the girls got fed up with the guys teasing and peeking at them, Virginia Johnson threw a metal folding chair over the sheets as a warning shot. "It scared everybody, but it worked!" says Abarca.

Mitchell wore tights to the first Dance Theatre of Harlem lecture-demonstration, but the audience of children giggled so loudly at him that he switched to trousers going forward. He'd lead the company through a typical ninety-minute-long class, beginning at the barre, where he'd enthusiastically break down the purpose and relevance of every position, then transition to center and partnering work. At the end, the dancers would perform parts of their repertoire in costume. "They would bus all these kids in, and they'd be ooh-ing and aah-ing when we would do a grand plié or a développé," says Abarca. "Mr. Mitchell would have the kids come up on stage to show him the latest street dance and then he would break it down into ballet moves."

As commanding as he was enchanting, Mitchell broke down ballet into images and stories that rang true to his unfamiliar audience's ears. He'd show how ballet technique could be found at the core of the camel walk dance, or the bus stop, or the pony. In the way a girl walks into her class party, knowing she's the baddest in the room. Mitchell, as cool as he could be silly, had a way of making children who'd never been exposed to classical dance believe that ballet belonged to them too. "He just took the whole mystery out of it," says Abarca. "He'd take kids from the audience to demonstrate and say, 'See! You're doing ballet!'"

There was nobody better in front of an audience of children than Arthur Mitchell. In a lecture-demonstration captured in the PBS documentary *Rhythmetron,* Mitchell addresses a group of young people, all on their knees, crowded around a stage, explaining to them the importance of a battement tendu relevé. Sensing that his audience is starting to fidget and drift, he turns to them and asks, "Now, how many of you own a cat?" Half the audience raises their hands. "Not bad, not bad. How many have seen a cat? Okay, that's good. Now, when a cat jumps and he lands, he doesn't pancake to the floor." He demonstrates by jumping and thudding to the floor on a heavy flat foot, and then jumping again, landing just one foot on the floor without making a sound. "He *alights,* he cushions himself down. And that step that you just saw, that battement tendu relevé, strengthens that metatarsal. It's just like what we see in jazz dancing. Here, I'm going to do a catlike walk." Mitchell slinks groovily across the stage, snapping his fingers, scatting. The kids howl in laughter. His beauty and charisma overwhelm, the light of him almost drinkable.

SHEILA ROHAN ALWAYS LEFT the studio at the end of their marathon days in a sprint. "I got to get the boat!" she'd yell to those behind her, by way of goodbye. The younger dancers would be plotting their evenings, taking a quick nap before hitting a disco or enjoying an hours-long soak in the tub with Epsom salts to baby their feet. Rohan had to race to the subway, which she took down to South Ferry, where she'd wait for the boat to take her back to Staten Island where, as she puts it, she had to make sure there was peanut butter in the cupboard for the day ahead. If she ever missed the midnight ferry, when it switched to running on the hour instead of every half, she'd try to keep herself awake by reading on a bench, inevitably passing out from sheer exhaustion. Mitchell had begun throwing multiple ballets at them to learn in a rush. Balanchine had graciously given Dance Theatre of Harlem the rights to use some of his most popular ballets, beginning with *Concerto Barocco,* so they had been meeting with City Ballet dancers to learn the choreography. "You guys were dancing for your lives," Rohan's youngest, Little Sheila, says now in a family conversation.

As their audience size increased, so too did Rohan's battle with stage fright. She questioned her talent compared to dancers like Abarca ("she had the beautiful face and body and extension"), Johnson ("so elegant and crisp"), and McKinney-Griffith ("her gorgeous technique"). Says Rohan, "I believed you really couldn't dance ballet unless you had complete control over it. I thought I wasn't ready or good enough to be on stage yet and Mr. Mitchell was pushing us before we were ready. I was terrified I was going to make a mistake or knock someone over or go on the wrong side of the stage." (Once during a performance in which she was dressed as a yellow canary, her worst fear came true. "I fell on my ass, and instead of just quietly getting up, I went *whoof!* on the stage," she says, laughing and covering her face. "It's bad enough to fall on your ass, but then the audience laughed! I played that one over and over in my head waiting for the ferry.")

Eager to develop tools to calm herself down, Rohan began reading about Buddhism and, along with several other company dancers, visited a downtown temple for meditation classes. She started chanting before shows—"Namu Myōhō Renge Kyō"—so that the vibrations might connect her to a higher level of consciousness. And she drew upon her fundamental sturdiness, which attracted the younger dancers to her. "She was our rock," says Abarca.

"We would all run to Sheila," agrees McKinney-Griffith. "I would always ask her, 'How did you get your inner peace?'" Rohan invited her to Chinatown one afternoon, where she would sometimes spend the night at Nanette and Romare's Canal Street loft. Inside one of the shops, Rohan presented McKinney-Griffith with three coins and showed her how to use them alongside the *I Ching*. "I used the book until I wore it out," says McKinney-Griffith. "Every time I threw my coins, it calmed my spirit, helped me think, made me breathe again."

Rohan's children were mesmerized by what felt like sudden stardom for their mother. They delighted in the occasions when they could watch her on television, like when she appeared in a one-hour Christmas Eve special *A Holiday Celebration with Ossie Davis and Ruby Dee,* dancing in an excerpt from *Holberg Suite*. Or on NBC on Thanksgiving morning, freezing alongside the other dancers in front of Macy's, performing *Forces of Rhythm*. The wind howled so fiercely, it wrapped a giant Snoopy's head around the cab of the helium truck, forcing organizers to remove balloons from the parade for only the second time in its forty-five-year history. They wanted a part in their mother's world.

So as she had done for their mother, Nanette paid for her nephew and nieces' arts training. She would meet them on the New York side of the ferry and travel with them up to Harlem, where Sheila's middle child, Charlene, was taking ballet classes. Their mother would have reminded them in the morning to address her as Aunt Sheila. If anyone asked, they were her nephew and nieces.

Charlene was eight years old when she first took a class with Arthur Mitchell. He'd spend half the time shouting at the children about the importance of alignment and posture and the other half lecturing about dance history and the personal dignity that flows from the practice of discipline. His classes were serious business, but as a teacher, he could be just as fun and funny as he could be mean. He was a tyrant, but she could tell that he was one of those rare adults who genuinely likes children.

After class, Charlene would linger to watch her mother and the rest of the company rehearse, drinking in the sight of her new favorite dancer, the young Lydia Abarca. "She was like our Barbie Doll," says Charlene. "Everyone wanted to be her. She was the beauty, and she got to wear the best costumes and dance the best roles."

It took over a year for Sheila to confess that those kids who'd been hanging around the studio on Saturdays were in fact hers. Dance Theatre of Harlem had been accepted as one of the touring companies by the New York State Council on the Arts and then the National Endowment for the Arts, a huge honor considering that the bylaws of both organizations demanded that a company have a minimum of five years under its belt. Rohan needed Mitchell to know that while he had her full commitment, she was a woman with obligations. After her confession, Mitchell stared at Rohan in disbelief from behind his desk before letting out a sigh of exasperation. "If I'd known you had mouths at home to feed, I would've paid you more!" he snapped, sending her back to class. True to his word, there was a modest bump in her salary the next paycheck.

Rohan sensed that Mitchell began sparing her from his nastiest temper too. "If I was ever late for rehearsal or for class, and he hated people to be late, he'd say 'Yeah, I see you over there creeping in!' One time I fell on stage, and he just rolled his eyes. Once I forgot to take off my brown leg warmers and wore them on stage during a performance of *Rhythmetron*. I thought he was really going to let me have it, but he just said, 'You're going to get fined for that.' He didn't really yell at me or come down on me like he did Lydia or the others. I think he must have respected the fact that I was a mother and maybe admired that I was trying."

AT THE 2016 PRESENTATION of Mitchell's archives to Columbia University, a guest in the audience made the mistake of addressing him by his first name. Mitchell narrowed his eyes before replying, "Young man, unless you woke up in bed next to me, my name is Mr. Mitchell."

At that same event, Rohan went up to greet her former teacher. "'Hey Arthur, good to see you!' I figured I'm older now. I'm a grandmother. 'Hey Arthur!'" She recalls Mitchell bristling at her informal greeting. "It's Mr. Mitchell to you," he reminded her sternly. As she sucked back a retort, Mitchell gave Rohan a once-over before asking, "Weren't you the one with all the kids?"

Throughout her time in Dance Theatre of Harlem, Sheila's mother, Eliza, who loved the Brooklyn Dodgers not ballet, remained skeptical of all the sacrifices her youngest daughter was making. "She had an immigrant mentality," says Rohan. "My mother saw me dance, but she wasn't sentimental. She didn't believe in art for art's sake. The fact that I had to leave my children to barely make a living didn't make much sense to her. And she worried about the fact that I was getting older. 'How long do you think you're going to be doing this? If you're not making money, why are you going on? You've got three kids. Go home to them.'"

She had no interest in meeting the great Arthur Mitchell, which was probably for the best. "If she ever heard him yelling at us the way he could, she'd have cursed him out," says Rohan. "She was the type of woman who would've stood up in the audience and laid him flat. Of course, he probably would've loved her. Because she was gutsy, and she would've gave him word for word. I think he would've respected her."

But when money was tight, Sheila would worry that maybe her mother was right after all. She and Ellsworth would look at their bills spread out on the kitchen table, and she'd float the idea of quitting Dance Theatre of Harlem to find work as a secretary. Every time Ellsworth would shake his head fondly and remind her of her purpose: "Sheila, you're one of the few people who get to do what they actually love. Do what you love to do."

Maybe she would've quit, if it weren't for her husband's support. Or if she hadn't trusted so completely in the purity of Mitchell's vision. Or if she hadn't been able to rely on the other dancers, who took turns crying on each other's shoulders and lifting one another's chins. "In rehearsals, Arthur would insinuate things about the other dancers," she says. "'Oh, look at her legs.' 'That's a fat one.' Just loud enough for them to hear. Or he'd be trying to start stuff between Lydia and Virginia. 'Oh, if you can't do that, maybe she can.' It hurt me to see my friends cry in the dressing room. But if this was what we had to put up with, so be it. The work was so hard that we had to come together as a force. We clung to each other. We were all in the same boat, and we had to survive this captain."

They lived in fear of the reflection of his square head underneath the EXIT silhouette at the back of a theater, where he would watch rehearsal. They feared, too, the shadow of his afro moving backstage before he stomped into view to deliver his corrections. "We knew that he loved us, but he was very, very stern with us," says McKinney-Griffith. "Everything was always upping the ante. 'Okay, you did this this way, you got to do it better tomorrow. You're fat today, lose that weight for tomorrow.' You were never good enough for him."

Still, when you pleased Mitchell, he could glow with the warmth of a thousand suns. McKinney-Griffith remembers one afternoon when she made him swoon. They were rehearsing *Fête Noire,* Mitchell's original neoclassical-style ballet, set to music by the Russian composer Dmitri Shostakovich. She was dancing in the adagio section. "It was a pas de quatre, and the man is walking around in the promenade, and then we stop, and we do it on the other side," she says. "Then he takes it one more time and throws your hand, and you spin around. Well, I did like six arabesque turns on pointe. Mr. Mitchell screamed at the top of his voice, and he came down and he hugged me, and he gave me a kiss, and then he says, 'Oh, I love that! I love that!'" The thrill of being in his favor was a rush beyond, but it was always short-lived. Losing it was like a little death.

How easy it would have been to go back home, or to college, or to nine-to-five lives. They stayed for the promise of the next curtain rising, on stages bigger and grander with every passing month. "In the dressing rooms beforehand, we might've all gone quiet because of some big alter-cation," says McKinney-Griffith. "And then you'd just snap out of it and put your makeup on and go wait in the wings. All that noise, if you could just slip through it, you'd be fine. Mr. Mitchell couldn't touch you when you were on stage."

5

By 1970, word had spread through New York City of Arthur Mitchell's mission to make ballet more inclusive. Over one thousand children, some of them white, had enrolled in the Dance Theatre of Harlem school. When reporters asked Mitchell about his intentions to integrate the company, he balked at the idea. "I don't want an all-Black company, but until other companies start to employ them, why should I take a white dancer and put a Black one out of work?" Of the major dance companies in New York at the time, American Ballet Theatre had yet to welcome a Black dancer to its ranks, City Ballet had one, and Joffrey Ballet had two.

Wherever Dance Theatre of Harlem traveled, Mitchell scouted for talent. When he recognized potential in a young person, even in someone as raw as a kid who'd just volunteered to join him on stage during a lecture-demonstration, he'd encourage them to move to New York so he could take over their training. DTH would pay for their education at New York's Professional Children's School. Sometimes, if a dancer struggled to find housing, Mitchell would move them into a spare room in his mother's Harlem brownstone, which he'd purchased for her. As far as he was concerned, nothing was going to stand in the way of a child with talent and drive.

THAT YEAR, when Dance Theatre of Harlem traveled to Cincinnati, ten-year-old Marcia Sells told her mother they needed to get tickets. She'd been the only Black student in her ballet classes since she was four years old. She'd never seen a Black ballerina perform before. This performance was about to change that.

Marcia's mother, Mamie, was her greatest defender. As a teenager, Marcia danced in the role of a snowflake in *The Nutcracker* with the Cincinnati Ballet. During intermission, Mamie, who had little patience for ignorance or unkindness, overheard a child whining to her parents about the "dirty snowflake" on the stage. "You've never seen candy dance either," she told the family. All ballet is fantasy—a graceful unspooling of wonder and enchantment. If the child could accept a snowflake coming to life, surely her worldview could expand enough to allow for a Black girl in the role.

Mamie was a teacher and had always been adamant that her students be educated in Black history far beyond the perfunctory bullet points on slavery that made up the public school system's newly created Black History Week curriculum. At the time, some of Marcia's teachers weren't even ready to acknowledge that slavery had been an operation built on evil. Mamie expected her daughter to educate her peers in ways her teachers weren't. By the third grade, Marcia was teaching kids in her class about W. E. B. Du Bois and Booker T. Washington, the journalist Ida B. Wells and the first Black female lawyer Charlotte E. Ray, and the singers Marian Anderson and Leontyne Price. There was greatness all around her to emulate, starting in the close-knit community of Black lawyers, doctors, teachers, and judges who composed their family's inner circle.

Mamie served on the board of the Women's Auxiliary for the Symphony and was a leader in the YWCA, a member of the Women's City Club, and in her later years, a columnist for the Black newspaper *The Call Post* and eventually for *The Cincinnati Herald*. Anybody who was anybody wanted to find themselves captured in "Mamie's Urban Scene."

A WOMAN'S JOIE DE VIVRE can exist independent of her actual physical vitality. Mamie lived with the debilitating autoimmune disease sarcoidosis, a rare inflammatory condition that wreaked havoc on her lungs.

When Marcia was five years old, she found her mother unconscious on the kitchen floor and had to use the hand-carved step stool that her uncle had made for her to reach the telephone and dial 0 for an ambulance. Mamie was saved that day, but the disease did eventually take her. She died in 1992 at the age of sixty-two, nearly the same age Marcia was when she joined the 152nd Street Black Ballet Legacy Council with history on her mind.

Mamie's autoimmune disease would land her in hospitals throughout her adult life, once for an entire year and half. A young graduate student moved in to the third floor of their home to help watch over the children and soon became like a treasured family member. Mamie was forced periodically to accessorize her elegant ensembles with an oxygen tank and was beholden to a strict regimen of steroids and medications. Her body was tender, her organs inflamed. As a young mother, she had lacked the energy for young children and looked for activities to occupy her children's bodies and minds, which was how Marcia landed in ballet classes in the first place. Marcia was a jumping bean of a child, often told to sit next to the pianist until she could regain focus. But when she complained to her mother that her teachers picked on her, Mamie would say, "That means they're paying attention to you. Worse would be if they ignored you."

Mamie missed many milestones in Marcia's life—her wedding, the birth of her daughter, Alix, her rise to serve as dean of students at Columbia University and then of Harvard Law School, her appointment in 2021 as the Metropolitan Opera's first-ever chief diversity officer. In her first season at the Met, Marcia Sells sat in on a rehearsal for a new production, an adaptation of Charles Blow's memoir *Fire Shut Up in My Bones*. The adaptation had been composed by six-time Grammy winner Terence Blanchard, the first Black composer in the Met's 138-year history. As co-director Camille A. Brown rallied the room full of Black artists, Brown encouraged them all to avoid thinking of their upcoming performances through the lens of the audience's gaze. "We are sharing experiences of Black life with the world," she said. "As it should be. They are not watching us. We are inviting them in to share and see how we live and engage."

Marcia Sells sat in the audience on opening night of *Fire Shut Up in My Bones,* longing to be there alongside Mamie, basking in the gift of Black excellence. "I could just see her," she says, her voice breaking. "My mother would've so loved that night. She'd have rocked the place. I would have had to stand back."

Mamie Sells didn't get everything she deserved in life, but she did get to be a mother, which she had been warned by doctors would take a miracle due to her sarcoidosis. A ferocious optimist, she wore a mustard seed in a glass pendant around her neck to symbolize her faith in Jesus Christ. Glory would grow within her, she trusted. She had married Halloway Charles Sells, Jr., her minister's son, and the two had moved to Michigan, where Halloway received his master's in social work. They had then settled in Cincinnati, where he got his Ph.D. in sociology and organizational development. Mamie gave birth to Marcia in 1960 and two years later to Marcia's brother.

Mother and daughter were each other's favorite dates to dance performances and cultural events throughout Marcia's childhood. They went to see *Swan Lake* when the American Ballet Theatre came through Ohio. They saw Rudolf Nureyev dance in Columbus. They went to see the Cincinnati Ballet perform *Winter's Traces* to a Verdi score, taking proud note of Black dancer Dwight Hughes in the corps. They swooned at the ferocious talent of Judith Jamison performing with the Alvin Ailey American Dance Theater. They saw the Joffrey company perform at Cincinnati's annual May Festival, in a production that included Black dancers Gary Chryst and Christian Holder. With every performance, Marcia's fantasies of her future grew more extravagant. She imagined herself dancing iconic roles like Odette/Odile, the Sugar Plum Fairy, and the leads in Balanchine's *Serenade* and *Concerto Barocco*. She daydreamed about greeting her fans backstage, her arms heavy with roses. She was still young and well-loved enough to believe that even though she hadn't seen it, she could still be it.

BUT THAT FIRST NIGHT, when Dance Theatre of Harlem came to Cincinnati, Marcia sat next to Mamie in a sold-out theater at the local university, both dressed to the nines. When the dancers first appeared on stage, the girl's jaw dropped and stayed that way until the very end of their chest-thumper of a finale, *Rhythmetron*. "I just remember when the curtain came up and Patsy Ricketts was standing in the middle of the stage wearing the most immense cape in a golden-brown color," she says. "And then the rhythm of the music began. And the dancing that was all on pointe but also completely different from any other classical ballet I'd ever seen. It was electric and the audience was going berserk. I remember saying to my mother, 'Look at this! Look at this!' " That night ballet revealed itself as something neither mother nor daughter had previously known it could be—dramatic, theatrical, spiritual, Black in both color and core.

"I've been the only Black girl in my ballet school for my entire childhood up until then," says Sells. "And now here comes Arthur Mitchell. A Black ballet company on the university main stage in my hometown. Lydia and Gayle and Sheila! Suddenly nobody will ever be able to tell me it's not possible for me too. Even if my ballet school doesn't imagine that for me, I can point to that stage and say, 'Right there—see! Those women, right there, already having an impact, even as they're just starting the company.'" It's a night she credits with changing the course of her life. "Because I don't think I would've gone forward if I hadn't seen Dance Theatre of Harlem in 1970."

After the performance, Mamie took Marcia backstage to congratulate and mingle with the company. The dancers were sweaty and exhilarated, the men as handsome as any she'd ever seen, everyone shining through the stage makeup they hadn't yet had time to remove. Arthur Mitchell preening in the center of it all. This was the backstage life Marcia had always fantasized about, but she'd never before imagined everyone in that fantasy could be Black. In front of her, collecting roses and words of adoration, was Lydia Abarca, who was even more radiant up close than she'd been on stage. Marcia didn't know whether to stare or look away. Mamie told her to go introduce herself, which struck Marcia as preposterous. She was so in awe of what felt like new dance royalty that she'd sooner approach the queen of England. "I remember I saw Lydia and, forget about it," she says. "I couldn't even talk properly. Even at ten years old, I knew a star when I saw one." She did manage to murmur some words of dazed appreciation to McKinney-Griffith, who smiled down at the child with her beatific warmth and spoke sweetly with Mamie about the excitement of being in the company.

Marcia hung close to her mother, who'd joined a circle of conversation with Mitchell, James Truitte, and Thelma Hill, the University of Cincinnati's new Black visiting dance professors, who'd been instrumental in bringing Dance Theatre of Harlem to town. They had been founding members of the Alvin Ailey American Dance Theater and a couple of Mitchell's early Harlem faculty hires.

Since they'd arrived in Cincinnati, they'd been keeping a watchful eye on Marcia Sells, the only Black girl in the college preparatory ballet program. As a teenager in the 1950s, Hill had been one of five Black students at the Metropolitan School of Ballet, where she'd earned the lifelong nickname "Mother" for her nurturing temperament. She knew how lonely it could be for a Black girl in ballet, so she always encouraged Marcia to take sustenance in the careers of Raven Wilkinson and Janet Collins, to see the ballet technique in modern icons like Jamison and Carmen de Lavallade, who'd partnered with Truitte in the 1950s at the Lester Horton Dance Theater. Hill regaled the eager young ballet student with stories of her adventures in co-founding and performing with the New York Negro Ballet Company, whose one international tour in 1957 was cut unceremoniously short when the dancers ran out of money. Hill wanted this bright-eyed girl, who hadn't yet known struggle, to understand that the road ahead would be hard. But it had been traveled before.

When Mitchell joined their circle, Truitte made the introductions. Mitchell nodded down at Marcia, telling Mamie that he had taken notice of her in her dance class. "It looks like your daughter has some skill," he said, which, coming from Mitchell, was high praise. Mamie insisted he join them at their home for a family dinner the following evening after he'd finished giving a master class for the university's dance department.

Mamie invited Mitchell over for dinner for the same reason that McKinney-Griffith's family had hosted the company when it came through their town, with a potluck supper of dishes cooked by her mother's friends from the Methodist church. For them, in the Black communities they'd been raised in, it was just what you did. You gathered and offered warmth and fellowship and a safe space. "When someone like Arthur Mitchell comes to town, you're supposed to invite them," says Marcia Sells. "Because in the old days in the South, a Black person wouldn't have had anywhere else to go. My mother was born in Alabama, and my father was born in Oklahoma. This is what you did." At the time, though, she was horrified. "Ten-year-old me didn't understand this at the time like sixty-three-year-old me does. So ten-year-old me found the whole thing nerve-wracking. It was like the principal of your school coming over—like, oh my God, what are they going to be doing in my house?"

The Sells family lived in a three-story house on a picturesque cul-de-sac with two cars in the driveway, a library with built-in bookshelves, and a bay window that looked out upon an enormous apple tree. Mamie sat Mitchell and Lorenzo James, the former personal secretary and rumored partner of Montgomery Clift who by then served as Mitchell's confidant and right-hand man, at her elegantly appointed dining room table. Throughout the meal of Cornish game hen, wild rice, and brussels sprouts, Marcia sat riveted by the fervor of Mitchell's storytelling and his bright-eyed attention.

Over dessert Mitchell, who'd already examined Marcia's feet in the studio, declared that the next obvious step was for her to move to New York City to begin training full time at Dance Theatre of Harlem. He already had a family in mind for her to live with, and she could complete her education at the Professional Children's School on West 60th Street. Mamie gave Marcia's father a sideways glance, a near-invisible shake of her head. No child of hers was leaving for New York City anytime soon.

After the meal, the children were sent upstairs so the grown folks could talk in peace. The adults moved to the living room, which held a piano and a couch long enough for Holloway, with his six-foot-five frame, to take Sunday afternoon naps. After getting into her pajamas, Marcia crept down the stairs and peeked through the rails of the banister at Mitchell sitting in one of her mother's living room chairs, deep in conversation with her parents.

That night, with Mamie leading the charge, the group sketched out the initial plan for Dance Theatre of Harlem's next visit to Cincinnati. Holloway was the executive director of Seven Hills Neighborhood Houses, Cincinnati's largest social service agency, serving a socio-economically disadvantaged community near the University of Cincinnati. Seven Hills would sponsor a five-day residency for DTH, during which Mitchell would direct master classes at the university, and the company would perform lecture-demonstrations for inner-city children at over a dozen public schools, then dance on stage at Cincinnati's big Music Hall for a heavily publicized one-night performance.

MARCIA LISTENED for a while as all that business was sorted out in the living room, then retreated to her bedroom. She unfolded the three-panel black-and-white program on thick shiny card stock from Dance Theatre of Harlem's performance the night before. The copy included a quote from a piece that *New York Times* dance critic Clive Barnes had published four months before Mitchell started DTH. "Few Negro children learn classic ballet," Barnes wrote about the exclusionary gates to the art form. "This is probably because there are few chances for Negroes to make their way in classic ballet, and unfortunately, those chances do not get any greater, because there are so few Negroes trained in classic ballet."

Alongside the text, the program featured individual photos of the company members, the women wearing black leotards and pink tights and pointe shoes, the men in fitted white T-shirts and black tights. She taped it to the wall between her twin beds, so that she could look at dancers like Lydia Abarca and Sheila Rohan and Gayle McKinney-Griffith as she fell asleep.

At ten years old, Marcia had already transitioned to pointe work in her ballet classes. "It's like foot binding," she says. "This tight little box squeezing your feet. It's all blisters and bruises and calluses and losing your toenails. You start at the barre with simple exercises—bourrées, relevés—then you graduate to doing a little center work. It's all incredibly painful, but you start building up strength in your ankles and calves and thighs. You get some momentum, and you're able to stand on pointe and do the pirouette. You feel the actual physics of it all. Suddenly you feel light. Like *oh my gosh, I'm now a ballerina.*"

Still, she wasn't ready to leave her family for New York, not that her mother would've let her. But the following summer, at age eleven, she attended Dance Theatre of Harlem's first-ever summer intensive program for talented ballet students. She was the youngest child in the Church of the Master studio, dancing on pointe alongside sixteen-year-olds. Mamie did volunteer administrative work for DTH while Marcia took classes. They stayed in Thelma Hill's apartment.

6

⁓

I n 1970, Dance Theatre of Harlem left on its first major tour, a swing through the Caribbean that included stops in Bermuda, the Bahamas, and the Antilles. For many of the members, it marked their first time ever on an airplane. Arthur Mitchell laid down strict expectations for company travel attire. From the moment they stepped out of their apartment until they found themselves on the subway back home, he wanted them dressed sharp, their hair and makeup perfect. "When you get to the airport, you'd better look like you're traveling in first class," he warned, "because they're going to be expecting you to come to the airport with fried chicken in your pocket."

When they arrived in Bermuda, and the dancers were checking in to their hotel, nobody volunteered to room with Lydia Abarca. A splinter seemed to have lodged between her and the other women. There were no petty squabbles or acts of sabotage, but Mitchell had placed her on a pedestal, creating a distance between her and the other dancers. "There was a clique and then there was Lydia," says Llanchie Stevenson. "Arthur was trying to do everything Balanchine did, so he had to have his principal ballerina. Lydia was the Suzanne Farrell of Dance Theatre of Harlem."

She was the chosen one. She got the best roles and the bulk of Mitchell's attention. There was a sense that she could conduct herself in ways that the other women never could, like missing the occasional company class for a modeling job. Abarca still remembers Sheila Rohan raising her hand during a company meeting to ask Mitchell why Abarca could miss class but the rest of them couldn't. Watching him brush Rohan off in response, Abarca wished for the studio floor to swallow her whole.

That first tour, though, Stevenson volunteered to room with Abarca out of pity for the younger girl. "I felt so sad for her," she says. "We're both ballerinas. We can room together. And that was the greatest thing I could've done because Lydia and I became sisters after that. And how can you dislike your sister?"

IN BERMUDA, the company premiered their first Balanchine ballet, *Concerto Barocco*, which had been coached on them by City Ballet's Melissa Hayden. There's a moment in the ballet in which the principal ballerina, here Abarca, declares with an aggressive placement of her foot that she is superior to the second ballerina, Stevenson's role. In a conversation with the Legacy Council, Stevenson asks Abarca how she felt about her when they would perform the ballet. "Did you ever feel, when you put your foot down like that, did you think like, *Boom, I am the prima ballerina here. You might think you're so great, but I am better*?" The specificity of the questioning confuses Abarca. "Because when you watch the New York City Ballet," continues Stevenson, "Suzanne Farrell puts that foot down, and she's saying *I. Am. The. One.* Balanchine put that in her. But I never got that feeling from Lydia. Offstage, she was always like *Okay, here I am, little Lydia.* It's like we actually enjoyed dancing together. When we smiled, we really were smiling at each other. But I still always wondered. Did you feel superior in that moment?"

Abarca grimaces, waving her hands as if to ward off the very idea. Sensing her discomfort, Rohan steps in. "You know what I really believe?" she says. "Lydia never knew she was on the throne."

A muse is a source, not a star. She's chosen to reflect someone else's greatness. It's a role assigned, and one that comes at a cost. Abarca was always shy about Mitchell's anointing of her, nervous that the other women resented her position. How could she not be, with her mother's voice lodged firmly in her ear, warning her to keep her guard up?

"You can't trust these girls," Josephine Abarca would always tell her. "They're all jealous of you." Her mother's paranoia made Lydia sick. "I would say, 'Ma, stop it. Just stop.' Because I was living with these girls, I was sharing my secrets. And my mom's telling me, 'I can tell she doesn't like you. Don't tell them your business. They smile in your face, but they really think, *Well, how come she got that part?* You can't trust anybody.'"

But Lydia's experience had already shown her otherwise. About a month into the company's existence, she and Rohan were alone in the dressing room before company class. She had been out sick for a couple of days, and when Rohan asked where she'd been, the normally reserved seventeen-year-old surprised her by bursting into tears. "I've been in bed," Abarca admitted. "I had to get an abortion."

Rohan received the bare brick of news with quiet tenderness. "I thought you might be pregnant," she said. Abarca was stunned by her response. She hadn't started showing yet. How had Rohan guessed? The older woman just shrugged and patted the teenager gently on her back. She didn't press Abarca for details or question her decision. If anyone understood how a baby could recalibrate a life, it was she. "You did what you had to do. Now you can move on," Rohan reassured her that morning.

Rohan would keep their exchange private all these years, until a half-century later when Abarca felt compelled to share the story of her abortion with the rest of the Legacy Council. The recent overturning of *Roe v. Wade* had convinced her of the benefit of transparency. Nobody should have to deal with the physical and emotional trauma she'd suffered back in 1968.

Abarca had messed around just the one time with her high school boyfriend, she told the women. A couple of missed periods later, she sobbed on her twin bed at night while her brother, Julio, slept. "By then I was so excited by everything Mr. Mitchell was planning," she remembers. "*What do I do? What do I do?* I was the oldest of seven. I knew how much work it was to raise a child. I couldn't give up this chance he was offering me."

She remembers being given a pill by a friend who told her it would end her pregnancy, but all it did was twist her stomach into an exploding fist. Then a stranger came over to the apartment. The violence of a metal hanger. The nightmare of having to go to the hospital where police interrogated her in her hospital gown. She shares with the women the terror, the trauma, the guilt, and also the relief she felt as a teenager who just wanted to return to dancing, and her dream of a bigger life. Unanimously, the women are as loving and accepting of Abarca's story as Rohan was fifty years ago. She is safe with them.

HER FRIENDS' GENEROSITY of spirit then and now doesn't mean that Mitchell's anointing of Abarca didn't inevitably set her apart. From the beginning, she was the chosen one. The question of whether colorism might have played a role in that status still makes Abarca uncomfortable. "I never took somebody's part," she says. "I never asked for a part. Whatever I had was given to me, without asking. And if it was trusted to me, I did my best to make it the best I could do to please Mr. Mitchell." But two things can exist at once: Abarca emerged as a magical force in the company, as did Virginia Johnson, another favorite of Mitchell's, *and* their light complexions played a role in his anointing of them. The indisputable fact of their artistry can live beside the dreary truth that Dance Theatre of Harlem wasn't immune to an early prioritization of Caucasian beauty standards.

Former principal danseur Mel Tomlinson described the bias he witnessed at the company in his 2018 memoir, *Beyond My Dreams*. "It was hard watching some brilliantly talented ballerinas be passed over repeatedly for roles because they were too dark in Mr. Mitchell's eyes," he writes. But in the very same chapter, he rhapsodizes over Abarca's singular appeal. "Everything about her," he writes, "from how she moved her little finger to how she moved the souls of everyone who ever saw her, created an awe in me that I have never felt for any other ballerina."

In his interview with The HistoryMakers, Mitchell brushed off the accusations of colorism that dogged the company's early years. " 'He only likes the light-skinned girls,' " Mitchell parroted when asked about the subject, his voice heavy with impatience. "I said, 'What are you talking about the light-skinned girls?' I said, 'Sweetheart, you've got legs like a piano, no.' "

Indeed, Llanchie Stevenson felt Mitchell's lack of interest in her had less to do with her dark complexion than with her weight. "Lydia had the perfect body," she says. "Even though I had the technique and bah bah bah, I knew I would always be second fiddle."

At City Ballet, Mitchell had absorbed Balanchine's stern preference for ballerinas with pea heads on top of wraith frames. Clavicles popping out of necks like bicycle handles; tendons long enough to stretch beyond human limitation; all those thin, interchangeable buns holding back colorless sheets of hair. In earlier eras of dance, ballerinas were allowed curves and muscles, but Balanchine's taste for whitewashed slips of muscle and bone changed the art form's aesthetic ideal. Ballet still hasn't righted itself from his influence.

In Harlem, Mitchell may have preached about the importance of inclusivity on a classical stage, but he could be just as narrow-minded when it came to the female form. "On the one hand he's talking about Blackness and Black culture and beautiful Black bodies," says Rohan, "but in rehearsals he's talking about 'I want skinny, Balanchine-looking girls. Your butt is too big. You could get your leg up if you could lose the fat on your thighs. Wear a tighter bra to hold your breasts in.'"

"He was always slapping thighs," says McKinney-Griffith. "He hated butts. He wanted everyone what he called 'bone thin.' He could tell if you gained an ounce." After her abortion, Abarca started taking birth control pills that made her breasts swell. Mitchell noticed immediately and told her she needed to lose five pounds—which she did.

AND SO IT WAS Abarca, not Stevenson, whom Mitchell chose to dance the pas de deux in *Agon*, the second ballet Balanchine gave Dance Theatre of Harlem. During rehearsals, Mitchell was exacting on every detail of her performance, down to the placement of her pinky fingers. "In *Agon*, there's a part where I had to take my partner's hand," Abarca says, holding her own wrist to demonstrate. In cascading fashion, she languidly curls her fingers down upon her skin one at a time. "He'd say 'Finger, finger, finger. The audience has to see and think about what you're doing, what story you are trying to tell. You never just take your partner's hand! It's loaded. Do it with purpose and feeling.'" However shy and self-conscious she could be in everyday life, Abarca possessed a toughness in the studio. She could absorb Mitchell's criticism, his badgering, the furiousness of his attention, without it leaving a mark on her soul. "Hours and hours of private rehearsals with him," remembers Rohan. "I don't know how Lydia took it." It was because she hoped that since Mitchell had transformed himself into a star, he might do the same for her.

Early in the company's existence, Mitchell was talked into performing *Agon* for a one-time engagement in Atlanta, on a splashy bill that included Judith Jamison dancing her iconic sixteen-minute solo *Cry,* which Alvin Ailey had created for her as a tribute to his mother and the spirit of Black women. Mitchell chose Abarca as his partner and rehearsed her to death leading up to their performance. McKinney-Griffith recalls how heavily Mitchell's ego hung in the studio as he readied his muse. "This was his dream with Lydia. To be able to say, 'This is my partner. I've trained her. I've made her.' "

The *Agon* pas de deux is a test of extreme partnering. An austere tangle of body parts is set to Stravinsky's rhythmically complex music. The costuming is simple—a fitted white T-shirt and black tights on the man; a black leotard for the woman—so as not to distract from the intimacy of limbs braiding and stretching apart in dynamic lunges and sculptural shapes. There's a moment in Balanchine's choreography when the male leads his partner in a semicircle as if showing her off to the audience. When he first created the dance on Mitchell, Balanchine told him to picture himself like a trainer leading his prize racehorse back to its stall. That night in Atlanta, Mitchell's prize was Abarca.

On stage, Abarca didn't feel nervous or intimidated. "When I danced *Agon,* I felt sexy, aristocratic, in charge," she says. She understood the honor of being Mitchell's first and only Black partner in a pas de deux that had been considered so scandalous when he'd performed it with white women. "But we weren't making a political statement together," she says. "It was just pure dance. The crowd loved it. Getting to do that with Mr. Mitchell was so special, even though as a partner he was a little pushy. Like, you don't have to hold my hand so tight. I got this!"

OCCASIONALLY THE DANCERS saved money by shacking up in the family home of two teenage sisters whom Mitchell had scouted the year prior on a visit to Spelman College and recruited to join the company. Abarca was getting ready to fall asleep on the couch, when one of the younger male dancers, who'd cleverly set up his pallet on the floor beneath her, started flirting with her. They stayed up late talking and giggling. Abarca nicknamed the seventeen-year-old "Frog Legs" because of his spectacular jumps. Soon they were going for pizza after rehearsals. Having a boyfriend soothed her anxiety. She thought it would quash speculation that there was anything going on between her and Mitchell outside dancing. She needed that to be true.

Not long before that, Mitchell had escorted her back to Harlem after another evening of accompanying him to a fundraising event. He'd surprised her by walking her inside the Grant Houses. Pausing under the fluorescent lights in front of the first-floor elevator bank, he stunned her by planting a kiss goodnight on her lips. Abarca remembers leaving her body, before mumbling a few words of polite gratitude for a pleasant evening and escaping into her family's apartment. She spent a sleepless night in bed, trying not to wake Julio. Staring up at the ceiling, she replayed the unexpectedness of his brief embrace. "It was like my dad kissing me," she told herself. "He probably just meant it as like, *Oh I'm glad you came with me.*" She felt sick.

Balanchine had a troubling habit of marrying his muses. Vera Zorina, Maria Tallchief, Tanaquil Le Clercq. He so lost his head over Suzanne Farrell that when she rebuffed his passions in 1969 and married another dancer, he exiled her from City Ballet for six years.

Mitchell often spoke about how he didn't have the stomach for such scandals and intrigue. The fate of Dance Theatre of Harlem was too precious, too precarious. "He wanted to be George Balanchine without the scandals," says McKinney-Griffith. "We knew he was never going to marry any of us. He wouldn't jeopardize his dream like that." In all their years knowing each other, Mitchell would never have a frank conversation with any of them about his sexuality. Though after his death he'd be claimed as an LGBTQ icon by some, no one in the Legacy Council knows firsthand whether the man was gay or bisexual. They thought of him as married to Dance Theatre of Harlem.

But Mitchell's unexpected kiss rattled Abarca. "I mean, this guy was my boss," she says. "I tossed and turned all night about it. This man is too important to my future for anything to go wrong between us." She was terrified that anyone might speculate that she'd earned his favor for reasons beyond the dance floor. She vowed never to speak of the kiss—to her mother, to the other dancers, and certainly not to Mitchell.

But when Abarca finally did share the memory of that night with the Legacy Council, it allowed her to admit how much pressure she'd felt as Mitchell's muse. How it had made her throw herself recklessly into the arms of boyfriends who weren't safe or worthy but would at least spare her the threat of gossip. She didn't want anyone to think she'd ever gotten anything in life she hadn't earned.

The other women seem stunned at her admission, unaware of how isolated Abarca had felt. "Even when Lydia got every role, I always thought, *Well, yes, she deserves it. Good for you, girl,*" says Rohan. Abarca puts her hand to her heart and smiles with gratitude at her friend. As if she's waited fifty years for such validation.

IN 1970 Dance Theatre of Harlem participated in a week of showcase performances at Jacob's Pillow Dance Festival. The opening night audience treated the dancers to nine curtain calls, with the remainder of their matinee and evening shows playing equally well to full houses. "And what was extraordinary was for some reason people came to see us, and they came very skeptical," says Virginia Johnson. "And you could feel their skepticism when the curtain went up. But you could also feel when their hearts turned, and they were with you. And when that curtain came down at the end, they were standing on their feet cheering. And that happened over and over and over again."

Critics began writing about Mitchell's young company with a genuine sense of astonishment.

The twenty dancers were at once belles of the ball and tourists in a strange land. Says Abarca, "I just remember Melissa Hayden [of City Ballet] doing a pas de deux and then cussing like a sailor backstage. I was like a sponge. I'd never been around ballerinas before. Like, ballerinas do curse, okay."

"And they smoke!" adds Rohan. "I just remember all the men and women coming off stage and smoking. In the dressing rooms, backstage, everywhere."

Inevitably, one—or several—of the women ended up in tears after a performance. No matter how late they'd stayed up rehearsing, or how well they thought they might have done, Mitchell returned to them with scathing notes. Karel Shook, mercifully, had more of a filter. "You know it wasn't bad," he'd tell them. "But it wasn't good!" They wanted the dancers better, stronger, thinner, perfect. Shook zeroed in on the finer points of their technique. Mitchell pushed for more "Zah!"—that extra tension in a step that shoots energy out of a performer's limbs straight into the audience. He wanted his dancers to take up as much space as possible on the dance floor, be able to cross a stage in two steps. Announce. Enlarge. Electrify.

But however hard he was on their progress, the critics and photographers who'd traveled up from New York City and nearby towns were sold.

Said one critic: "This company of nearly twenty performers has obviously been beautifully trained, and we rather suspect, relentlessly. Good dancing isn't come by easily; and superb dancing such as this comes of long grueling hours of stress, strain, trial, and error until the fine finished product emerges."

Another reviewer marveled: "In a few years the Dance Theatre of Harlem will be able to mop up Leningrad, Moscow, London."

Dance critic Anna Kisselgoff declared, "No young company has made such progress in so short a time. . . . The troupe's members—some in their early teens—already have a performing presence rarely seen elsewhere and very much their own."

After reading reviews that referred to the miracle of his success, Mitchell was circumspect. "It is absolutely a miracle," he said. "But it's a miracle of purpose and dedication, not something that just happened and makes no sense. It is not a miracle for Black people to be fine classical artists. I have to laugh when people get excited about our dancers, as though a Black girl in toe shoes is a creature from outer space. Some of the reactions to us when we go out on the road are just incredible. People come expecting *Super Fly* and switchblades because, after all, it is Harlem. And then they see disciplined young dancers and they can't believe it right away. But it's not incredible at all. There were always Black classical dancers in America. They just never got on stage."

.   .   .

IN JANUARY 1971, Mitchell felt the time had come for Dance Theatre of Harlem to make its formal New York debut. Their three-night engagement at the Guggenheim Museum was sponsored by the heiress and philanthropist Alva Gimbel, of the Gimbels department store fortune. The elderly white woman had become an ardent supporter of Mitchell and his mission after attending an open Wednesday rehearsal at the Church of the Master. Sitting in the observation deck next to the actress Benay Venuta, she worried over the inadequacy of the cramped surroundings that the company had clearly outgrown. Afterward she summoned Mitchell and his treasurer De Rose to a private meeting in her suite at the Pierre Hotel. "What I want you to do," she told them, "is go out and find a building that you like and bring the information back to me."

Explaining why Dance Theatre of Harlem had become her favorite cause, Gimbel told *The New York Times,* "One of the reasons I wanted to help Arthur Mitchell is that I felt this was one solution to getting these young people in Harlem to have an inspiration in their lives. If they're going to be good dancers, they cannot run around, they cannot take dope, they cannot lie around, but must keep in perfect condition and work very hard." She invited the entire company to her two-hundred-acre garden estate in Greenwich, Connecticut. Clumsily eager to make her Black guests feel at home, she served a lunch of fried chicken and watermelon, which the women still laugh about today.

But Mitchell was going to take the money however it came. On a freezing January morning, a tip from a gypsy cab driver led Mitchell and De Rose to an abandoned garage and warehouse with two stories and a basement on 152nd Street between St. Nicholas and Amsterdam. As they walked through the hovel of a building, rats running over their feet, Mitchell said they'd finally found their permanent home. When he brought the news to Gimbel, she handed over a check for $110,000, saying, "I want you to cash it before my accountants know that I've written it." A $75,000 grant from the Rockefeller Brothers Fund went toward hiring architects; Mitchell booked the dancers for $70,000 of added performances. The renovations would take months to complete, but Mitchell could finally stop worrying about rising rents and hassles with landlords.

·   ·   ·

AT OPENING NIGHT at the Guggenheim, Gimbel preened like a hen, her silver-top cane in hand as she held court with her fancy flock of friends. A half-moon stage had been built in the museum's rotunda. There were raised seats surrounding it for the audience, and spectators could position themselves around the apple-peel galleries overhead as well. The dancers had been rehearsing in the museum all day, as Mitchell restaged their performance to fit the round stage.

"This was make or break," says Rohan. "Our launching. Mr. Mitchell was intimidating us, telling us how many important people were there, money people. 'This is it! I got all these reporters here. You guys are dancing for your lives.' We understood we needed to make the audience take us seriously."

When it was time for them to take the stage, the dancers had to walk through the audience, padding nervously on their ballet shoes across the cold marble floor. McKinney-Griffith's nephew Todd, dapper in his new three-piece suit, cut through the tension when he hung over the parapet of the museum's spiraling ramp and waved at his aunt and her friends down below. "Look, there's Patsy! Hi Patsy!" he called out to Patsy Ricketts, who was bunking with McKinney-Griffith on Maxine's pull-out couch at the time.

The company performed three pieces, all of them Mitchell's—*Tones*, the premiere of *Fête Noire*, a party-setting confection choreographed in Balanchine's neoclassical style that was dedicated to Gimbel, and the crowd-pleaser *Rhythmetron*, which highlighted Mitchell's intention to produce dancers who were as fluent in classical idioms as they were in contemporary- and African-diaspora-influenced styles of movement.

After the performance, the roar of the audience's approval shot up the spiral of the building. Rohan remembers that the largely white crowd was so enchanted that they reached out to touch them after their bows, as if to see if the dancers were in fact real, their wonder almost fetishizing. "These white people were treating us like we were touched in gold," she says. "'You're so beautiful! Ooh, look at your legs!'"

Rohan has a picture taken of her and Walter Raines, the elder statesman of the male dancers, beloved by all, in the dressing room beforehand. They're sitting next to each other backstage, both dressed in their simple pearl-gray costumes for *Tones*. His weary head rests on her shoulder, the front of his leotard soaked in sweat, while she sits drowsily upright, one of her arms resting on her knee. At the cocktail reception afterward, Raines broke down in tears, realizing for the first time that the company was going to make it after all.

TWO MONTHS LATER Dance Theatre of Harlem debuted its first Broadway engagement, at the ANTA Theater, which included a premiere of another ballet from the City Ballet repertory, Jerome Robbins's *Afternoon of a Faun,* set to a Claude Debussy score. "From the time the curtain lifted until it fell for the last time, there were vibes in that theatre that I've never felt before while watching ballet," wrote Colette Dowling for *Playbill* magazine, of the experience of sitting in a theater whose audience she estimated was about 25 percent Black people. "In short, the place was *alive.* This was no passive reception of sights and sounds but a kind of living, breathing participation, so strong was the involvement between audience and dancers. Among the bravos that followed each ballet were shouts of, 'Don't stop!' and 'Right on, brothers and sisters!' "

Abarca danced *Afternoon of a Faun,* a pas de deux about an intimate encounter between two dancers alone in a dance studio. Ripe with the bloom of beauty and youth, the man and woman gaze at themselves through an imagined mirror played by the audience. Robbins's ballet is as much about desire as it is about the curious fascination at finding oneself desirable.

To help Abarca unlock her character, Mitchell had asked his friend Cicely Tyson to help her feel the emotion beneath the choreography. Tyson urged the young woman to practice the movements at home in front of the bathroom mirror, taking notice of where and how her eyes moved throughout the piece. When she got in front of an audience, Tyson wanted the girl to be conscious only of her own imagined reflection.

Abarca was further helped along by having the ballerina who had originated the role with the City Ballet in 1953 as her personal coach. Tanaquil Le Clercq's spectacular career had been cut brutally short after she'd contracted polio in 1956 while on tour with City Ballet in Copenhagen. She remained paralyzed from the waist down, still living in the Apthorp apartment she'd shared with Balanchine until he'd left her to chase after

Suzanne Farrell. She hadn't been inside a dance studio in years until one day, she and Mitchell crossed paths at a restaurant in their shared neighborhood. Sensing that his former partner was floundering, he insisted she bring her knowledge and experience up to Harlem. After some initial resistance, she handed herself over gratefully, promising, "Whatever you want me to do."

Every day when Le Clercq arrived, the male dancers would lift her wheelchair and carry her up the narrow staircase where she would teach surprisingly ferocious classes, zooming around the wooden floor, demonstrating the steps with her one mobile arm. Even in a wheelchair, she had the darting energy of a hummingbird. When she noticed a break in a dancer's line, she'd whip her chair to their side, take hold of the dancer's leg, and roll backward with it until they were in full extension.

In *Afternoon of a Faun,* a documentary about Le Clercq's life, Balanchine's longtime assistant Barbara Horgan speaks to the emotional importance that returning to the studio had for her. "Frankly, the person who saved [Le Clercq] was Arthur Mitchell," says Horgan. "Balanchine never wanted her to teach at the School of American Ballet. She would have loved to have taught at the school. She would've been wonderful, could've done variation class. He didn't want her near the school. It would've been an embarrassment for him; he didn't want the wheelchair in the school. Arthur Mitchell is the one who said, 'Come on, come and teach for us.'"

In advance of the Broadway performance, Le Clercq was joined in leading rehearsal by Jerome Robbins himself, who loomed so large in Abarca's imagination from *West Side Story.* A photographer came to the studio to shoot them rehearsing as well. Antony Armstrong-Jones, Earl of Snowdon, then husband to Princess Margaret and a professional photographer, had adopted Dance Theatre of Harlem as one of his favorite subjects after attending an Open Wednesday. He captured an iconic shot of Robbins demonstrating how the man in the ballet is romantically obsessed with the woman. Abarca sits on the floor on her knees, dressed in pale tights and a black turtleneck over her leotard, her hair scraped into a high ponytail. Robbins crouches on his fingertips beside her, brushing her cheek so passionately with his lips, it's like he's trying to inhale her. Ignoring Robbins's kiss, she gazes upon her imagined reflection with erotic indifference.

Lord Snowdon was so smitten with Abarca that he later arranged for a photo shoot outside her projects, pulling up to the Grant Houses on 125th Street in a limousine. "All we knew was somebody by the name of Lord Snowdon was coming over," says Lydia's sister Celia. "Didn't know his first name. Suddenly he's just in our little kitchen surrounded by a bunch of us, looking around like he'd never been to a place like ours before. My dad didn't give him much thought. He didn't know about kings and queens and Europe. All he knew was that his daughter danced." Abarca has a Polaroid of herself sitting in between the queen's brother-in-law and her daddy on their family room sofa. Lydia has a shy smile on her face, holding her hands relaxed at her side with her legs crossed. Francisco, his mustache so trimmed it appears penciled on, stares unsmiling at the camera. Snowdon, dressed head to toe in dark denim, looks warily at Francisco, as if sizing the other man up and finding his own self lacking. He would spend the morning shooting Lydia walking up and down 125th Street for a European fashion magazine, while his driver gave her younger siblings a ride to Corpus Christi School on 122nd Street in his limousine.

Lydia felt like she was on the threshold of the life she'd long dreamed for herself. She began slipping out of her family's apartment at the crack of dawn in the morning after a big performance to race to the newsstand at the end of her block. "I'd tell the guy, 'Let me look for my name?'" Then she'd squeal and read the reviews aloud for him whenever she found it. On the day after the ANTA, she held her breath as she found her name again and again in the morning's pages.

"Especially entrancing as the girl who stirs a narcissistic ballet student (Clover Mathis) from his daydreams was Lydia Abarca, 19, a native New Yorker who has been dancing for less than two years," read the review in *Time*. "Lithe and feathery, she exuded a quality of virginal nubility—and she displayed the eye-commanding presence that is the mark of a potential star."

Abarca held the magazine to her chest, the wheeze of the downtown bus and squeal of the bodega's metal gate rolling up for the day like music to her ears. She couldn't wait to show her mother.

7

The company was on a sprint into public consciousness. After the Guggenheim and their Broadway engagement at the ANTA, they made a second swing through the Caribbean. Then came a two-week residency in Chicago. A day of free lecture-demonstrations on the campus of Columbia University for over three thousand inner-city schoolchildren, which was such a resounding success that the administration invited the company to return for an ongoing series. A transcontinental tour of the United States. All they did was dance, or travel from place to place, piled on top of each other on buses and planes, to dance some more. "I remember when we went to Buffalo, New York, in the winter," says Gayle McKinney-Griffith. "There was like six feet of snow, and we had to get off the bus in the night, unpack the bus with all the big bins of costumes and lights, then get back on the bus to check into our hotel where Mr. Mitchell says, 'There's a ten o'clock class in the morning, goodnight!' That was our reality day in and day out."

In May, George Balanchine extended a historical invitation to his former protégé Arthur Mitchell. He wanted City Ballet to share the stage, during its annual spring gala benefit at Lincoln Center's renowned State Theater, with Dance Theatre of Harlem. For the first time in the history of his company, Balanchine would present his dancers in tandem with another company's, a group of Black artists who'd been performing for less than two years.

In preparation for the event, Balanchine and Mitchell teamed up as co-choreographers of a new ballet, *Concerto for Jazz Band and Orchestra,* a piece that fused classical ballet idioms with boogie-woogie jazz steps. *The Tonight Show*'s bandleader Doc Severinsen and his jazz musicians would play upstage while the New York City Ballet Orchestra played in the pit. Twenty-four dancers from each company would meet and merge on stage: City Ballet male dancers would partner with Harlem ballerinas and vice versa. "That night was the turning point that made others consider us big league," says Charles De Rose. "After that is when the Bolshoi started coming to our rehearsals to see what everyone was talking about. A new level of competition had arrived on the scene—dancers with athleticism and technique and exuberance and freshness and something to prove."

IT WASN'T BEING strapped to the rocket ship of Dance Theatre of Harlem that tore at the seams of Sheila Rohan's marriage, though the demands of company life did cause a strain in the household. "He would have to pick up the kids after school or from the babysitters," remembers Rohan. "Sometimes I would try to cook in the morning, but if I didn't, he would have to cook. And he was doing heavy duty work as a janitor during the day, he wasn't sitting at a desk. There was tension, but we managed."

Ellsworth loved her dancing. He never once asked her to quit, not that she would have. "I was proud of myself," says Rohan, of making it as a professional dancer. "I was accomplishing something. I wasn't out in the street or working in McDonald's. The whole neighborhood was rooting for me."

But the childhood sweethearts had a history of separating and getting back together. Ellsworth had a wandering eye. When Charlene was four years old, she remembers her daddy coming to pick her up from her grandmother's house so he could walk her over to his new apartment. And when Ellsworth assisted his brother-in-law Romare on a work trip in California, he ended up staying for almost a year, missing the Guggenheim, the ANTA, and Lincoln Center. Rohan was tasked with holding down the fort on Staten Island with the three kids and a tour schedule that wanted to send her to Europe that summer for over two months—the company's first transatlantic tour. She had to find a way to make it all work.

The kids were divided up among family and neighbors. Gary went to one of Rohan's sister's houses up the street, Charlene to another sister. Little Sheila would sometimes stay with her Nanny Eliza or Ms. Barbara, the neighborhood babysitter, who lived so close by that the families could practically share a clothesline. The Markham Homes were Ms. Barbara's whole life. Until she moved to Cincinnati to live with her daughter in her eighties, she'd never been off Staten Island, not even to take the ferry into Manhattan. She was a tiny, feisty woman who never let the kids in her charge switch the television from her soap operas to cartoons. "We had to play outside rain, sleet, snow, or hail," says Little Sheila. "Ma would pay Ms. Barbara with Pall Malls, a six-pack of Meister Brau, and maybe some baloney and cheese sandwiches and tomato soup to feed all us kids." (Rohan objects to this recounting, insisting Ms. Barbara was paid in cash as well.) Continues Little Sheila, "Ms. Barbara would sometimes send me to the bar on the corner. My skinny little body, six years old, would open the door and head straight to the cigarette machine. 'It's for Ms. Barbara!'" Ms. Barbara was the only grownup who ever washed Little Sheila's mouth out with soap. Her picture still hangs today on Rohan's bedroom wall, next to photos of her grandchildren and great-grandchildren.

Rohan knew her kids were safe, but leaving them still scraped at her stretched heart. Wherever she went in the world, she worried about her children back home. She remembers one painful goodbye when Charlene, down with a cold, begged her to stay. "Don't go, Mom! Don't go!" her daughter cried. Rohan grimaces as she recalls the scene today, in a conversation with the Legacy Council, and her friends can now empathize with her struggle for work-life balance in ways they never could as young, childless dancers. "At the time I was coming to Dance Theatre of Harlem for the summer intensives," says Sells, "I didn't know then about Sheila having family and being a working mom. A ballerina having a child isn't such a big deal anymore, but it was huge back then!" The other women applaud. "You were a pioneer," says Abarca. "Somehow you made it happen."

AS THEIR TRIP to Europe approached, Rohan wasn't the only one in a flurry preparing to fly across the ocean for the first time. "We were all packing our bags, getting our outfits," says McKinney-Griffith. "This was the most exciting thing that had ever happened in my life." From the moment company members stepped out of the cab at the airport until they were safely out of Mitchell's sight back in their New York apartments, the dancers were expected to come correct, dressed in stylish clothes, with impeccable hair and makeup. "When we go on tour, people think the dancers are a group of models," Mitchell said later in an interview. "They're so beautiful. They have good taste. They dress, but they don't overdress. They have beautiful, marvelous bodies and can wear just about anything. Sure, I criticize them. I guess I'm against both the garret and garish looks. Poverty is where we come from. If you're beautiful, don't cover it up."

Cicely Tyson joined them for a portion of their tour, casting herself in the role of the younger dancers' academic tutor. Between Mitchell and Tyson, two celebrities whose entire careers were spent in service of breaking barriers in the arts so as to lift up their race, the dancers stayed on their best behavior for the entirety of the tour. "She was like the mother of the group and Mr. Mitchell was like the father," says McKinney-Griffith. "They were all eyes on us." Mitchell liked to brag that his young apprentices in the company had risen from D to B+ academic students once they'd come under his demanding gaze. Tyson was a rigorous tutor and, though she was encouraging of the dancers, an intimidating one. "You never stopped feeling starstruck around her," says McKinney-Griffith.

For the most part, the dancers took to the glamour of Europe immediately, but Abarca quickly crumpled upon their arrival in Italy, their first stop, pining for the safety of her family. Not even having her boyfriend, Frog Legs, on the tour with them could soothe her. "Oh God, once we left New York City, give me about two days, and you'd find me in a bathroom somewhere crying my eyes out," she says. "I would get so homesick. 'Where's Lydia?' 'In the bathroom crying.'" Mitchell called Abarca's mother in Harlem complaining that her daughter was depressed, and they needed to revive her. Unbeknownst to Abarca, he told Josephine to get a passport for someone in the family. They needed to come to Italy.

Not long afterward Mitchell told his dancers that the company's wardrobe mistress Zelda Wynn's knee had given out and she needed to return to New York for surgery—all true. Prior to her life at Dance Theatre of

Harlem, Wynn had become famous for designing gowns for the likes of Josephine Baker, Dorothy Dandridge, Ella Fitzgerald, and Mae West, as well as collaborating with Hugh Hefner on what would become *Playboy*'s iconic bunny waitress ensemble. She joined DTH when she was well into her sixties, running the department out of 152nd Street's brightly lit basement, where she always kept a percolator of hot coffee running and was occasionally known to sleep on her large fabric-cutting table. Wynn, so deeply beloved by the dancers, despite her habit of sticking them with her pins and then saying it was their fault for moving, served as the company's main costume designer for thirty-one years, until she died in 2001 at the age of ninety-six.

Mitchell took it upon himself to shepherd Wynn safely back from Italy to the United States, promising his dancers he'd return in no time. Unbeknownst to them, he would return with family support for his sagging prima. Josephine had chosen her son, eleven-year-old Julio, who was out of school for the summer and didn't have a job, to make the trip to Italy. Mitchell met the two outside the gate at JFK before their flight to Rome. Josephine would later tell her son that when she watched the plane pull away from the gate with her only boy, she was so nervous that her knees gave out. Julio, for his part, was terrified for the entire flight, sitting next to Mitchell, trying not to bleed his anxiety onto his sister's boss. "I'm not even the kid who was into roller coasters at the park," he says. "So I'm thinking to myself, *What am I doing thirty thousand feet in the air for seven and a half hours with this stranger?*"

The company's tour was set to begin with ten performances at the fourteenth annual Festival of the Two Worlds, a major cultural event that draws thousands to the ancient Umbrian town of Spoleto. The town sat on a foothill of the Apennine Mountains—as far from the Grant Houses or Staten Island or Maxine's spare sofa as the women could imagine. Cobblestone streets, women with silk scarves in their hair, handsome men winking at them from convertibles, gelato stands on every corner. "It was like being on the set of an Italian movie, it was so glamorous," says Rohan.

Abarca was in rehearsal one day, upside down, stretching her legs on the floor of the theater, when she heard a high-pitched ooh-ing and aah-ing in the hallway. Just as she righted herself to see what all the commotion was about, Julio burst through the door. She started sobbing at the surprise of having him in her arms, and her brother and Mitchell, who'd trailed in just behind him, sniffled right along with her. "I told Mr. Mitchell, 'You have no idea what this means to me,'" she says. "There was no way in hell my family could have ever come see us in Europe, and now here was my baby brother standing before me." Says Julio, "Everybody in that room was crying. They were so happy for me and Lydia. Although I was probably crying with happiness because I was just so glad to be off that plane."

For the rest of the trip, Abarca survived on peanut butter sandwiches, reserving her tiny stipend for Julio so he could enjoy restaurant food. He bunked in a *pensione* with Abarca's boyfriend, who at two years younger than her, was only seventeen. The boys would spend their summer jockeying for Abarca's attention. "Two's company, three's a crowd type of thing," says Julio.

THE FESTIVAL BEGAN soon after Julio's arrival. With Tania León conducting her first orchestra, the company performed *Tones* to a sold-out house. Recently Charlene found her mother a bootleg copy of their performance on the internet, and it remains Rohan's only recording of her dancing with the company. At the end of their performance, the crowd surged to their feet for a twenty-minute standing ovation, their voices united in a rhythmic chanting of *"Bis! Bis! Bis!"* Says McKinney-Griffith, "We thought they were calling us 'beasts,' but quickly learned it translated into 'More!'"

European audiences, so much less reserved than American balletomanes, waited in throngs to greet the dancers at the stage doors for their nine subsequent performances in Spoleto. They showered them with bouquets on stage or had them delivered to their dressing rooms. Some of the women took to wearing their flowers in their hair, thinking it made them look like Billie Holiday. "We were feeling like we were on top of the planet," says Abarca. "We felt so good, so special. Like real ambassadors, you know what I mean? It was like, wow, this is what happens when you demand a hundred percent of yourself."

After Spoleto, the company traveled by train for performances in Turin, Verona, and Florence, then up to Amsterdam and Belgium, before returning to Italy for vacation days in Rome. "I was on the adventure of a lifetime," says Julio. "We stayed in an apartment near the Spanish Steps. I threw coins into the Trevi Fountain. Went to the Colosseum, saw Michelangelo. We'd go on scooters down to the ocean where my sister bought me a little blow-up canoe. All those pretty girls in the dance company. I was infatuated with one of them, I tell you.

"But the best part of it all, to tell you the truth—hold on a second," says Julio gruffly, as he breaks into tears. "Sorry, every time I think about my sister dancing it makes me cry. The best part of it was getting to see her dance. She was so freakin' beautiful. I would watch her from backstage. You wouldn't think an eleven-year-old boy would be into ballet, but that's how special she was. She was the gift. Everywhere we traveled was just the ambience." His big sister was like liquid magic on stage, so pure and effortless under the lights. In between ballets, he'd watch her jam her inhaler into her mouth, desperately trying to open her lungs, then go right back on stage for another ballet. He'd never seen anything so heroic in his life.

To this day, whenever Lydia and Julio are together, the conversation inevitably turns to the surprise of getting to experience Europe together. The trip marked Julio's first and last time on a plane. He grew into a man so afraid of flying that he won't go anywhere that he can't get to in the comfort of his own car.

WHEN ELLSWORTH LEARNED the kids were being cared for under separate roofs while Rohan was on tour, he finally came home. "When my dad came back to Staten Island, he moved back into the house," says Charlene. "To my knowledge, my parents were back together. And that's when I remember the real shift in the home. Dad became the primary caregiver while Mom was traveling and dancing. I always say I learned to cook, clean, and sew from my father because he took care of us when my mom was touring. That was his sacrifice. He saw that my mother had a vision for her life, and he wanted her to do it. And he loved to watch her dance."

Some nights after local performances, Ellsworth would pick Rohan up at the theater in his old BMW. He never resented the beautiful men who spent so much time with his wife, embracing and lifting her up on stage. "Why would I feel jealous? I can't dance," he says. Through it all, he remained convinced of the value of her work. "A lot of that came from Sheila's family," he says with a laugh. "Eight women? I mean they'd have whupped my butt if I got in the way of her dreams. No, nunh-unh. It would have been ill-advised of me to try and stymie that kind of creativity. She had a true talent, and it had to be used."

On the weekends, their three kids continued their regular trips to the studio, at the company's new home on 152nd Street. The building had undergone extensive renovations, thanks to the grant from the Rockefeller brothers and donated performance fees from the dancers. "We needed everything," Mitchell would later recount to a group of students at Radcliffe College. "We couldn't afford to buy costumes, so I asked Singer to give us some sewing machines. I got the usual 'We aren't allowed to do that—you'll have to write a proposal' routine. I suggested they just loan me a dozen machines, which they did and which I still have. Then I went to several textile mills and discovered that they threw away the ends of bolts of material—sometimes as much as a hundred yards a swatch. I got them to donate the leftover fabric. With the machines and the cloth, we started a sewing and tailoring program. We also trained our own electricians, our own sound people, our own lighting technicians."

"Tell me I can't, and I'll show you I can" was Mitchell's motto. He had built himself a three-story response to all the naysayers who said what he dreamed couldn't be done. The company rehearsed on the top floor of their new home, in Studio 3, which mercifully had a fire escape where the dancers could catch a breath of air or dry their tears of frustration.

During rehearsals, they danced to the pulsing beat and slap of basketball and handball games on the Battleground playground courts just outside the brick-walled studio's giant windows. Mitchell claimed a narrow space tucked into a former elevator shaft for his office, just across the hall from Studio 3. Younger students rehearsed in two smaller studios on the ground floor, and then in the basement, Zelda Wynn set up her workshop, where neighborhood housewives joined her students on the rows of loaned Singers. The locker rooms were in the basement too, as was Karel Shook's office, from which smoke poured like out of an oven. "Sometimes he'd work in there in the dark, so you didn't always know he was in there," says Sells. "But then if I was sneaking in late to class, I'd see the ember of his cigarette light up, and the vapors of smoke, like out of some film noir."

The building allowed Tania León to finally create a music department at the school. Rohan would go up early on weekend mornings for rehearsals, Nanette meeting her kids at the ferry later as they'd grown accustomed, and escort them up to 152nd Street. There they'd hang out for the day and make the journey home later with their mother. Rohan's son, Gary, took León's percussion classes. Little Sheila, meanwhile, just six years old, got herself kicked out of ballet for her habit of running her mouth and swinging on the barre, but she studied violin and guitar with León. Though she spent the bulk of her energies asking for pony rides on Mitchell's shoulders, hiding under the company's designer costumes, and sitting on the ballerinas' laps in the dressing rooms, messing up their makeup.

"We just kind of had an all-access pass to roam the whole building," says McKinney-Griffith's nephew Todd who, alongside his brother, Kevin, started taking León's music lessons when he was six years old. "Which is really reflective of how safe of a haven Dance Theatre of Harlem was. The dancers took all the little kids under their wing and were always so happy to see us."

Sheila Rohan's older daughter, Charlene, had kept up with her ballet classes. She loved her mother's world so much that she took to spending entire days in the theater when the company was in season, listening to Mitchell yell—"Right! That's what I told you! You have to use your head!"—at his dancers. She saw how the other women would gravitate toward Gayle McKinney-Griffith in the hours leading up to a performance. "She never seemed to get agitated by Mr. Mitchell when he was barking," says Charlene. "She seemed to have this ability to calm the other dancers."

She and her cousins would watch rehearsals from the wings of the theater, nap in the shadows, and then wake up in time to watch the performance from backstage. Every season Aunt Nanette bought her a ticket to one performance so she could watch from the audience. Charlene's proudest moment was the first time she saw her mother dance in the role of the bride in Geoffrey Holder's *Dougla,* which depicts the elaborate wedding ritual between partners of African and Indian descent. "Mom was the one being showcased as the prima in that particular ballet," says Charlene. "The guys carried her onto the stage. Two men had her by the arms while she was in an aerial split, and they twirled all the way around. It was heaven."

When Charlene went to high school, though, she let ballet go. "There was always a level of angst in the room," she says. "You could tell the dancers loved Arthur, but they were constantly trying to get his eye and stay in his favor. That quest for perfectionism takes an emotional and physical toll." Today Charlene is a wellness practitioner working on her first book, about Black teachers in the yoga space. Her art is in the pursuit of peace, not perfection.

AT HOME, Sheila Rohan had started reading Dr. Spock, the author and pediatrician who was making headlines for encouraging parents to talk more openly with their children and show them affection. But Ellsworth wasn't interested in evolving his parenting style. He'd bang on the walls to wake the kids up in the morning. Set their alarms for early Saturday morning to start their chores. "My children thought I was kind of hard," he says now. "We made it work though. I think the one special thing about us is that no matter what we've gone through, we are family."

Sheila Rohan would go on to divorce Ellsworth when his running around with other women in the neighborhood caught up with him. Today he has eight children by four different women. At the same time that their mother started her Legacy Council Zooms, Little Sheila and Charlene organized weekly Zoom sessions with their five half-sisters, who've become like true extended family.

Through it all, Sheila and Ellsworth found a way to stay forever partners. The health of the family unit took precedence over any heartbreak. "We started as friends, we fell in love, and we continued as friends," says Rohan. "Family is the most important thing in our life. He's one of thirteen. I'm one of eight. Children are the roots. So regardless of whatever was going on with us, we kept the family together. We're soulmates."

After the divorce, they went on performing together at local events around Staten Island. Charlene remembers an event at P.S. 18, when she watched along with all the kids in the school as her father sang the Beatles song "Something" as an accompaniment to her mother dancing.

Something in the way she moves . . .

"Did she tell you how long I been chasing her?" Ellsworth asks on speakerphone, during a family dinner at the New Jersey home Rohan shares with her sister Delores. Their three adult children sitting around the kitchen table lean closer into the receiver, charmed by the flirtatious note in their father's voice. "I've been chasing Sheila since she was sixteen years old, when she sauntered into the backyard in that pink dress."

8

~~~

Three years in, feelings at Dance Theatre of Harlem still lived hot on the surface. Arthur Mitchell's stress level never came down. On top of his time with the dancers, he was learning how to keep schedules and record choreography and do payroll and continue producing the grants and proposals they needed to help meet their ballooning budgets. Every day was a fight to keep pace with the company's growth.

Now that the company was settling into its permanent home on 152nd Street, founding member Bill Scott, a young, brash, beautiful twenty-one-year-old dancer and choreographer who fancied himself a younger Arthur Mitchell, volunteered to step up as ballet master, the person charged with helping to manage the daily rhythms of company life. Impressed by Gayle McKinney-Griffith's calm demeanor, he asked her to join forces as his assistant. For her part, she would have preferred to concentrate only on her art. But the ask had been made, and the need for extra hands was so apparent. She split herself in two for the sake of the company.

Mitchell knew McKinney-Griffith was blessed with the ability to learn and memorize steps quickly, as well as having a little Juilliard training in styles of dance notations—a language to document human movement in symbolic representation. Even as she feared that he was overestimating the breadth of the skill set that she'd developed over a couple of college classes, he tasked her with capturing the choreography of all the new ballets he was throwing at the company. Suddenly, for large portions of the day, she found herself tucked into a narrow metal desk at the front of the studio with stacks of notebooks, feverishly recording choreography as it unspooled from the minds of Mitchell and the other great artists who worked with them.

As time went on, the constellation of her new role's demands continued to expand. She took over scheduling. She helped organize company rehearsals, ran them, and maintained the dancers' schedules. If Mitchell was displeased with a ballet's casting or a woman's weight or a dancer's bad attitude, he'd charge her with communicating that news to them. In her personal archives, for instance, McKinney-Griffith has a telegram from Hutaff Lennon in the costume department, sent while the company was on the road. "Dear Girls, Mr. Mitchell has instructed me to hold up on the issuing of pointe shoes. Please try to make do with what you have already been issued." Dancers on tour run through shoes like brushfire. When the shoe box wears thin, the dancer bears her full body weight on her unprotected toes. McKinney-Griffith pushed back on Mitchell to reconsider the seriousness of the ask, and he went ballistic. "He was just screaming at me," she says. " 'Do you know how much this all costs and you're complaining?' " He was too proud to let her know that when the company operated on a deficit, he was forced to dip into his own pocket to cover the dancers' salaries.

She was always being asked to do more, more, more. McKinney-Griffith remembers a time on tour when Mitchell burst into Bill Scott's hotel room, where the two were fine-tuning the day's rehearsal schedule. Mitchell exclaimed that he'd been invited to meet with some possible fundraisers at the last minute and was unprepared. "He said, 'I need to get some clothes! I need a haircut!' " McKinney-Griffith says. "Bill went 'Oh, Gayle will cut your hair.' Um, thanks, Bill. I cut some of the boys' hair sometimes, so I had my scissors with me. I tucked a pillowcase around Mr. Mitchell's neck. And I told myself, *Gayle, if you make a mistake, this is the end of your life.*"

Mitchell loved being described in an early profile by *The New York Times* as "a controlled maniac," and he never stopped referring to himself as such. And McKinney-Griffith could handle him in ways that the more outwardly ambitious Scott couldn't. When the egos of the two men clashed, she served as the breeze between them. There's a gentleness to the soft-spoken McKinney-Griffith that's not to be confused with fragility. She knew what was worth fighting for—the greater health of the company rather than anyone's singular grievances, including her own—so she spared herself power struggles that she knew she couldn't win. When Mitchell was on a tear, she didn't engage. When she needed him to look at a problem from a different point of view, she came at him indirectly, so that he wouldn't feel she was questioning his authority. "Arthur would never say, 'Oh you're right,'" she says. "But he might say, 'Well come back and we'll go over it again.' As soon as he said, 'I'll think about it,' I felt like I had won."

And there were wins, extraordinary ones. The women in the company had long relied on relaxers or on Murray's and Vitapointe and Dax to grease their hair up into high buns, which they'd then cover with do-rags to make lay flat. But the natural movement was in full, glorious swing. Black women on the street and in cinema had started embracing their curls and afros as sexy and free. "Cicely Tyson was wearing braids and afros," says McKinney-Griffith. "The rest of us said, 'Hey, we want to wear afros too.' We were tired of putting the grease in, and the spray and the pins. We talked to the guys in the company first and said, 'We want to see how our hair is naturally.' They were all for it, though behind our backs they were probably like, 'They're going to get killed.'"

McKinney-Griffith brought to Mitchell the idea of the women all picking their hair out. She pointed out that Rohan danced with her tiny afro and hadn't faced any blowback from the audience or press. But the idea of an entire company of ballerinas wearing their hair natural was too much for him. "Mr. Mitchell was like, 'No, no, no, we're not going to do that!'" she says. "I don't think it crossed his mind that we could wear our afros *and* be elegant. But we stood our ground. I told him 'It's not permanent, we can change it. We just want to see how it looks.' Plus, we were having lecture-demonstrations, and I was saying it would just be really great to relate to the students because they know afros." And so for a couple of years, the women of Dance Theatre of Harlem wore their hair free, though eventually they reverted to Mitchell's preferred chignons. He always won in the end.

WHEN SCOTT MOVED ON from the company, eventually landing for a brief stint as assistant artistic director at Washington's Capitol Ballet, McKinney-Griffith was left to manage Mitchell alone, taking on the role of the company's first ballet mistress. Within his office's narrow brick-lined walls, she bore intimate witness to all of his stresses and furies. Whatever triggered his upset—the perceived failings of one of the dancers, a board member daring to suggest how he should run a company that he'd built from the ground up, or the world in general for refusing to bend to his will—would rouse him from his desk, and he'd mount the hand-carved spiral steps that were bolted into the wall behind it, leading nowhere. Looming over her, he'd bellow about his various frustrations and condemnations, and McKinney-Griffith would silently endure his purge. Then she'd have to stand alongside him in the studio or theaters as he complimented the dancers or the visiting donors to their faces, and afterward she'd follow him out of the room and listen as he ripped them to shreds, often before they were out of earshot.

Whenever Mitchell was in a particularly ugly mood, McKinney-Griffith would beg someone else on staff to be a third body in the dungeon with her. She'd shoot the company manager, Richard Gonsalves, a World War II veteran who'd served in the Merchant Marine, a pitiable stare. Mr. G was the beating heart of the company, a fix-it-all who traveled with the dancers and took care of their rooms, luggage, crew, costumes. If somebody lost their tickets, he'd handle it. When someone was sick and needed to go to the hospital, he'd sit patiently alongside them. Tall, thin, and gentlemanly, he dressed conservatively in slacks and button-up shirts and spoke to the dancers in a soothing baritone and was always ready to stand with McKinney-Griffith when she needed him. If Mr. G was too busy to save her, she'd turn to Zelda Wynn, or Tania León, or Shirley Mills, Mitchell's beloved younger sister, who worked in administration and kept her temperamental brother in check by referring to him as "Junior." Should any of them "happen" to appear in Mitchell's office during one of his rampages, McKinney-Griffith knew to act like their mollifying presence was a coincidence, lest her boss feel ganged up on, which would surely turn his mood even more sour.

Through it all, she had to find a way to hold on to the joy of dancing for Mitchell, even as he revealed to her the darkest sides of himself. But listening to him speak so caustically about dancers whom she'd come to think of as her brothers and sisters wore at her spirit. "I was privy to a lot of conversations about casting, and it was just horrible sometimes," she says. "I cried for people. I would never tell anyone the disparaging things he'd say. Sometimes it was too much for me, and I would just become stone, listening to him with a poker face. 'This one's too fat!' or 'If she can't lose this weight, I'm taking her out of this!' I would have to try to make him see reason. I'd have to say in my most diplomatic voice, not too aggressively, 'Well, we only have a certain amount of people. You can't take them out.'" She'd studiously record his demands in her notepad, already strategizing how to convey his messages to her fellow dancers as diplomatically as possible.

Whenever dealing with Mitchell became too overwhelming, McKinney-Griffith would run to Walter Raines, Mitchell's first hire in the company, to ground herself. Raines was as kind as he was elegant, a contemporary of Mitchell's rather than his creation. He was the rare dancer in the company who called the boss by his first name. Raines had traveled the world before landing at Dance Theatre of Harlem. He spoke German and French. He knew everybody, traveling in the same elite circles as Mitchell, and he had a way of adapting his personality to meet the needs of every individual lucky enough to call him a friend. He and Rohan thought of themselves as the seniors in the company, the mom—or "Mamacita," as Tania León called Rohan—and pop to the younger kids. Raines also took on the role of patient tutor to León, helping her with her English on her assignments for NYU, where she was still a student. And he provided a stiff shoulder for McKinney-Griffith to cry upon whenever she needed it, while offering wise counsel on how to deal with their mercurial leader.

"Walter would listen to me rant on and on and on. He'd say, 'You know, Gayle, just go on and do what you feel. If you think that he's wrong, then he's wrong. Don't let him try to insult you. Don't argue with him. Just say your piece and leave.'"

OF ALL HER DUTIES as ballet mistress, the one she dreaded most was having to communicate to the other women Mitchell's dissatisfaction with their weight. "If I didn't tell this person that he said they were too fat for the role or that their costume didn't fit so therefore she had to lose weight, he'd say 'Well, what are you doing?'"

She watched helplessly as one of the dancers binged and purged herself into oblivion, the young woman believing that if she could lose her body's natural curves, Mitchell might consider her for principal roles. Even as the dancer shrank herself to ninety-five pounds, sucking on lemons and pickles for sustenance, he remained unimpressed. "She really thought that if she was thinner than Lydia, he would choose her," says McKinney-Griffith. "And I was like, 'No, no, no, there's a whole bunch of other stuff that comes with all of this. You're just depleting yourself. How are you going to get up there and do one of Lydia's pieces like this?' She was so thin and weak, she couldn't dance. I was trying to slap some sense into her, but she was too far gone."

On Dance Theatre of Harlem's first London tour, Mitchell discovered to his horror that the hotel had supplied each room with a tiny oven and delivered complimentary croissants to the guests each evening. "So one night he knocked on my door and said, 'Get your pad! Get your pad!'" says McKinney-Griffith. "I had to walk around the hallways with him while he went sniffing at the doors of each of the dancers. He could smell if the bread was being baked, and he would make me write down who was cooking and who he didn't want eating. 'Oh no, this one can't have that.' I just made scribbles; I didn't write anyone's name down. But I had to break from my time to go run around the halls of a hotel with him." The women quickly outwitted Mitchell anyway—they took their precious carbs to the men's rooms, where they could indulge in peace.

And being Mitchell's faithful ballet mistress didn't exempt McKinney-Griffith herself from his scathing tongue. Her sister, Maxine, remembers attending an open house performance when Mitchell commented admiringly on her petite frame. "Now, why can't Gayle have your body?" he asked Maxine, to which she responded with a withering stare. Her baby sister might have to tolerate this man, but she sure didn't.

Every day Mitchell used McKinney-Griffith as a vessel in which to pour his foulest moods in private. Then she'd leave his office and rejoin the company and think pragmatically about how best to help whoever was under his guillotine. "I would take it, and swallow it, and try and find my own way to help that dancer," she says. "'No, no, no, no. You've got to stand up. You've got to work harder on this. You've got to stand in the center.' I'd rearrange everything in rehearsals so that he could see he was wrong in his thinking, and that all these dancers were special."

She wasn't naïve. Not everybody could be the star, no matter how much their ego whined for recognition. "You felt for some, but you also understood that this is show business," she says. "This is a professional company that does not care about certain feelings. You can't get jealous of somebody else when you're in the company and you're doing your dream work and you're trying to better yourself. Your job is to be a part of the ensemble. Yeah, it was kind of disappointing when he always chose Lydia for the big roles, but I learned early on to tell the others, 'If you do really well, then you might be able to step into that part one day. Keep moving in the back of class when it's not your turn. Keep practicing relevés. If you need to bourrée in the center, then you better be bourréeing while you're waiting in the back.' "

McKinney-Griffith became a champion for the second and third casts, successfully arguing with Mitchell that more dancers deserved opportunities for advancement. "I would go in to him and say, 'Well, these people should get a chance to do it too.' But the first cast always got the rehearsal, while the second cast had to dance in the backside, never getting a chance to come forward. So he'd say, 'Well that'll be your job to get the second cast ready, and if they're not ready, then it's on you.' But at least I knew that I had the dancers' attention, and I had them thinking they can produce."

BEING DANCE THEATRE OF HARLEM'S first ballet mistress was one of the great honors of McKinney-Griffith's life. But it cost her too. Maxine still remembers the evening she found her sister sobbing on her apartment terrace after yet another brutal episode with her boss. That evening she wrote Gayle a poem she entitled "Consider the Source," reminding her that this man, while a visionary and a hero, was not her father or her God.

> *I can see you're discouraged sister,*
> *by a certain mister who directs*
> *The group of which you are a part.*

Maybe less is what he needs
to make you feel,
so he can feel greater than he
truly is on earth.

IT WASN'T JUST the emotional turmoil of working so closely with Mitchell that took its toll, though. It was the way the job cut into her own art. In the evenings, when the rest of the dancers packed up their bags to head home, McKinney-Griffith could finally pull herself away from her role as ballet mistress and remember that she was a dancer first. "It was so nerve-wracking, because I couldn't always rehearse with the group that I was supposed to be performing with the next week," she says. "I would always have to beg the men to stay late with me. 'Please, let's just run through our pas de trois or our pas de deux.'"

When asked now if her tenure as ballet mistress cost her opportunities as a dancer, McKinney-Griffith goes silent for a beat. While she considers her response, the other women chime in, flanking their friend's younger self. "No, she was too good," says Abarca.

And yet so much of her energy did go toward taking care of other people's business. And in acting as the liaison between the dancers and Mitchell, she would often become the target of his ire. Marcia Sells is adamant that the dancers would've united on McKinney-Griffith's behalf had Mitchell ever tried to punish her over tensions that arose between them. "He couldn't have done it. She was too good, like Lydia says. I have to believe if it ever really came to that, there'd have just been too many of us that would have stood up for her." Echoes Karlya Shelton, "He couldn't have denied Gayle. She was a technically amazing, beautiful ballerina with all these incredible nuances."

Smiling graciously at her friends' support, McKinney-Griffith is sanguine on the matter. "I didn't feel denied, but I was so involved with the present of everything we were doing. Sometimes when we were casting, I would feel like I could have done one of the ballets that he never considered me for." When she'd suggest herself for a role, he'd usually cut her off with a quick "nah," without even looking up from his paperwork. She pleaded with Mitchell to consider her for *Le Corsaire,* in the pas de deux that's one of the most famous in the classical ballet repertoire. Each time he'd brush her off, insisting she wasn't yet ready. He had it in his head that the purple tutu that the dancer Laura Brown wore in the role wouldn't suit McKinney-Griffith. "He wanted me in harem pants instead for whatever reason," she says. "So that's how he kept me at bay. 'I've got to get this new costume.'" When Mitchell finally surprised her with the opportunity to don Brown's purple tutu for a matinee show in front of a small audience, she remembers fumbling her performance. "I'd been trying to rehearse at night, but my partner, Paul Russell, didn't want to stay late," she says. "He was such a great partner that I hoped it wouldn't really matter. But that day I messed up my solo. Brilliantly."

Ultimately, her greatest roles never came from Mitchell, but rather from outside artists who recognized her potential and had no qualms about potentially distracting her from her ballet mistress duties. James Truitte and Carmen de Lavallade, the original stars of Lester Horton's *The Beloved,* set the ballet on Dance Theatre of Harlem. They chose McKinney-Griffith as their star. De Lavallade, a dancer of such refined elegance and the wife of Geoffrey Holder, worked with her on the role of the abused wife wrongly accused of infidelity, while Truitte and Raines dissected the role of the rageful husband who ultimately chokes her to death. Her gentle friend Raines brought a Method approach to the part. "I remember coming up to Walter before showtime, and he was stalking the backstage. I touched his arm, and he yelled, 'Do not bother me! I do not want to see you until after the show!' I backed away from him slowly, thinking he was going to kill me." On stage, he pulled and threw McKinney-Griffith violently around by her arms. It was a beautifully choreographed piece, the memory of which would haunt her in the future.

But of all of McKinney-Griffith's roles, her friends hold up her pas de trois in *Forces of Rhythm* as a perfect union of artist and material. Louis Johnson, who'd studied at the School of American Ballet with Mitchell, was a genre-crossing choreographer for Hollywood, Broadway, and the classical stage. The former ballet dancer, who taught by flowing, bounding example, was coming into the studio to cast what would become one of the company's signature ballets for years. "Mr. Mitchell told me that we were going to have a new piece, and Louis Johnson was the chore-ographer, and I was to do all the notation," she says. So she assumed her familiar position at her desk, ready to record his choreography.

But to her shock, Johnson called her to the center when he was casting what would become the ballet's iconic pas de trois. "I wasn't warmed up. I was just sitting there writing away. But then Louis said again, 'Gayle, come on over here.' My heart was fluttering. A dancer always walks on eggshells because sometimes a choreographer will say, 'Step in here and do this,' and then change course. 'Okay, no, not you. You over there, come step in.' You don't want to ever get too attached."

She glanced over at Mitchell before setting down her pen and note-books. Johnson paired her with two of the male dancers, Homer Bryant and Derek Williams. He looked at McKinney-Griffith through his squint-ing eyes and told her, "Your character is searching, searching. I want you to run over to this side of the room, and pause, curious, then run over to the other and do the same." Something in her grace and yearning spoke to him. He had found his ballerina for the pas de trois, which he set to Donny Hathaway's version of "He Ain't Heavy, He's My Brother." The song is a bath of feeling, from the opening strains of piano to the stroking vel-vet of Hathaway's voice. *The road is long, with many a winding turn.* "Her style, Hathaway's voice, it was the perfect pairing," says Shelton. "Soft, delicate, and so strong at the same time."

In video clips, there's an exquisite sense of hesitation and longing to McKinney-Griffith's performance, as her character struggles to choose between two different paths in life, represented by her partners Williams and Bryant. She flutters like a sparrow in a simple white leotard and bal-let skirt, gently careening back and forth between the men as the music throbs to its crescendo. With one last longing look at Bryant, she turns away from him at a run and jumps. She appears to levitate backward as Bryant comes in underneath her and lifts her by her seat straight over his head. After that one gravity-defying motion, she perches delicately in the air, sitting upright atop the palms of Bryant's hands like a cloud. The famous sit lift tested her core strength—she had to somehow lean backward, with arms outstretched, without toppling over her partner's backside—as much as her courage. "We rehearsed that until we knew it in our sleep," says McKinney-Griffith. "Once the guy locks his arms in, you can lift up and open your arms. But before that you can't do anything. I've seen a dancer go over the head onto the floor before. But Homer never dropped me, not once."

McKinney-Griffith's nephew Todd, who by then had moved from León's music classes to the downstairs dance studio, went to all his aunt's New York performances. He remembers waiting breathlessly in the audience each night for the sit lift. "That was always the applause moment," he says. "The music would swell, and all of a sudden my aunt Gayle would be up in the air, and you wouldn't know how she got up there. She'd just be this ballet angel goddess sitting on top of a guy's hands. You would hear the whole audience gasp, and everybody cry 'Ohhhh!'"

To this day, McKinney-Griffith can't hear "He Ain't Heavy, He's My Brother," a song of gratitude for worthwhile burdens, without choking up. It transports her back to the wings of a theater, where she'd wait for her pas de trois. "I always felt my heart bursting out beforehand because it felt like the women on stage were calling me. Then I'd have a lump in my throat the whole time I was dancing from the weight of what was being sung. The verses. The lyrics. Louis knew how to combine classical music with contemporary so that it touched your soul. And he could dance every part. If he could've had a strong enough partner, he would've done the sit lift himself."

In 2020, Louis Johnson, acclaimed choreographer, dancer, and director, died at the age of ninety after testing positive for Covid. For all his professional triumphs, Johnson never got the opportunity he deserved to display his talent as a ballet dancer. Upon his acceptance into the School of American Ballet, the administration warned that they would never let him into City Ballet. "I don't talk about it much," Johnson once told a reporter. "But I knew it was because I was Black. I would love to have danced ballet more than I did because that was what I did so much of my life, and never got a chance to do it for the public. You say to yourself, *Gee, I wish people could have known I did that, and I really did do it well.*"

McKinney-Griffith, for her part, still remembers the nervous thrill of hearing Johnson call her name that day in Studio 3, rousing her from her scribbling. "I'll never stop being thankful for it. Because that was it for me—the epitome of dancing. I was okay after that no matter what. I'd made it. I was in heaven."

9

"The evening's honors went to Lydia Abarca, a lovely young dancer who could easily be a fashion model should she so desire. Well-partnered by Derek Williams, her Balanchinesque body, long-limbed and slender, easily assumed the proper line of the choreography."   —*Evening Bulletin*

"Abarca appears on stage like a Modigliani creation, combining a child-like vulnerability with finishing school gentility."
                                                                          —*New York Woman*

"A siren to stop all traffic."   —*Chicago Sun-Times*

"When Miss Abarca, an alluring young ballerina, appeared on stage, her artistic charisma electrified the audience."   —*Daily Defender*

"Undoubtedly, Miss Lydia Abarca is the unbilled prima ballerina here, displaying incredible fluidity, pin-point perfection in her bone-cracking extensions, as well as a lovely sensuality, too. Pure visual joy."   —*Philadelphia Daily News*

L ydia Abarca had to do a double take when she passed the news-stand on her way to the subway. It was January 1973, and she was on the cover of *Essence* magazine. She had signed with a model-ing agency named Black Beauty and was booking regular print jobs. But

Essence had hired her as a hand model for an inside article in its special issue celebrating Black love. "But then I'm walking down the street and I see me on the front of the magazine," she says. The cover showed her bare back and the profile of her face in a romantic embrace with a male model. "So I called the agency and I said, 'Excuse me, can you call *Essence* and ask if I get any extra money for that?'" They paid her an extra $300, which to her felt like gold.

Abarca didn't grow up like so many of the other middle-class girls in the company. They had doctors and dentists and professors and engineers for parents. "They grew up in homes with an upstairs and a downstairs," she says. "To me that meant you were rich. I remember the first time Gayle invited me to her parents' huge home in Connecticut for the weekend. When we walked inside the door, the first thing I blurted out was, 'You have an upstairs!?'" When she went on a road trip from New York to Florida with a few of the women in the company, they stopped along the way in Augusta, Georgia, to stay overnight with one of the dancers' families. "We went down this long driveway, and I'm looking at the building and I say, 'Well, where's your apartment?' And she said, 'No, that's my house.' I was so embarrassed. I didn't know people had houses like that."

Abarca wanted that for herself and for her parents, who had given her everything they could for a shot at a bigger life than theirs. "We never wanted for anything growing up," she says. "But here's Lydia with these dreams in her head, always wanting more. I wanted to buy my parents a house. Get us out of the projects. I wanted a car, you know, regular stuff. I didn't want to have to live with roommates for the rest of my life."

But five years into her career at Dance Theatre of Harlem, with all the accolades that had piled up at her feet, she was making only $25 a week more than what Mitchell first offered to pay her if she quit the bank. She didn't have a nickel for a savings account. Even when Revlon selected her as one of its original Charlie girls—alongside the first female jockey, Mary Bacon, and Alice Cooper's girlfriend Cindy Lang, whom *Interview* magazine dubbed "America's First Lady of Rock and Roll"—Revlon paid DTH instead of her.

"It was only when I was dancing that I felt like a star," she says. "Then to come off the stage to my little life was always shocking. I'm in the first successful Black ballet company. We're doing legitimate ballets, not some made-up dance recital stuff. But nothing changed. Maybe if I'd had a publicist or a manager who could have looked at me and said, 'Okay, we can do something with her. She's a commodity.' But the commodity was always Arthur Mitchell. This was his dream. And I understood that. My allegiance was always to him and to Dance Theatre of Harlem. But couldn't I have high hopes for myself too?"

Not according to Mitchell. His stated agenda was to lift the whole company rather than spotlight an individual. If there was going to be a star of Dance Theatre of Harlem, it would be him. To separate her ambitions in any way from him or the company could be seen only as a betrayal.

MEANWHILE, LLANCHIE STEVENSON'S DREAM was to have Mitchell look at her as he gazed upon Abarca. She yearned for a shot at the *Agon* pas de deux—"that's the prima ballerina role," she says—but Mitchell never let her do it. She was over thirty years old by this point, tired of the travel and the hustling and the knowledge that the best roles would stay out of her reach. "The other dancers were all up to my level and past me now because I started getting lazy and tired of the whole ballet thing," she says.

And yet it was then, when she was feeling her most invisible to Mitchell, that Stevenson revolutionized the way Black ballerinas looked on stage forever. Traditionally ballerinas had always danced in tights and shoes that were the palest of "European pink," meant to enhance the illusion of women dancing on their toes without any shoes. At the time, ballet shoes came in just two shades—Capezio Pink and Freed Pink. Stevenson had taken to dying the straps of her tutu brown while she danced in the National Ballet, so the pale slashes of fabric wouldn't interfere with the line of her neck and shoulders.

At Dance Theatre of Harlem, she took it one step further, layering brown tights with the feet cut off on top of her ballet pinks in class until her muscles warmed up. The result, however unintentional, was stirring. "Wait, my arms now match my legs!" says Stevenson. "All of the sudden, I'm connected. I'm a whole body instead of half of one. Soon I couldn't rehearse without them. I couldn't do the three pirouettes on pointe if I wasn't in my brown tights!" The other women in the company were delighted with the visual effect. "Brown tights pulled our lines out," says McKinney-Griffith. "It made us look slender. Llanchie and I used to talk, saying 'Look at my thighs! Look how great!'"

Mitchell so admired the uninterrupted lines of his dancers that he would eventually adopt brown tights and shoes as company-wide practice. They began a European tour in pink tights and completed it in flesh tones, declaring to the world that the lines of the Black body deserved the same care and respect as those of their white peers.

Once they were back home, the dancers began a ritualistic process of going through Wynn's meticulously calibrated colors of dye and tea leaves to find their own unique shade. Before every performance, they would use makeup powder on their shoes to ensure they still matched their tights exactly, just in case a snatch of pink was sneaking through the dye. After every show, they would spray shellac or Future floor wax inside their shoes and around the box and shank and let them dry and reharden overnight. Expanding the aesthetic of ballet wasn't an abandonment of tradition, they realized, but an act of vital expansion and inclusion.

But Stevenson, who was never credited publicly by Mitchell for her innovation, was stalling out in the company. "I thought if I had Gayle's feet, I would be so much stronger," she says. "Or Sheila's strength and how she could jump and leap. If I had Lydia's extension and body, maybe Arthur would look at me more." She convinced herself the problem was her weight. "So many dancers came into the company, and he'd tell them to lose ten pounds immediately. I thought if I was thinner, I would get more roles."

She turned to Nation of Islam leader Elijah Muhammad's book *How to Eat to Live,* thinking it would help her lose the weight and catch Mitchell's eye. But what it did instead was introduce her to a different higher power. She started attending Nation of Islam meetings, whose tradition prohibits women from dancing uncovered in public. She fell in love with a lawyer who accompanied Dance Theatre of Harlem on tour as a tutor, and after he converted to the Muslim tradition as she had, they married.

Today Stevenson, now Aminah Ahmad, speaks of quitting Dance Theatre of Harlem in 1973 with a sense of palpable relief. "With Arthur, it was never perfect," she says. "The pressure that was put upon us was so intense. No matter how well you danced, there was something else he thought you could've added. You never got to feel like *Oh, I made it!* He kept our egos down by wanting so much more and more and more all the time. I'd realized there was a superior entity that was above all that. When I did an arabesque, it was this entity that was holding up and helping me. 'You're not the one making me do the arabesque or three pirouettes on pointe. You're no longer the end-all, be-all master of my life.' In that case I couldn't accept Arthur's criticism anymore. So that was the end for me."

THAT SAME YEAR, on the Sunday before Valentine's Day, twenty-three-year-old Lydia Abarca married Frog Legs, Julio's nemesis from their summer in Europe. In interviews from around this time, she'd begun acknowledging the "pressure being one of the few Black ballerinas" and the need to always play the part of "poised prima." She hoped marriage could provide a stabilizing anchor to her life of constant striving. "I just wanted what my mom had," she says. "I wanted someone that loved me like my daddy loved my mother. She'd give him a can of SpaghettiOs, and he'd say 'Oh, your mother is such a good cook.'"

With Mitchell standing up as the best man during the ceremony, the young couple married at the Convent Avenue Baptist Church. Abarca borrowed her cousin Iris's wedding dress from the previous year, and her five sisters reused Iris's floor-length red velvet bridesmaid dresses. Abarca has a picture of the modest reception that was held in Studio 3, in which she's sitting on a chair between Mitchell and her new husband. She looks so radiant and full of hope, her face framed by her cousin's veil. The men stare past her at each other, smirks for expressions, as if deciding between themselves who has the right to remove her garter belt. Years later Celia would confess that she heard Mitchell remark to another guest at the reception, "I should've married her instead."

After the wedding, Abarca moved with her new husband into an apartment up in Riverdale. But just a few months later, he dropped out of the company to work full time for his father's trucking business, which moved people's residences from New York to Florida. He started leaving for weeks-long stretches on the road. On one of his returns, he brought home a German shepherd puppy named Bruno that scared Abarca and aggravated her asthma. She began and ended her days after that by being dragged around their apartment building by a dog she'd never wanted.

Soon her husband began returning from his trips itchy with resentment and insecurity. He wanted to know how she spent her time when he was on the road. After one trip, he met her back at the apartment and demanded to know why she hadn't answered the phone the night before. When she told him that Hutaff had taken her out dancing at a gay bar, he hit her in the face. "It was a big hard slap," she says. "I guess he thought I was supposed to be sitting at home and taking care of the dog while he was gone."

In the morning Abarca went to stay with her grandmother. She was done. The next time he left for Florida, she moved all her stuff out of the apartment. The marriage had lasted less than a year, though it would take her another two years to save up the money for a lawyer's fee to pay for a divorce. "Honestly, I was relieved," she says. "I hate how it ended, but it was never going to last." Abarca had been looking for a port in the storm, a sturdy and reliable force against the tidal wave of pressure that came along with being the prima. She'd wanted someone like her father. But this man was no Francisco Abarca.

And how Francisco loved his daughter, even as he didn't understand her new world. He came to see her dance just once. The company was performing at Brooklyn College, where Francisco worked as a custodial engineer. Abarca was dancing the principal role in William Dollar's *Le Combat,* playing a warrior during the Crusades who conceals her gender as she seeks to avenge her brother's death. In the climactic scene, Abarca and her partner, Paul Russell, who would soon leave the company over creative clashes with Mitchell, engage in a swordfight that mortally wounds her. "I'm on the floor, and I take my helmet off and throw it," she says of the drama on stage. "Paul's character has fallen in love with me so when he realizes it's me, he's like, 'Oh my God, what have I done!' He picks up my body. I start quivering and finally die. Devastated, he starts swinging my limp body around. I'm telling you, every time the audience just went crazy."

As his daughter died on stage, Francisco gripped Josephine's arm, his cheeks damp with tears. Later, he would nod solemnly at Abarca: "Very good, Mama."

But of all Abarca's family members, it was her sister Celia who most loved to watch her dance. "I don't think I ever missed a performance," she says. Before Dance Theatre of Harlem, she knew nothing about ballet or classical music, beyond her parents' record of George Bizet's *Carmen*. Seeing her sister on stage opened a whole new world to her. Every time she'd go to the theater, she'd look for Lorenzo James in the lobby, who'd be waiting for her with a loose ticket in his hand. She'd take her seat by herself in the audience, where she'd only have eyes for her big sister. "To see Lydia on stage? I can't express the pride I felt. After it was over, I'd hear people yelling behind me, 'Bravo! Bravo! Bravo!' She'd be the last one to come out and take her bow at the very end. 'Bravo! Bravo!' And I would see her looking for me in the audience, because she knew I was out there somewhere. And every now and then she would find me, and she would lock eyes with me and give me a wink or a little smile. I'd be saying to myself, *They're all loving her, all these people. And she is mine. She is my sister.* Then we'd get on the train together to go home from the City Center or wherever, because we didn't have money for cabs, and she'd still have all her makeup on and be carrying her bouquets of flowers. And it'd just make me so proud. Here I am with this beautiful person on a train full of bums."

Celia went to the ballet because she loved her sister. What she didn't expect was to fall headlong in love with classical music. She started taking the train down to the Lincoln Center library on Saturdays, where she'd check out CDs of the music she'd heard at the theater. During the week, when she wasn't in classes at the John Jay College of Criminal Justice, or working at her new job at the hospital, she'd listen to Tchaikovsky's *Allegro Brillante* and *Serenade for Strings* on repeat over and over and over, transported by the sweep of his overtures. She'd go on to raise a daughter who studied the classical violin for fifteen years, a lived lesson that Arthur Mitchell was right. Ballet is for everyone. The classical arts belong to all of us.

BY 1974, Dance Theatre of Harlem was working six days a week, forty-eight weeks out of the year. Mitchell decided his young company was finally equipped to face critics and audiences in England. "I didn't bring them to London before because I did not think they were ready," he told *The London Times* before their debut at Sadler's Wells. "It is a very young company, many of them only started to learn dancing five years ago. We have a girl only just fifteen, and a boy who has been dancing only one year." But clearly they were ready now. For DTH's three-week season, the theater was sold out to the rafters at 113 percent attendance. After breaking its box office record, Sadler's Wells invited the company to return to London for another week on the back end of its tour, following performances in Oslo, Helsinki, and Belgium.

And then that November the company returned to the UK for a spectacle above all the others. They performed excerpts from two ballets, Mitchell's *Spiritual Suite* and Holder's *Dougla,* in the Royal Variety Show before the queen mother at the London Palladium. The dancers performed in between sets by the comedian Ted Rogers and the singer Perry Como. Much to their awe and excitement, Josephine Baker, one of the marquis performers on the bill, visited with the women in their dressing room during rehearsals, treating them to an impromptu concert of songs in different languages. "She told us how beautiful she thought we were," says Sheila Rohan. "She also wanted to borrow a hairbrush, which I immediately jumped up and gave her mine. She returned the brush with a few strands of her hair. I took them out and put them away. I kept them for a long time. Before the show, I remember she was standing in the wings waiting for her cue, leaning against the wall like an old lady. As soon as the music came on, she stood up, put on her famous headdress, and walked out on the stage like a goddess." Less than a year later, Baker would slip into a coma during her sleep and die at the age of sixty-eight.

Everywhere they went seemed an opportunity for new wonders, but the pace of their touring schedule was putting Abarca's asthma to the test. Ballets like *Le Combat* and Balanchine's *Concerto Barocco,* in which Abarca danced in all three acts, had her lunging for her inhaler backstage. "I call my asthma 'Miss Wheezy,' and if she showed up during a ballet, I would try my best to ignore her," she says. Sometimes Abarca would come off stage almost retching, unsure how she would muster the strength to return for her bows.

Her struggle continued once they were back in Harlem. She remembers one Sunday Open House at 152nd Street performing in front of a community audience that included her grandmother, feeling weak and hot, her legs noodling beneath her. She fell during a lift. She thought it was her asthma acting up again, but overnight her fever rose to 103, with a headache so bad it had her seeing stars.

At Columbia Presbyterian Hospital, doctors diagnosed Abarca with bacterial pneumonia. In between bronchoscopies and breathing treatments, she had no choice but to let herself rest. Lorenzo James, acting as Mitchell's emissary, brought flowers to her hospital room. Cicely Tyson visited at her bedside, leaving a copy of the children's novel *Sounder,* the movie adaptation of which had earned her an Oscar nomination, on the side table.

The situation had Mitchell in a panic. The company's New York season was fast approaching, and he'd lost his star ballerina. McKinney-Griffith was able to settle him with the promise of reserves at the ready. "He was tearing his hair out. I kept telling him, 'We have it, we have it. We can do this. I'm here, Virginia's here, Sheila's here, Susan Lovelle is here. We can all go in, and we're ready, because I've rehearsed all the casts.'"

Abarca stayed in the hospital for a month, then eventually rejoined the company on tour in Mexico City. "I made it through *Concerto Barocco,* but it felt like my lungs were screaming," she says. "Mr. Mitchell came backstage and turned me upside down. He put my legs over his shoulders, and he starts bouncing me up and down like a baby, trying to help me breathe."

How intimate and vulnerable they must have appeared to the other dancers. A terrified father desperate to revive his favorite child. A ballerina gasping for air, helpless in his arms. An audience out of sight, waiting, expectant.

But no matter how he cared for her, Abarca knew that if she didn't improve enough to perform, it was only a matter of time before she lost her spot. Mitchell regularly threatened his dancers about the ephemeral nature of the job. "He used to say, 'Dancers are a dime a dozen,'" remembers Abarca. "Any time a new girl was coming, he would always say, 'Wait until you all see this new girl. She's got legs and feet! Just wait until you see her.'"

The show had to go on. She wasn't ready to be replaced.

10

⌒

In 1975, *Dance Magazine* put a Black company ballerina on the cover for the first time in its forty-seven-year history. Hailed as "the dreaming soul of dance," the close-up image of Lydia Abarca dressed in character for George Balanchine's *Bugaku* feels lifted from a fairy tale. Her long, elegant fingers flank her angelic face. A sprig of silk cherry blossoms lies tucked into the side of her smooth high bun. "A for Abarca places this dancer first on the roster," the writer raved inside the nine-page spread dedicated to Dance Theatre of Harlem. "And there she belongs! Her looks, her style, her manner have the harmony of sheer perfection."

Across the country, in her local Denver dance shop, teenager Karlya Shelton stared in disbelief at the sight of this sylph with twin oceans for eyes on the cover of her favorite magazine. Shelton, the only Black dancer in the Colorado Concert Ballet, had never seen the face of a Black ballerina other than her own, staring back at herself in the mirror.

The feature rhapsodized over this thriving company of Black artists, describing Gayle McKinney-Griffith as "a doe-eyed dancer-actress of beguilingly various moods" and Sheila Rohan as "a cool, exact, enigmatic beauty." Shelton read about the company's record-breaking visit the previous year to London's Sadler's Wells, its command performance in Oslo for the king of Norway, and its sixteen-day triumphant season in Mexico City. "Everywhere DTH is feted at Embassy receptions as ambassadors of American culture," the reporter wrote. And yet somehow, across the country, this was the first time Shelton had learned of its existence.

She raced home, eager to share the magazine with her mother, Jean. Together they pored over the photographs—Abarca, leggy and sumptuous; Rohan, gorgeous and regal as the Bride in Geoffrey Holder's *Dougla;* Arthur Mitchell, dashing and chiseled, holding court in the company's 152nd Street studio. Jean found herself exhaling as Karlya clutched the magazine to her chest. "My God, Karlya's been bringing home that magazine her whole life, and I've never seen a Black person on it," Jean remembers of the moment. "Perhaps there's a glimmer of hope for her after all."

When her daughter was young, Jean had to make a conscious decision to support her passion for ballet, despite her fear that it would run Karlya into a brick wall. "Black dancers weren't here in America," she says. "You didn't see them. You didn't hear about them. I just figured, oh my god, this child is really going to be disappointed. Maybe she could dance in Europe. Not here in this country. But I told myself, this is the road she wants to travel, and she's got to go her own road."

Karlya was four years old when she got her first and only case of stage fright. It was during the Christmas performance of *The Nutcracker* at Denver's Bonfils Theatre. When it was time to go on stage, her teacher, in the wings, put her hands on Karlya's back and urged the little toy soldier out into the light. Karlya refused to budge. Out in the audience, Jean was startled by her absence. When she went backstage after the performance, she found Karlya sitting calmly by herself. "You didn't want to do it?" Jean asked. Karlya shook her head no, unapologetic. Jean squeezed her child's hand. "Well, you know, your brother, your cousins, your aunt and uncle, everyone's coming tomorrow night," she said. "Do you think you'll dance tomorrow?" Karlya thought seriously on the matter, then nodded in stoic agreement.

The following evening Jean waited until the family were settled in their seats before going to check on her daughter backstage. "I sat with her, and I kept saying, 'Now are you sure you're going to go out?'" she says. "And Karlya would nod. No smile. No nothing. I didn't know what was going to happen." Jean rejoined the family in the audience, waiting nervously with flowers on her lap. After the lights dimmed, and the curtain rose, Karlya appeared on cue. She beamed from the stage, pleased to find herself exactly where she belonged.

Nobody was prouder in the audience that night than her father, Lloyd. "Whatever his baby girl did had his buttons popping," says Jean. "And Karlya was just the same. She was a Daddy's girl. She would ask me something, and I would answer the question, and then she'd look at her father and say, 'Is that right, Daddy?'" Lloyd Shelton was a navy veteran, a towering man of substance, a hero to all who knew him. He rose before dawn for the early shift at the post office, came home for an afternoon nap, then headed out again in the evening to work a second job at the liquor store or as a janitor. Karlya and her little brother, Kyle, would ride their bikes with their friends for hours after school, never worried about getting lost. The mountains were always west, so if they could see them, they knew the direction home. When the streetlights came on, Lloyd had a powerful whistle that seemed to travel miles.

Karlya describes her childhood as blessed. "We were not wealthy," she says, "but we didn't want for anything." Says Jean, "Karlya would come home before another production of *The Nutcracker,* saying 'Mom, I need twelve new pairs of pointe shoes!' I'd tell her 'Kar, nobody orders twelve pairs of shoes.' Well, we'd go to the ballet shop, and my husband would say, 'Whatever she needs, that's what she needs.'"

On the weekends, before dance completely took over her schedule, Lloyd would take Karlya fishing down at the Cherry Creek Reservoir, where his own father had once worked to build the dam. When Lloyd wasn't fishing with his daughter, he could be found under the hood of the family car with Kyle. Their driveway became a kind of emergency room for neighborhood kids' bikes and skateboards and roller skates. Lloyd was a man who could fix anything. He was so good with his hands, so capable of focus, that he developed a hobby of carving intricate faces into the heads of toothpicks with an X-Acto knife. He'd sit in his chair or out on the patio making tiny little shavings until a recognizable visage appeared in the centimeter of wood.

Every summer the family went out into the bigness of the world together, packing up the station wagon with their suitcases and a cooler of drinks and fruit and sandwiches. Lloyd set a strict departure time of five in the morning, and they'd hit the road to visit relatives in his home state of Iowa, or to take in the Grand Canyon, or they'd head to California or Tennessee. When Karlya was fourteen, her parents realized that their growing children were aging out of the family tradition. As a last hoorah, they handed over control of the final journey to their kids. They could stay with family along the way or, if the kids were lucky, at a hotel with a pool. The siblings chose a route that had them driving up to Michigan, into Canada to Niagara Falls, then down through New York City, where Karlya announced to her family that she would one day make the city her home.

A DIFFERENT MOTHER might have pushed Karlya to walk a path already cleared. Jean had been one of Denver's first Black debutantes. Lloyd was president of the Owls Club, the Denver chapter of Black men who put on the debutantes' ball. But their daughter didn't have the time or interest in such pomp and circumstance. Karlya was committed to her twin passions of music and ballet. By the time she was a teenager, she had risen to second chair in the all-city orchestra on the viola. Her music teacher resented that ballet took time away from her practice, complaining to Jean that she was stretched too thin and needed to make a choice between the two. Her mother smiled at the man, telling him it wasn't for either of them to interfere. "She knows what she wants to do," she said. "My job is to help further that."

After Karlya broke her left wrist in a car accident at sixteen, the decision was made. She set down the viola. But she knew her music teacher had been wrong—she didn't really have to choose between dance and music. "When you're dancing, you are the music," she explains. "The music is everything. I would always think, *Okay, today I'm going to be the violin, and I'm going to accent that part. And right here, where there's a cymbal, I'm going to give a turn of my head.*"

Somehow between his various jobs, Lloyd found the time to chauffeur her to years of ballet classes. She learned to drive coming home from the studio. Those car rides offered a brief respite for them both in a rapidly changing world. In middle school, the city slashed Karlya's neighborhood in half, busing her side of the street to the white school across town. Karlya, who was used to being surrounded by whiteness from her dance classes, aroused suspicion from the protesting Black students at her new school for, as she calls it, "fraternizing so easily with the enemy." Occasionally they'd accuse her of being an "Uncle Tom" or an "Oreo," which was bad news for them because she was never one to back down from a fight.

But Karlya's parents were worried that their daughter was losing touch with her community. What with dance and now school, church was her only experience with Black culture. They lobbied the school board to let her attend the primarily Black neighborhood high school where two of her uncles were on the faculty. Even back on her home turf, she felt out of place. She felt she had to defend her eagerness to call out the right answer in class and the fact that she always chose ballet over pep club and football games. Sometimes a white boy who danced with her would give her a ride to ballet, which inevitably led to accusations that she had a white boyfriend. At ballet she was the only. At school she was the outlier.

Early into her high school years, the Colorado Concert Ballet invited Karlya to join the company on a swing of Wyoming, New Mexico, and Colorado dates. The tour was down a couple of dancers because of sickness and injury, and Karlya's teachers trusted she knew the repertoire well enough to step in. She relished the opportunity to prove herself on a grander scale. Her legs had jump in them that would draw gasps from the audience. The other young women in the company were pleasant with her, even if their fascination with her hair and compulsion to touch it grated. Even though her whole ballet world was white, it never occurred to her that she didn't have a place in it too. She could do five turns in pointe shoes, so how could she not?

Shelton speaks of her time at the Colorado Concert Ballet with affection. The white artistic directors did their honest best to support her dancing, but they had their own limitations. Karlya would never dance the role of Clara in *The Nutcracker,* for instance, or the Sugar Plum Fairy, which she attributes to a failure of imagination. And she wouldn't cross the unspoken divide that lived between her and her white peers. There would be no talk of the civil rights movement in the dressing room or on the bus. Nobody ever mentioned Dr. King's assassination.

One Fourth of July, the Sheltons attended a cookout with other Black families in a nearby neighborhood. Kyle and the other kids were playing in the front yard when they saw a parade of Ku Klux Klan members streaming down the street. They ran to tell the adults barbecuing in the backyard about the specter of Klan members in hoods and cloaks. "My Daddy and the other men came out with pans and skillets and whatever else they could grab in their hands," says Karlya. "My brother was going too but my mother held him back. The men chased the Klan down the block and then some." It never occurred to her to share the story with her white dance friends. When asked why, she sighs. "I think it would have made them very uncomfortable," she says. "I don't think they would've wanted to get that far into my world."

Her dancing life in Colorado was kind, but lonely, and compartmentalized. When the majority in the room aren't curious, and then sturdy in that curiosity, "the only" learns to protect her vulnerable core.

WHEN KARLYA SHELTON WAS seventeen years old, a teacher named Dolores Kehr, a former soloist with the Ballet Russe de Monte Carlo with strong ties to the School of American Ballet and the Joffrey Ballet School, took over training her and the other advanced ballet students. The worldly woman asked her new students about their plans upon graduation. It was Karlya who took the first step forward. "I'm going to be a professional dancer," she announced, with the same matter-of-fact authority she might have told the woman the spelling of her last name. Kehr looked at her through narrowed eyes. "How old are you, dear?" she asked. When Shelton responded that she was seventeen, the teacher gently winced. "Well, you're almost too old," she said. After that Kehr met with the dancers' parents and convinced them to send their teenage children with her on a trip to New York City to make the rounds of the country's best ballet companies.

It was only days before that trip that Shelton discovered Dance Theatre of Harlem in *Dance Magazine*. Suddenly she was desperate for a chance to meet Arthur Mitchell and his company of dancers. She called Kehr to ask if there was any way her teacher might arrange for an audition. It turned out Kehr was friends with Violette Verdy, a principal ballerina at City Ballet who had danced with Mitchell. She told the girl she would try to take advantage of the connection but couldn't make any promises. That was enough for Shelton, who got busy in the bathroom mirror trying to style her bun exactly like Abarca's on the cover, biting her lip in frustration at the one puffy section on the top of her head that refused to lie flat.

IN NEW YORK, the group from Colorado checked in to the Empire Hotel across from Lincoln Center on a brisk spring afternoon. Kehr marched them through a three-day whirlwind tour of the ballet world. Their first stop was Balanchine's School of American Ballet.

As Kehr escorted her giddy students through the venerated halls, the group passed the legendary Jerome Robbins in the hall. Kehr called a cheerful hello to the choreographer, asking if he might have time to greet some eager fledglings. As if batting at a cloud of gnats, he waved them off with an impatient grimace. His testy dismissal chilled Shelton. But she was here to dance. The kids shed their outer layers in the hall and joined three somber adults in a room. There was nobody at the piano, no music. They were told to line up at the barre and stand in first position. One of the women came around with a stick measuring the lengths of their necks, arms, legs, and torsos, and their hip-to-foot ratios. "What about talent?" asks Abarca, horrified by Shelton's retelling. "They can't measure that!"

After the dispiriting audition, Shelton looked for the dressing room to change out of her dance wear into her street clothes. She asked a couple of students in the hallway where the visiting Colorado dancers might change in preparation for their audition. When one of the SAB dancers pointed Shelton in the right direction, her friend shushed her, wrinkling her nose at Shelton. "Don't talk to her," the girl hissed, taking her friend by the shoulder and turning their backs. Shelton still gets steamed talking about it. "'Don't talk to her!' Might it have been because I was Black? Or was she just that easily threatened by the idea of new competition?" She knew then and there that this wasn't the place for her. "I would have been in fights all the time. The whole atmosphere was unfriendly. I was still naïve at that age, but when you grow up Black, you know what racism looks like, what it feels like. It almost has a smell to it."

Happily, on their last day in town, Kehr announced that she'd managed to get Shelton an audition with Dance Theatre of Harlem. The company was busy preparing for their first season at Broadway's Uris Theatre, so she was going to have to join the company class on stage. When they arrived at the theater, Kehr and Shelton's classmates found seats in the theater to observe. Shelton assumed a spot toward the back of the stage for the company class and found herself getting choked up standing in such a large group of Black classical dancers. For the first time she allowed herself to feel just how alone she'd been on so many stages throughout her childhood. "I remember wanting to cry out to my white friends in the audience," she says. *"See? See! I'm not alone! There's a whole company of Black ballerinas and danseurs."*

And then in came Arthur Mitchell. One always sensed him before he appeared. The threatening urgency to his approach announced itself like a crack of thunder. "You can always hear Arthur Mitchell coming into the studio or backstage because you hear the thunder of his heels going boom, boom, boom," says Shelton. "So everybody would stand up and then when he enters, he's got this whole force field around him. He was just so powerful. And it made the whole thing real for me, like here is that guy from the magazine before me."

Mitchell surveyed the stage, taking in the unfamiliar girl, then led the company in class. Shelton remembers there being a single white person on stage with them, a small man in glasses named George who normally played the piano but this morning was shadowing Mitchell with a stick to keep time. After the class, Mitchell looked at Shelton holding her breath and told her to go put on her pointe shoes for center work.

While kneeling in the wings to lace up the pale ribbons of her shoes, Shelton noticed Gayle McKinney-Griffith and Sheila Rohan sitting on the steps applying brown makeup to theirs. As her eyes traveled up from their feet, she took in how the brown of their tights matched the hues of their skin. In all her years, she'd never considered that she might have a right to bend the art form to meet her, as these women were. "For so long I'd looked at myself in pictures knowing something's broken," she says. "The line is not right. 'Is that my leg? Because it's not the same color as my arm.' I didn't do anything because nothing was ever offered as a solution."

Oh, this is where I belong, Shelton said to herself. She finished tying the ribbons of her pink pointe shoes, already knowing she'd outgrown them, and returned to the stage. Mitchell ran her through one of his center variations—échappé, échappé, passé, passé, changement to fourth, then two pirouettes—to see how quickly she could get up on her legs. Shelton repeated the variation four times for him, while the company stood back appraising her. Then he asked her to show him two pirouettes; she did three.

The next day she returned home to Colorado, where three scholarship invitations would soon arrive at her house. "I had offers to Joffrey and School of American Ballet. But after I saw Dance Theatre of Harlem, it was like knowing the difference between Godiva chocolate and Hershey's. I felt like those other companies were going to be just like where I had been. I would be limited, and I didn't trust that they would let me climb. There were going to be roles that I was kept from because of the color of my skin. They were going to keep me in the corps de ballet. Arthur Mitchell was offering me a chance to dance in a company where it would feel good to dance again."

WHEN THE LEGACY COUNCIL talks now about the individual ambitions they had as young dancers, an obvious generational difference emerges. The first generation spent their childhoods training with a sense of possibility that the founders lacked. Rohan can't relate to Shelton's tour of ballet companies. "Didn't your mother tell you that no white company was going to take a Black ballerina?" she asks. Shelton responds, "Why would she? Because I already was dancing with a white company from the time I was twelve." Or when Sells tells the story of being called "a dirty snowflake," in *The Nutcracker*, Rohan says, "Didn't your mother warn you that would happen?"

Rohan grew up thinking of ballet as an art form that intrigued her but a tradition that purposefully excluded her. "Sure, I had read about companies in Europe—the Ballet Russe or the Paris Opéra—and that there were Black ballerinas over there. But I wouldn't even bother to pursue dancing with a white company." Sells, nearly twenty years Rohan's junior, considers this for a moment. "I think my mother thought, *Maybe there's going to be a change.*"

By twelve years old, Marcia Sells was dancing in the corps with the Cincinnati Ballet. At fifteen, she was awarded a prestigious Ford Foundation national scholarship to attend the School of American Ballet's eight-week summer program in New York. City Ballet soloist and SAB teacher Richard Rapp auditioned her himself. She was the only dancer from the region to be awarded the scholarship.

Mamie took succor from the example of Debra Austin, the brilliant dancer who'd been hand-picked by Balanchine, at just sixteen, to join City Ballet in 1971. But while Austin's accomplishment was indeed cause for celebration, the telling of the woman's triumph would bruise Marcia's spirit. Her white peers at SAB took a careless delight in repeating to her how after the light-skinned Austin danced for Balanchine in her audition, he was thought to have said approvingly, "Who is the girl with the tan?" His assistant was tasked with informing him, "Her tan is permanent." "As the lone Black girl in the school at that moment," Sells says now, "I immediately realize I'm in trouble. Because I'm a lot darker than Debbie Austin. You can tell I'm a Black woman from one hundred feet away."

Near the end of the summer term, SAB's associate director, Nathalie Gleboff, pulled Sells into her private office, ostensibly to discuss her progress and future with the organization. Sells had felt well respected in her classes, often chosen by her teachers to demonstrate technique for the other students. Having a private meeting with Gleboff felt like an honor. But the air in the room felt chilly as soon as she closed the door behind her. The Russian émigré wasted no time getting to the point. "The teachers like you," she said. "You're quite competent. But you'll never be in the company." Sells sat absorbing these conflicting statements, her face flushing with confusion and embarrassment. The arbitrariness of the rejection landed like a smack. She was too tender and too proud to ask for an explanation. She needed to escape the flatness of this woman's gaze. In the doorway, Gleboff lobbed one more grenade. "Your rear end," she told the prepubescent girl who stood frozen with her back to her, "you'll probably have to have some surgery to have part of it removed. And your nose too."

Marcia spent the rest of the day in a daze. She cried for hours to her mother on the phone. But then the next day she woke up and remembered that she was the daughter of Mamie Sells, and she'd spent the last several years sleeping beneath the guiding lights of Dance Theatre of Harlem's founding dancers. This old Russian woman wouldn't have the final say over her future. The following week Sells reported to 152nd Street for her final summer intensive, which she'd attended every summer since first seeing them perform in her hometown. The following summer, when she was sixteen, Sells finally would join her childhood heroes in the company of her dreams.

THAT SAME SUMMER that Marcia Sells studied at SAB—and was met with the harsh reality of how truly little the larger world of ballet had evolved—Karlya Shelton moved to New York City. Jean and Lloyd left Denver in their Pontiac Catalina, the trunk packed full of their daughter's belongings. They stopped at the Briansky Ballet Center in Saratoga Springs, New York, where Shelton had been chosen as the first African American to represent the United States at the international Prix de Lausanne competition. Then they drove their daughter into Manhattan, to a women's boardinghouse in Hell's Kitchen, where they'd rented her a single room for thirty-five dollars a week. "Paying for the Webster House was our version of a college payment," says Jean. But while the lobby may have appeared grand, stepping out of the elevator onto the fourth floor felt like sliding sideways into an entirely different, far grimmer building. Shelton and her mother—men weren't allowed upstairs, not even fathers—were shown to a room the size of a walk-in closet painted the sour shade of hospital green, with a tiny window looking out onto a warehouse.

The next morning Shelton emerged from the lobby smiling with a couple of other girls, whom she'd met at the Webster's daily breakfast and had been delighted to learn were also Dance Theatre of Harlem dancers. They all piled into the Catalina, the girls talking merrily over each other like old friends, as Lloyd drove them uptown.

The only impressions Shelton had previously had of Harlem were from media scare reports and popular Blaxploitation movies that painted the community as a blighted wasteland, corrupt and hollowed out by crime and drugs. "I expected these dark, dirty streets lined with people up to no good," she says. Instead, she found herself enveloped into a bustling community that treated the dancers with genuine pride and affection. Mr. Austin, a gentlemanly neighbor in a car coat and porkpie hat, served as a kind of cheerful sentinel to the 152nd Street studio morning and night. As the company's self-appointed doorman, he'd go on to greet

Shelton every day, urging her to be her best, occasionally regaling her with stories of his own prowess back in the day dancing the Lindy Hop.

But that first day, Shelton hugged her parents tight outside the studio, clinging hardest to her father. "Daddy, can I call home every night?" she said as Lloyd patted his baby girl on the back, assuring her, "You can call as often as you want." Jean promised she would write and indeed would mail a letter to her daughter every single day for the first two years, all of which Shelton has saved in an old Capezio bag, and care packages of her favorite treats, drinks, even a birthday cake. And with that, they were off, trusting they were leaving their brave girl right where she belonged.

OR SO SHE THOUGHT. Shelton was sure she'd been accepted into the company, but now the front desk was telling her she'd be training in the downstairs studio with dancers Mitchell envisioned becoming part of a second company rather than up in Studio 3. She didn't make a fuss. She joined the preprofessional group to which she'd been assigned. But she knew one thing for sure. "I didn't know how I was going to get there," she says, "but I was going upstairs where I belonged."

For three months, Shelton labored dutifully downstairs, training with teachers like Mary Barnett, who would go on to be the associate artistic director at Alvin Ailey American Dance Theater. Barnett taught her an important lesson about the pragmatic value of surrender. "One time this guy and I were doing a lift, and he let go of me and I fell," says Shelton. "Ms. Barnett looked at us both and said, 'You need to learn to fall!' I was like, 'Excuse me?' But she was right. Most people tense up and hurt themselves when they fall. She was telling me to just collapse into it, so I wouldn't hurt anything. Surrender! Which is a very hard thing to do."

At a Sunday Open House, Shelton finally had the opportunity to show Mitchell what she could bring to the company. Barnett had given her some allegro choreography that highlighted the power of her turns and jumps, and she executed it beautifully. The next morning an administrator called Shelton out from the downstairs studio and told her to report to Studio 3 for company class. Mitchell had decided to bring her in as an apprentice, another test she was determined to pass. "You know how tennis players yell 'Come on!' when they win a hard point?" she says. "That was me. So that's how I'm getting upstairs. Finally!"

The pace of company life hit Shelton like a fire hose. Lecture-demonstrations began as early as eight in the morning. Then came a two-hour class to keep the body stretched and primed for the day ahead. A theoretical lunch break followed, but ballerinas were trained to think of lunch more as a time marker than as an invitation to eat. Splibs, as apprentices were called, were expected to work in the studio through lunch, practicing their pointe and partnering skills, before a mandatory four o'clock class with Karel Shook. During the dinner break, the male dancers might enjoy a Jamaican meat patty or chicken dinner from the open grill on the corner counter storefront with a hand-painted sign that read FOOD or brisket from Sherman's Barbecue up the block. The women seemed to get by on Tab soda and Tropicana orange juice and cups of Yoplait yogurt in the lobby, where the ashtrays overflowed with Newport cigarette butts. Then back into Studio 3 for a two-hour evening rehearsal.

One of the first things Shelton learned upstairs was how to walk with the DTH tip. Ballerinas typically walk with a certain stiffness, an inaccessible chill. "Imagine trying to walk on half-point toe, without moving your hips," says Shelton. "That's not the way women naturally walk." Mitchell encouraged his dancers to bring the heat. He taught the women to walk high on demi-pointe in diagonals across the studio, as if the floor beneath them were lucky to bear their rolling steps. "It's a very feminine walk, elegant and regal," explains Shelton. "The hips are allowed to move naturally. It's also a cultural thing, maybe learned unconsciously from watching our parents. It's like when we're dressed and know we're looking good." Shelton remembers watching Abarca and McKinney-Griffith incorporate the DTH tip in ballets like *Agon* and *Forces of Rhythm*, thinking they were the epitome of Black Girl Magic. "I would point my feet on each step," Abarca says now, "stay up on half-point, and slightly sway my hips to make it sexy."

During the company's New York season, Shelton and some of the other apprentices were told to stay behind in Harlem to train with Alice Elliott, an imperious woman of Ghanaian descent who had trained at the Bolshoi. Elliott and the pianist, Svetlana, had a way of speaking and laughing with each other in Russian that let the dancers know they were being skewered. One afternoon Shelton had to pause in the corner while practicing bourrées and pas de bourée couru, a series of fluttering tiny steps on pointe. "Carol," Elliott said to Karlya, purposefully misidentifying her, "why are you stopping?" When Shelton complained that her toes had started bleeding, the unimpressed woman demanded proof. "I took off my shoes and showed them to her, and she said, 'Too bad! Put them back on and try again.'"

Every night Shelton took the train back to Hell's Kitchen, having long since missed the dinner service that was included as part of her rent. She'd walk down Ninth Avenue with another dancer, the hookers catcalling them affectionately, and buy fruit from a bodega to split for dinner. In her first year at the company, Shelton dropped fifteen pounds, prompting Mitchell to call her out in Studio 3 one afternoon in front of everyone. "Yeah, that's what I'm talking about," he remarked. "Before your behind was like two watermelons!" Shelton still flinches at the nastiness of his words. She'd had her fair share of personalities in teachers before, like an instructor in Colorado who taught while holding a hamburger and a cigarette in one hand and a drink in the other. But she'd never had someone try to humiliate her in the studio in front of her peers. It was the cruelty in his voice that could cut. "Some people could take his insults and let them just roll off like water. But for me it got into my core."

McKinney-Griffith had begun to take a special notice of Shelton, though—both her talent and the way she seemed to shrink from Mitchell's gaze. "Karlya had this spark and energy and strength that all the dancers who came up with her didn't have. But I worried she was shy." As ballet mistress, she worried that the new girl's deferential habit of standing at the back of the studio during class was doing her talent a disservice.

One morning McKinney-Griffith pulled Shelton aside before class started and told her to switch places with her. "Gayle told me, 'He needs to see you,'" she says. "She wanted to make sure that everyone that deserved to be seen was at least given an opportunity. She put me in her spot for the center portion of class. From that day forward I claimed it with pride and told myself to always work hard to do it justice, in gratitude for how much this gesture of kindness meant to me."

Privately, McKinney-Griffith urged Mitchell to give the new girl a shot.

One of the women in *Forces of Rhythm* was injured, and the ballet mistress believed the young apprentice was ready to take her place. "I think Karlya's the best dancer to put in there because she's strong," she told her boss. "She remembers the choreography. She's perfect." She was careful to keep the tone of her voice even, lest Mitchell find her pushy and say no out of spite.

But Mitchell just nodded impatiently, his attention elsewhere. McKinney-Griffith moved Shelton into the ballet, and the apprentice did her proud. After the girl's first performance, McKinney-Griffith took her aside and praised her dancing and told her she looked like she'd been in the company for years. But then she gently explained that her Maybelline blue eye shadow wasn't her best option.

Apprentices were typically given a year to prove their stuff before Mitchell brought them on as full company members, which meant an increase in both status and salary. Throughout her first year, Shelton elevated the corps of every ballet in the repertoire—the precision of her dancing, the muscularity of her turns and jumps, the obvious joy she brought to the stage. But when that year passed, she received no word about her progress. She finally got up the nerve to approach Mitchell about whether she was a full company member. He looked at her, seemingly annoyed to be reminded of the missed timeline. "Oh, I thought you already were," he said.

From that point on, she told herself she wasn't dancing for his attention or approval. Earning it seemed like an impossible, wrong-headed goal. "I decided my job wasn't to make Arthur Mitchell like me, or to dance with the expectation of his praise," she says. "He wasn't out there when we were performing. So why would I dance for him? I danced for myself, and for the joy of it, and for the pleasure and challenge of trying to make it perfect."

11

The women and men who built Dance Theatre of Harlem from the ground up were more than colleagues and peers. No professional identity could possibly encapsulate what they meant to one another during that first pivotal decade. In a perfect illustration of their intimate bond, a few dancers spontaneously put together a family tree, assigning everybody roles under the patriarchal branches of Arthur Mitchell and Mr. G. Dancers were claimed as mothers and fathers, husbands and wives, brothers and sisters, sons and daughters. "We were young and being thrust into the public eye and the critics were all writing about us," explains Gayle McKinney-Griffith, who took on Karlya Shelton as her little sister and considered Sheila Rohan her mother. "Mr. Mitchell was getting all the funding and putting his whole life and career on the line. But if the reviews weren't good, the weight was all on us. That's why we developed the family system—just to feel like we could run up under somebody's wing. We were a unit. One weak link, we all fall. So we had to build each other up."

To blunt the harshness of their temperamental father figure, they would remind one another of their greatness. The dancers devised group rituals, like the prayer they'd recite over and over on stage before *Dougla*:

> *I believe in God,*
> *maker of heaven and earth,*

and myself.
The whole world stinks.
But I am lovely.
I am gorgeous.
I am divine.

Whoever was playing the Groom in the ballet would call out each line of the prayer, and the other dancers on stage would repeat after him. "Then the curtain would rise," says Shelton, "and the audience would see us standing there like African royalty. So straight and tall and proud."

The company began a tradition of leaving what they called power notes and little gifts of stuffed animals or trinkets in the dressing rooms for new members or for dancers stepping into a new role. The women of the Legacy Council have held on to theirs for decades. Shelton has a power note from McKinney-Griffith written in different-colored markers. "Bright Eyes," it reads. "Wake up and dance beautiful. Smile. Remember our short talk? You know what to do. Love, Gayle." And she has one Abarca wrote to her on a napkin: "Hey McKinney! Just relax and sell it! You'll be beautiful as always." It's taped in her archives next to a treasure from Walter Raines. "Dear Gayle," he wrote, about a performance of *Concerto Barocco* in England in which Mitchell finally let her dance a principal role. "I suppose you might call this a 'fan letter.' Your dancing in London has been something quite extraordinary. In many ways, you've surpassed yourself. For me, it has been a joy to behold. All I can say is, with best wishes and very much love. Your husband."

They bolstered themselves not just against Mitchell, who could turn on them or withhold his approval, but against the world itself, which stayed doubting, uncertain, and surprised by every one of their successes, every overturned stereotype. "Ballet for Blacks?" queried the headline of a 1971 *New York Times* article written by the dance critic Clive Barnes. And a year later, another Barnes piece ran under the headline "Black Ballet— A Good Idea?"

"I think that Arthur from the beginning to the end was always trying to prove that we could do ballet," says Shelton. "That was just always there, no matter how good we were. We had to keep proving it over and over and over."

"Not to each other though," says Abarca. "We knew how good we were." The women all nod and smile, remembering how perfect it was for a time.

They were there. They were there. Singing "We Are Family" on transatlantic flights at the top of their lungs; crammed together on buses pulling into strange cities after dark; crying together in the dressing room or on the Studio 3 fire escape; powdering their shoes one last time before stepping into the rosin box; running back on stage for another encore—they were there.

SO WERE their beloved partners. No Legacy Council conversation passes without some wistful attention paid to the men who danced alongside them—their brothers, husbands, fathers, and sons in the company. "They were princes, and they treated us like queens," says Shelton. "We felt like the most precious thing on Earth whenever we went on stage with them."

McKinney-Griffith speaks of the male dancers with equal reverence. "They were *danseurs*," she says, as the other women close their eyes in dreamy remembrance. "They had that stance, that pride. And they knew how we relied on them. I always felt protected by them, on stage and off. It was like having older brothers. Although some of them were so handsome you wished that they were your boyfriend."

The men helped them stretch out their feet before morning classes and hide the food Mitchell didn't want them eating. They made the women better dancers by teaching them the mechanics of partnering. They saved them at parties and receptions from boring conversations and unwanted advances. They were men who took seriously the noble calling of a danseur, which is to offer the sturdiest possible scaffolding for a ballerina from which to fly. On stage, they were the women's other halves.

"You know what was so great about all the guys?" says Abarca. "They were generous. They weren't men who were thinking it all had to be about them." Which is not to say they didn't sometimes try the women's last nerves. "Of course, we had arguments," says McKinney-Griffith with affection. "'No, you're holding me too tight,' or 'You're smelly,' or 'I don't want to dance with you because you're laughing all the time and you're going to drop me.' We were petty sometimes, but that's family too. They loved us."

And of all the men, not a one was more gallant and adored than Walter Raines. After every performance of *Agon,* standing in the wings before final bows, Raines made sure to bring a sense of grandeur to the moment. "Paris Opéra, ladies!" he'd call to the women, reminding them to preen.

"Walter was my heart," says McKinney-Griffith. "He was handsome as all get-out, and he knew everything. Whenever he would ask me to go to a museum event or a cocktail party, I was always like yes! before running off to get a new dress, because you had to be dressed when you were with Walter." She remembers one afternoon when he invited her to go shopping with him downtown at Bergdorf Goodman. "I said, 'But Walter, my little purse here—' And he said, 'No, no, no. Don't worry, we're just going to look!'" While the two milled around the hats section, making each other laugh trying on overpriced items, McKinney-Griffith heard a woman's voice cry out "Walter!" And Shirley MacLaine bounded up to Raines with her arms outstretched. "That's just who Walter was," says McKinney-Griffith. "He was in with the in-crowds, but always made you feel like the most special one on his arm."

Rohan grew up in a culture that cast gay people as fundamentally corrupt. "My upbringing was such that 'gayness' was a bad thing," she says. "Even though we had gay men in our community in Staten Island, it was looked down upon. You were supposed to stay away from them. I didn't really encounter gay men so much until I started studies in Manhattan. Then I just let them be and tried not to judge." But such polite avoidance denies the possibility for real connection, and she wasn't going to survive Mitchell's astronomical expectations, let alone the intimacy of company tours, without leaning into a shared spirit of empathy and understanding. "I had to make the shift," says Rohan. "Being gay was supposed to be a wrong thing. Christianity, you know. But these men were nice to me. They were wonderful. They were my brothers. We helped each other. We worked together. At first, I just accepted them. I didn't like it, but I accepted them, and we didn't talk about it. I had to work on myself with that. As I grew more, I got better. I realized—oh, we're all just human beings."

These were disco days, platform heel days, soul train days, do-the-hustle days. And the women had at their disposal the best, most handsome partners in town. "I mean, the men *escorted* you on nights out," says

McKinney-Griffith. She and fellow founding company member Samuel Smalls, praised for his work in ballets like Mitchell's *Holberg Suite,* would hit the Latin clubs for high-level salsa. "At these clubs, you had to have your own partner and you couldn't change throughout the night," she says. "Well, I'd always do this strut in with Sam, knowing I've got the best partner. Holy moly, if I stumbled, he would say 'You can't make mistakes! This is serious.'"

Sometimes when the spirit hit just right, the dancers would pull out moves from a ballet like *Dougla* on the disco floor, treating the room to that good DTH tip. "You can't help but tip in heels," says Shelton. "Oh girl, we took over," laughs Sells, who would go with a couple of the older dancers to Peter Rabbit, a Black gay bar in the West Village where she experienced cross-dressing culture for the first time. "I still remember going to the unisex bathroom and realizing the people in dresses are standing up," she says. "You know how they say, 'I'm not in Kansas anymore'? Well, I had left Cincinnati."

Company members met at the Saloon across from Lincoln Center, or Leviticus downtown. Champagne flowed like water, sips of cognac like smoke. Anything to prolong that high of a performance and keep the ringing of applause in their ears. Shelton remembers striding into Leviticus one night on the arm of wunderkind dancer Ronald Perry. Earlier on the phone that night, they'd planned their outfits together. She wore a white jumpsuit and Perry had on a jet black one. The two were there to hustle, and the crowd backed up. They cleared the floor, the rest of the people in the club making a circle around them, recognizing the magic that was about to go down.

Perry had first come under Mitchell's tutelage back at the Harlem School of the Arts when he was thirteen. The boy lacked formal training, but Mitchell recognized a raw brilliance in him. Perry had everything— feet, balance, height, flexibility, technique. Once he joined the company, he danced the lead roles in *Bugaku, Afternoon of a Faun,* and *Firebird,* before moving on to American Ballet Theatre. In 1981 he melted the hearts of critics and audiences as the *danseur noble* in Balanchine's *Themes and Variations,* though he had been brought into the company at a lower ranking. ABT never promoted Perry to principal dancer. Frustrated, he eventually left the company for Europe.

But while he was still at Dance Theatre of Harlem, everyone wanted to partner with Perry. Shelton, knowing Mitchell reserved him for Abarca and Virginia Johnson, settled for dancing with him at lecture-demonstrations. But on summer weekends she'd escape the city and take the train out to Long Island, where Perry lived in his mother's house along with the dancer Mel Tomlinson. They'd hop in his silver Volkswagen Bug and drive to Southampton beach, where they practiced lifts from *Rhythmetron* and *Le Corsaire* on the sand.

ON SELLS'S FIRST summer intensive in New York, her younger brother walked up to one of the male dancers outside Church of the Master and asked, "Are you a sissy?" The man said, "What do you think a sissy is? What does that mean to you?" All her brother could do was shrug his little shoulders. And so the dancer replied, "I spend time with girls. But there are men who spend time with men. It's all good."

Sells was lucky enough to have Perry assigned as her company father. "If you stood behind Ronald in class," she says, "you would forget what you were supposed to be doing because you'd be like, 'Damn, look at that.'" McKinney-Griffith, ever the wise and gentle ballet mistress, had to break it to her that he was gay.

"Growing up, nobody had ever really explained homosexuality to me," says Sells. "We had a copy of James Baldwin's *Giovanni's Room* in our library at home, and my mother told me, 'If there's anything in there you don't understand, you can come to me.'" But in Harlem, Sells was gifted a window into what it meant to be Black and gay at that time in American history. "The kind of conversations that I was able to have with some of the male dancers were not the ones people were having in the seventies," she says with appreciation.

As the youngest of the Legacy Council, Sells may have been up for an open dialogue the others didn't feel the right, or the wherewithal, to initiate. Dance Theatre of Harlem was a family. And as in all families, there were subjects skipped over and truths half-spoken. An unsafe world taught gay men to keep their intimate lives private and compartmentalized. "They purposefully didn't tell us, and we didn't ask," says Shelton of their partners' romantic identities. "It was like a boundary."

"They had their own community," notes McKinney-Griffith. "We weren't a part of that community. We could be close to them and cry with them and laugh with them. But there were things we didn't talk about. It was a whole different world."

It was the world. It was the time. It was Harlem, a neighborhood with a church on every corner. It was Arthur Mitchell himself, a man of enormous contradictions. "This was the generation that believed private lives should stay private," says Sells. "He knew he was a Black man in America who had to figure out which battles he could fight. I just don't think he felt like he could take on a whole other cultural battle."

They leave questions of Mitchell's sexuality to others. What right, they say, do they have to know anything about a person that he himself wasn't willing or able to share?

"If Arthur was gay some of the time, all of the time, or just once or twice, all we knew is he didn't want it around him," says Abarca. "Back then everything was still in the closet. He knew we were being looked at by the public, and he didn't want anything representing his company in a way he didn't like." Mitchell's mandate of his male dancers was forceful and direct. Keep it behind closed doors, he would tell them. "I don't care who are you going to bed with, or who you're whatever," paraphrases Shelton. "Just don't do it around here. When you go on stage, you are masculine and it's all about the woman. You are to show her off in every way." Outside Mitchell's presence, some of the men would make light of his rigidity by trying on exaggerated poses of machismo or mincing. "The guys would be backstage or at rehearsal messing around," says Abarca. " 'Look how we'll walk for Arthur today.' "

Mitchell's internalized homophobia dictated what he expected of them not just in the theater but out in the world. "He would always give dress attire lectures to the men before we went on tour," says McKinney-Griffith. "You couldn't be too 'leisure' in public. No short-shorts, even when it's blazing hot. No neck scarves." The men were to dress in a fashion that didn't call their sexuality into question. "It wasn't said, but yes," says McKinney-Griffith sadly. "The men's paychecks would get docked for the way they dressed outside the company. They couldn't be flamboyant. They had to be 'presentable,' so to speak."

Mitchell made a life for himself on stage and then stayed there. "Arthur was very determined to *be* Arthur Mitchell," says Tania León. "He was a visionary, so he had so much responsibility. He had to be on stage all the time." And now that he had built a stage for these kids, he wanted them to stay on it too, forever.

That meant you could never doubt him. You could never argue with him. You could never leave him.

But one by one, of course, the women all would leave. Because that's what children do. The leaving was often ugly, because Mitchell didn't know how to let people go. And that's when a new work began, the task of defining themselves as women apart from Mitchell, apart from Dance Theatre of Harlem. But who would they be if they weren't his ballerinas?

Act Two

Sheila

In 1975 I got the company schedule, and it was outrageous. Touring all over the United States, Canada, Europe. My children were getting older. Charlene was getting ready to start high school. I knew I wouldn't be able to do it. Not with my children becoming teenagers. Mr. Mitchell understood. Plus, I was suffering from sciatica in my left hip. He said, "Come and teach the young kids in the school." So Mr. Mitchell didn't really lose me, or at least not right away.

I learned how to teach, which it turned out I loved. I was reading technique. The other teachers were mentoring me. If somebody in the company was out, I could fill in for Forces of Rhythm or Rhythmetron as a swing.

Dance Theatre of Harlem was the highlight of my life—without it everything would've been more minor key. I was saddened to leave. I had a lot of respect for Mr. Mitchell, but he didn't hold power over my life. I never looked back. I wanted to stay dancing, so I kept learning. I wanted to get my technique together so the choreographers would know I was competent. I didn't need to be the star of a place. I was aiming to be an artist, a dance artist, not just a performer. I didn't care if I ever performed. I was just living my life.

I started full time at the Nanette Bearden Contemporary Dance Theatre around 1977. At first, I was a principal dancer, then ballet mistress, and then school coordinator. I worked with a variety of choreographers—George Faison, John Jones, Keith Lee, Walter Rutledge. One of the more famous ones was Talley Beatty, who is considered one of the icons of the modern jazz

*dance genre. He set two works on the company. Talley was known through-
out the Black dance world as a very difficult person to work with. He could
be arrogant, mean, and disrespectful. He used to throw chairs. He had a
bad temper and would throw a dancer out of rehearsal on a whim. They
could get away with it back then. Not today. Arthur did see me dance again.
I was doing Bill Scott's* Every Now and Then *with Bruce Hawkins at my
sister's company. There's a part where I go over for a penché and I didn't
make the six o'clock* [an extreme arabesque, in which a dancer's legs point
straight up and down, like the hands of a clock]. *I purposely didn't do it
because this was a jazz piece, and I didn't think it was necessary. Afterward
I saw him, and he says, "Well, you know you should've made that six o'clock
penché. There's no reason why you shouldn't have made that!" Well, okay,
nothing about the ballet itself or the artistry or anything.*

*We dancers had to make a living however we could because performing
didn't pay very much in those days. It was common to know dancers who
were with two or three companies and taught at several different schools.
Nanette would sometimes pay my rent or my utilities. She always took care
of me. In the 1980s, I auditioned for Alvin Ailey. Oh my god, there were
thousands of dancers lined up out the door, down the street. I went in there
like a ballerina, and they want to see you get down—but with technique. So
yeah, I made a fool of myself. I should've just stayed home. But they were
looking for ballet teachers. I started in the adult dance department in the
evening, and then I moved to teaching day classes in the school.*

*I was also an assistant to the choreographer Louis Johnson. It was a task,
but I loved it. Louis was unorganized and could be difficult. He would plan
a rehearsal and then cancel it the same day. Louis was a ballet dancer at
heart but choreographed in modern, jazz, and Afro-Caribbean techniques
as well. Louis was well loved throughout the Black dance world. When he
wanted dancers, they would come from all over to work with him. Louis
and Arthur were contemporaries, both in the New York City Ballet lineup
together when they were younger. But Balanchine took Arthur. Louis always
thought he himself was the better choice and that Arthur got picked because
he was better-looking.*

*In 1986 I went on a tour of China and Korea with the Myung Sook Chun
Dance Company, a modern dance troupe, for over a month. We got to live
with the people. No hotels. We went to Beijing, Shanghai, up toward Man-*

churia. And we weren't always dancing on wonderful stages. Sometimes we were in barns in the backwoods. The people loved us. It was like God gave me this wonderful adventure to prepare me for what was coming.

Ellsworth met me at the airport. He told me that my son and my son's wife got busted with drugs—this was crack in the 1980s—and that I was going to be taking care of their four children. One was a baby. Well, we managed. We got bunk beds. The city had a foster care program so that I, being their grandmother, had some money to take care of them. That was a big concern. How're we going to feed these kids? It was trial and error, but we all stayed family because family is the most important thing. I dragged the children to museums and Dance Africa and whatever else I could, anything to keep them tied to their culture. They thank me for it now.

I thought I was done with ballet, with all the kids. But then I got cast in Martin *[Gordon Parks's 1990 ballet film in which, at fifty years old, Rohan danced on pointe in the lead role of Rosa Parks]. The choreographer Rael Lamb contacted me about the production. He'd come to Dance Theatre of Harlem at times and knew Mr. Mitchell. Rael had also come to Nanette's and set a piece on us, so we knew each other. I wasn't nervous about my age. I never thought,* Oh, I'm too old. *I was in good shape and had never really stopped dancing, whether it was ballet, modern, jazz, or African. I was just surprised to be asked to perform a lead role.*

Mr. Parks was a quiet, distinguished gentleman. He produced, directed, and wrote the music. He wanted mature dancers. John Jones, who danced Martin Luther King, Jr., was even older than me but still in good shape. I remember one day we were filming the first act pas de deux. When we took a break, I noticed that the ribbon on one of my pointe shoes had come loose and was sticking out. This is a real no-no for a ballerina. I asked Mr. Parks if we could do the scene over. He just looked at me for a moment and said no. After the film came out, I was pleased to see that he must have edited over it or whatever they do. For years, PBS aired it every Black History Month. People would call the house and say, "I saw you on Channel 13!" I liked my performance too. This was the major dance role of my entire career.

The only thing I value more than art is family. Here is a story I haven't talked about before, about my lowest point in life. One of my granddaughters got pregnant when she was sixteen and had twins. When the twins were about three years old, she took up with an older man whom we didn't like.

But she was an adult, so I could protest only so much. I offered to give her a house I had at that time, thinking it would be more stable for her and the kids. Upon moving in, I got into an altercation with the man. We were arguing, and the bastard called the cops, and they arrested me. I was handcuffed and fingerprinted and given an order of protection, which meant I couldn't come within a certain distance from them. Not long after, I went to a Fourth of July barbecue at my sister Delores's house next door to where they were living. My granddaughter and this man called the cops on me again because I was too close. This time I had to spend the night in jail because there was no court that day. The police who arrested me and those who processed me were all very kind and sorry that this was happening to me. I was put in a cell by myself. I prayed. I was scared. It caused a big rift in my family. But you live through the hard times. As for my granddaughter, I've forgiven her. We're now very close. She finally got away from the man, and she and the girls are doing well.

But that night in my cell I talked to some young girls who were in the next cell, in there for a number of reasons—drugs, prostitution, stealing. They were young street girls, and I could hardly understand their language. I had to ask them to talk so I could understand. They called me Auntie and asked what I was doing in jail because I was so old. I felt sorry for those young girls. I still do. They were lost. One told me she couldn't read or write. Another didn't know her house address or how to spell it. They were so interested when I told them I was a dancer and used to dance on the stage. And I stayed dancing too, even after that.

When I was in my seventies, my good friend Hope Clarke, who's very well known in the theater and an award-winning Broadway choreographer, dancer, and actor, approached me with the idea of starting an ensemble of performers over fifty. In 2019 we decided on the 5 Plus Ensemble, made up of all seasoned and professional performers. It was me, Hope, Audrey Madison, Darryl Reuben Hall, Michael Leon Thomas, and Carmen de Lavallade as choreographer. We did two salons at DTH. Virginia [Johnson] welcomed us and was very enthusiastic about the project. We got space at City College's Aaron Davis Hall in Harlem for a performance. People were becoming very responsive to us, but it was too much work. The rehearsals were exhausting. We had to run around New York looking for affordable places

to practice and find money to pay everyone. But all in all, it was a lot of fun.
We laughed a lot.

THE FILMMAKER AND contemporary dancer Gabri Christa was in the audience of 5 Plus Ensemble's performance at Aaron Davis Hall. "All I could think was *Why ever have younger people on stage?*" says Christa. "This wasn't like, *Oh, here is this cute group of older people dancing.* It was amazing dance! And I couldn't keep my eyes off Sheila. All that wisdom, all the years of living, every littlest thing she did was so deep and powerful. That's the beauty of her and the gift that she gives."

In 2022 Christa's experimental documentary short *Sheila,* a wordless, dreamlike homage to Rohan's literal body of work, premiered at the Harlem International Film Festival. At the start of the film, we see Rohan under haunting light, sitting in a wooden chair, massaging her shoulders, rubbing her hands, stretching her ankles, before delicately sliding into a pair of soft ballet shoes. Wearing a simple black leotard and skirt, her salt-and-pepper locs pulled back from her face, she slowly begins to dance, and as she does, every time she touches her body, a different archival image of her is layered upon her skin—a shot from *Dougla* on her back, a scene from *Martin* at the ghostlike end of her fingertips. Generations appear in the background behind her, her great-granddaughters, who she once went to jail to protect, her best friend, Sajda Ladner, who passed away a month after filming.

"Sheila has touched so many people in her life," says Crista. "All these generations who've looked up to her, who she gave permission to dance and to see themselves in her. I wanted the film to honor her labor as a dancer, as a mother, and as a Black woman."

Once when on a visit with Rohan in her New Jersey home, she served bowls of homemade vegetable soup, and as we sat down for the meal, closed her eyes and bowed her head. *Do you know why I do that? I want to say thank you to the universe, to whatever, to myself. I want to make sure I stay thankful for what I have. Many, many people don't have this bowl of soup. Sometimes I stop in the middle of whatever I'm doing and say thank you. Now, it's not to any god, anybody in the sky, not any Jesus. It's just thank you. I don't know what happens when we die. I haven't settled that. One of my thinkings is when you're dead you're done. The energy we give out, our natural energy just goes back up. Anyway, thank you for this food I am about to receive for the nourishment of my body.*

Her gravitas earned her the nickname "Pearls" in the Legacy Council. "Sheila doesn't always say a lot, but when she does speak, it's always in these pearls of wisdom," Shelton explains. "Maybe it's because of her age, or her experience, or her spirituality. Sheila's plane is very high. We all look up to her."

12

Just as Sheila Rohan was making her exit, so too were some of the top donors who'd kept Dance Theatre of Harlem afloat since its inception. "When we started in the late sixties, it was the right social time," says Charles De Rose. "But little by little Black causes became less and less important to donors, even though the quality of dancing was getting better and better. When you base your budget on unearned income, you're asking for problems. Just because they helped you six years ago doesn't mean they're going to help you now. All of a sudden you have to pay a touring company to book you, and you have a problem with cash flow. So these things started multiplying. Every cent Arthur ever came by went into Dance Theatre of Harlem—this was his whole existence. When his mother died, I was in the hospital holding her hand, because Arthur was out hustling. I would try to manage a little bit of money for him. I would get his savings up to $100,000, $110,000, and he'd say, 'How much money do I have? I need the money. I can't make salaries this month.' 'Arthur, what're you doing?' 'These children have no money, Charles, and I'm not going to take your financial advice. This is my life. This is my thing. And I'm going to do it my way.'"

Gayle McKinney-Griffith could always tell when Mitchell was spiraling over budgets. "When he would come back from these fundraising meetings and they didn't give him the money or were stalling somehow, he could be very vulnerable," she says. "He never really wanted to show that, but he would say, 'I'm exhausted. I got to put my head down.' I'd think *Oh my god, he's letting me see he's human.* And that was touching. But I would never hold him or say, 'It's okay.' He would've slapped me! 'Girl, get out of here! You look like you're putting on weight!'"

When Mitchell caught wind that the dancers were keen to unionize, he threw a fit. The company was heading into a new season, and the grueling rehearsal schedule had pushed them to the brink. The male dancers were grumbling about their lack of standard union protections, leading one of the danseurs, Paul Russell, and McKinney-Griffith to investigate the benefits of joining the American Guild of Musical Artists. Mitchell was furious to learn they'd started collecting votes to unionize behind his back.

Privately, McKinney-Griffith tried to calm her boss down with assurances that they weren't asking for much. The dancers wanted him to abide by the union rules of a ten-minute break for every hour of work. Mitchell loathed the idea of such coddling and interference. Relentless when it came to his pursuit of perfection, he'd hold rehearsals for hours on end, forcing dancers to sneak panicked trips to the hallway drinking fountain or the fire escape for a shot of fresh air. "Oh no, we're not going to have any unions in here!" he yelled at his ballet mistress. "I'm the one who's going to be in charge, and I will tell you when you have your breaks!"

As the company's first union ambassadors, McKinney-Griffith and Russell pressed for months for him to sign the paperwork. He could get sued if a dancer got injured, they argued. Or if one of the company's underage apprentices was ever found to be touring without the required guardian and tutor. A lawsuit stating negligence would take down the company he'd fought so hard to build. For months, their pleas bounced off his stubborn ears. "He was always like, 'I'm rehearsing! I'm rehearsing! I can't talk about this now!'" says McKinney-Griffith. But she held the line, and with some helpful prodding from Mr. G and Mitchell's sister, Shirley, he eventually caved. The dancers received contracts with health insurance coverage and modest safety provisions. Now when grievances arose, like when Karlya Shelton and the other apprentices balked at their seventy-five-dollar weekly salaries, even though Mitchell had them working in demi-soloist and soloist roles, there was a path to negotiation. Still, the dancers held their union meetings in the costuming house that had moved across the street from the studio, out of fear that if Mitchell listened in, he might threaten to fire them all on the spot.

"Arthur was scared of losing control," says De Rose. "It wasn't megalomania so much as Founder's Disease. He was the parent, and this was his baby, and he was not going to let anybody else steer it for him or take any credit for it. There was a constant turnover on the board because Arthur could be very difficult to deal with. He would insult you; he would embarrass you. He would come to a board meeting, and he would upset the whole thing. 'Nah, you're wrong! We're not doing that! That's not right!' But people join your board because they're respected for their expertise in an area in which Arthur has no education or expertise. He couldn't let go. And that was him. Burn the boats."

LIKE CHILDREN UNAWARE of their parents' financial realities, the company wasn't privy to their own precarity. All they knew was to keep dancing, keep touring. On July 4, 1976, back in England, Dance Theatre of Harlem performed at the Manchester Opera House for an audience that included Mick Jagger. After the show, a member of the crew struck up a conversation with Jagger, who was delighted to learn that the dancers were staying at the same hotel as he was. He'd rented out an entire floor there, and he invited some of the ballerinas to come up and say hello. That night a handful of the women—including Shelton, McKinney-Griffith, and Abarca—joined Jagger in his hotel room, where he was already deep into partying with John Phillips from the Mamas and the Papas. Jagger suggested that they continue their evening at a nearby club. "We're all dressed up and Mick is wearing a white suit with a giant white hat," says Shelton. "We walked into the club and the whole room just stopped."

At the end of the night, everyone returned to Jagger's room, where the party went on until morning. "He was high up the wazoo, dancing on the bed and sofa," says McKinney-Griffith. They played backgammon, and the women tried to teach him how to play Bid Whist, a card game popular in Black colleges. Jagger had been sweet on Abarca throughout the evening, eager for her attention. But she said goodnight early, too nervous about what would happen if Mitchell, a man whose one vice was a nightly pint of ice cream, found out that they'd been smoking pot with one of the biggest rock stars in the world. "I tried to get Mr. Mitchell to drink a glass of champagne once, but he wouldn't do it," says Shelton. He didn't even drink coffee. Laughs McKinney-Griffith, "God no, he would've exploded."

PARTYING THE NIGHT AWAY with Mick Jagger was exactly the high-octane environment that Marcia Sells's grandmother had feared when her only granddaughter joined the company. She couldn't believe Mamie was letting an unchaperoned sixteen-year-old loose on the big city. "My grandmother was so worried that New York was going to turn me into a hoochie-coochie dancer that she threatened to stop talking to my mother if she let me go," says Sells, who, despite her excitement over joining the company, cried the entire flight from Cincinnati to LaGuardia after saying goodbye to her mother. She was going to stay with family friends in Brooklyn, where for months Marcia came home every night to an anxious message from her grandmother on the answering machine.

Dance Theatre of Harlem had arranged for Sells to continue high school at the Professional Children's School, which had a flexible schedule that allowed for full days of dancing. She enrolled as a junior, but because of her high test scores and credits from her magnet program back in Cincinnati, she was told that she could graduate by the end of the year. The report cards of younger dancers always went straight to Karel Shook, who was tasked with keeping an eye on their academic lives. "So you got that B in history?" he'd tease Sells while she was warming up at the barre. "Your mother said you used to get A's."

When Sells first moved to New York, she was placed downstairs with the ensemble, a ten-person preparatory group that took company class but hadn't yet been called up to join its ranks. Walter Raines, who ran the ensemble at the time, created a ballet to *Peter and the Wolf*, casting Sells as the Bluebird. The ensemble toured the ballet throughout New York City's public schools, performing in front of thousands of students. "Mr. Mitchell saw when I danced the Bluebird at a Sunday Open House," says Sells. "Then he started to bring me out, because I was the baby, at the lecture-demonstrations. He'd use me, saying things like, 'Okay, she's going to keep her leg here, see, it's not going to move.' It felt like he was noticing me."

That October, two months after moving to New York, Sells was catching her breath in the locker room after a full day of classes when an administrator burst in the room looking for her. "Marcia, you have to go upstairs to Studio 3 right now. Mr. Mitchell wants to talk to you." As she got herself together, Sells worried that she was in trouble, but upstairs, there was good news. "You are now an apprentice in the company," Mitchell announced. "You have to learn *Divertimento No. 15* tonight. Bring your pointe shoes and get ready. Rehearsal is at six o'clock."

Balanchine's *Divertimento No. 15* is choreographed for eight principal dancers, five women and three men, with a corps of eight women. Sells was told that one of the eight corps members had exited the company, just as Sara Leland, a former City Ballet principal entrusted with staging Balanchine's ballets on companies around the world, was wrapping up her final evening of instruction. Mitchell was in desperate need of an eighth for the corps, and he'd decided Sells was his best candidate.

"Fricking terror!" she says of being so abruptly thrown into Studio 3. "But I didn't have any time to get too insane with worry. Plus, I was already thinking, *Well, this is why I came here.*" Leland directed Sells to her spot on the floor, where McKinney-Griffith and a couple of other dancers demonstrated a few steps for the section. Waiting for the pianist to dive into the Mozart score, Sells reminded herself that she had a history of meeting the moment, like when she'd been thrown at age twelve into the Cincinnati Ballet's *Concerto Barocco* after one of their dancers had injured her knee. By the end of rehearsal, Sells, a fast study with a photographic memory, was caught up with the rest of the company. "I remember someone going, 'Wow, the baby is smart. She picked this up really quick!'" The following month they performed a section of the new ballet at a Sunday Open House.

As ballet mistress, McKinney-Griffith pushed Sells to focus in rehearsals. "Marcia would be chatty and laughing, and I'd have to tell her, 'Marcia, sit down!' She was a baby, so Mr. Mitchell wasn't going to choose her for a lot. But I told her to learn all the parts that she could and be serious about it." Sells still thinks that a large reason Mamie let her leave home in the first place was because of the kind impression McKinney-Griffith had made on her mother backstage in 1970. "If she hadn't met Gayle and thought, 'Oh, this is a really good woman, I can trust her with my child,' there's no way I'm in New York at sixteen." McKinney-Griffith was protective of all the younger girls who entered the company. Remembers Sells, "Gayle would forever be saying 'Okay, we have to make sure the baby is taken care of. Don't anybody scare the baby.'" Says McKinney-Griffith, "I felt a responsibility to watch out for Marcia while she prepared to learn the repertoire and travel on tour. I didn't want to disappoint her mother!"

Nonetheless, Sells was quickly baptized into a world of glamour and celebrity. While promoting his hit album *Songs in the Key of Life,* Stevie Wonder stopped by Dance Theatre of Harlem on a scheduled tour uptown. On the afternoon of his arrival, the entrance of the 152nd Street studio was crowded with eager staff and dancers. McKinney-Griffith escorted Wonder up the narrow metal staircase to Studio 3, and as the two made careful progress, he told her that he liked the sound of her voice. Upstairs, the studio had been set up as if for a scaled-back Open House, with enough chairs to accommodate Wonder and his team. As the company and the newly formed DTH Choral Ensemble crowded around the piano, Wonder serenaded the room with "You Are the Sunshine of My Life."

Not long after that, in Dallas, Dance Theatre of Harlem delivered four performances at a salute to singer Marian Anderson, hosted by Cicely Tyson. The actor LeVar Burton, fresh off his starring role in TV's *Roots,* narrated Mitchell's new ballet, *Dance in Praise of His Name.* At the gala following the performance, the ballerinas wore beautiful gowns designed by Mitchell's friend Halston. Burton took a fancy to Shelton and invited her out to dinner. Shelton asked Sells to tag along as a kind of chaperone. "I felt a little like a third wheel," remembers Sells with a laugh. "Mostly I was just dazzled that here's this guy who played Kunta Kinte who of course wants to date Karlya because she's so beautiful."

Sells got to take part too in a *Dance in America* nationally televised special honoring Mitchell's triumphant company, performing in soft shoe parts in *Forces of Rhythm* and *Dougla.* And then on Mother's Day, she performed in a specially choreographed concert performance at Avery Fisher Hall with George Benson, the thirty-three-year-old jazz musician whose album *Breezin'* had hit number one on the pop, R&B, and jazz charts. During rehearsals, Benson was playing his guitar in his dressing room when Shelton and fellow dancer Stephanie Dabney passed by. They followed the music inside the doorway, slid down the wall, and listened to him practice, basking in the intimacy of the moment. Mamie was in the audience that special evening, having come to New York to watch her daughter on the big stage.

Life was grand, as far as Sells was concerned. But then, right before what was supposed to have been her first New York season, came a rumble of trouble. Dance Theatre of Harlem's board of directors made the hard decision to cancel the company's scheduled spring 1977 season at the Uris Theatre. The announcement in *The New York Times* explained that the company "cannot afford a deficit which might jeopardize existing funding," and it urged the public to donate "the price of the ticket you would have purchased, had there been a season."

Mitchell didn't explain to the dancers why the season was canceled or if they should worry about job security. "Think about a general on the field of combat that loses a battle," says De Rose. "He's thinking about the war. It was always 'We go forward.'"

DESPITE THE CANCELLATION of their New York season, the company marched on with their robust touring schedule. During a West Coast swing that summer, the dancers were invited to appear in the film *A Piece of the Action,* directed by and starring Sidney Poitier, alongside co-star Bill Cosby. In the scene filmed at the Royce Theater in Los Angeles, the dancers perform in front of an audience, including Poitier and Cosby's con man characters, who are out with their dates for an elegant evening at the ballet. As the cameras rolled, Sells was preparing to sauté under an arch of dancers' arms when, to her horror, she felt the snap of her pointe shoe ribbon. With her strap flapping hopelessly, Poitier was forced to call cut.

"I was dying up there on stage," says Sells. "I thought I'd sewed it well enough, but it was just one of those terrible moments. I ran and got new pointe shoes on really quick, thinking, *Mr. Mitchell is going to kill me.* Like okay, this is it, I'm done. And Mr. Poitier, who was just a lovely, lovely man, came over to me and put his hand on my shoulder and said, 'It's okay. We'll just start filming again.'" The women shudder at the recounting of her narrow escape from Mitchell's certain wrath. "He beat Mr. Mitchell to you!" says Shelton.

Later that evening Sells called home to Mary Lane, as she did every night. "I met Mr. Poitier!" she exclaimed to her mother. "And he touched me!" When *A Piece of the Action* was released later that fall, Sells went to see it in the theater with her mother and younger brother. "When I do my grand jeté on screen," she says, "my brother stands up in the middle of the movie theater and yells, 'That's my sister!'"

AFTER FILMING, the company moved onward to San Francisco, where Karlya Shelton performed in front of four generations of family—her mother, her grandmother, her great-grandmother, and her younger brother, Kyle. "I hadn't ever seen dancing as political, at least not in the sense that we speak of it now," says Kyle. "But when I saw all the other women dancing, I thought, 'Well I'll be darned, they're all Black.' Because all those years I'd been going to see Karlya dance, I always knew when my sister was on stage. I couldn't help but see her because she was the only Black person up there! Now I got to see her with all these others and know she wasn't the only one. That filled me with a real sense of pride."

On a break before rehearsal, Sells and Shelton left the theater to grab breakfast. As they sat down with their plates of food at a window table in the crowded restaurant, Mitchell startled them by appearing on the other side of the glass. He pounded at the window, pointing down at their waffles and then gesturing at his behind, warning them not to eat. Shelton refused to look at him, the food in her mouth suddenly hard to choke down.

Sells knew she was on the curvy side for a traditional ballerina. "I had a butt" is how she explains it. But she was still so thin that, at sixteen, she hadn't even had her first period. "It's not like we were ordering French fries and cake and soda. But I was freaking out," she says. "Karlya was trying to school me and telling me to relax. 'Just look straight ahead. Don't let anybody know he's talking to you. No matter what, we have a right to eat.' Even when we walk back to the theater, she was still saying, 'Don't turn around, don't look at him. Just ignore him.'" Sells can laugh now telling this story, but Shelton doesn't crack a smile.

THEY HAD ONE DAY OFF while they were in San Francisco, and Sells spent it at a correspondence school, taking her final three exams so that she could graduate from high school. No senior prom for her. No cap and gown. She completed her exams and then overslept the following morning. She had a hotel room by herself because she hadn't been able to handle how anxious her assigned roommate had been about whether Mitchell liked her. So there'd been no one to throw a pillow at her head as she slept through her alarm. She woke to an empty room, realizing with terror that she'd missed the company bus to Berkeley, where they were scheduled to perform that evening. She took a taxi across the city, in a panic about how badly Mitchell was going to fine her, if not worse. When McKinney-Griffith saw her sneaking into the theater, she helped Sells gather money to pay the cab fare and distracted Mitchell while the girl got changed into her dance clothes. Sells made it on stage in time for company class without him being any the wiser, wondering aloud to the other dancers, "Nobody noticed I wasn't on the bus?"

That night when Sells called home to Mary Lane, Mamie greeted her with unexpected news. A thick envelope had arrived addressed to her from Barnard College. "You applied to college?" Mamie asked Marcia. The head of the Professional Children's School, a Barnard graduate, always urged her students to take the SATs and apply to one or two schools, regardless of their professional ambitions. "I guess I forgot to tell you," Marcia told her mother. "Well, go ahead and open the letter."

As her mother read her the acceptance letter, Marcia replied, "Okay, that's nice. But I'm not going." She'd been in the company less than a year and had barely been given a chance to dance on pointe yet. She thought she was just getting started.

FOR MCKINNEY-GRIFFITH, though, that tour of the West Coast was her last. At twenty-seven years old, she'd been feeling for some time that she had reached the apex of opportunity in the company. "At that time, we thought twenty-seven was old and that we were at our end," she says. She'd always loved watercolors and drawing and now wanted to explore stage design. She invited Mitchell out to lunch in San Francisco to share the news that she would be leaving the company. "I was telling him it's come to a time that I think I should start looking around about what else I can do."

The previous day she'd gotten a call in her hotel room from Louis Johnson. He'd been hired for the movie adaptation of the hit Broadway show *The Wiz*. He was putting together a skeleton crew of dancers to set the choreography on during a summer of preproduction. "Louis said, 'I need you. I need you,'" says McKinney-Griffith. "I was the only one he was asking from Dance Theatre of Harlem, and I had always danced in his ballets. I always thought, *I'm his favorite.* I told him we were on tour, and I'd have to think about it, and he said, 'Well, we're going to start soon so let me know.'"

Desperate for Mitchell not to feel like she'd been looking for work behind his back, she asked what he thought of her taking Johnson up on his offer. "And I remember he said, 'Oh Gayle, this is an opportunity for you! This would be good. You can branch out.'" After all, Mitchell had done Broadway and movies in the past. He knew not to squander good work when it came around.

They settled that she would leave the company immediately upon return to New York, but the door would remain open to her in the future. "We agreed on it, and he wished me luck," says McKinney-Griffith. "I didn't have any papers signed because I didn't think I needed it."

Rohan sucks her teeth listening to her friend's recounting of such a cordial arrangement. "Oh my God," she says. "That's back-stabbing." Because they all know now what would come next—Mitchell would erase the memory of their parting in his mind, casting McKinney-Griffith in the role of the abandoning child who betrayed her faithful father.

13

The *Wiz* was adapted from the seven-time Tony Award–winning 1975 Broadway musical of the same title, itself a Black reimagining of L. Frank Baum's *The Wonderful Wizard of Oz*. The Universal-Motown film, with Sidney Lumet directing his first musical and Quincy Jones serving as music supervisor and music producer. The movie starred Diana Ross as Dorothy, a naïve Harlem schoolteacher dropped into the Land of Oz; Michael Jackson, making his theatrical film debut as the Scarecrow; Nipsey Russell as the Tin Man; and Ted Ross as the Cowardly Lion. Lena Horne and Mabel King play Glinda and Evillene, and Richard Pryor, wearing a twenty-five-foot-high silver head, was the Wiz himself. Though considered a box office disappointment at the time of its release, *The Wiz* endures as a treasured cultural touchstone for Black audiences. Here finally was not just a big, splashy song and dance movie but a declaration that the archetype of home could hang just as naturally on a rural Kansas town as it could contemporary Harlem and the comforting breast of Black family life.

Lumet hired Louis Johnson to choreograph *The Wiz* because he was a fan of his ballet, *Forces of Rhythm*. Speaking to a reporter leading up to the movie's release, Johnson recounted, "[Sidney] told me up front he's never done a musical before, he said he knew I had the scope, and the eye, for a picture on this scale. He left me alone to do my own thing, but he'd pop in the studio all the time and watch rehearsals and say, 'Louis, you're right on it.'"

In preproduction, Johnson created choreography for elaborate production numbers like "Emerald City Sequence" and "Brand New Day" on McKinney-Griffith and the rest of his skeleton crew, who would later be charged with helping set it on the cast. During a summer of early rehearsals in their oven of a studio space, Johnson, a former high school acrobat, led with the churning energy of soda trapped in a shaken bottle. "Louis would do all the steps, all the flips, the tricks, the pirouettes, everything," says McKinney-Griffith. "He'd tell us, 'Do it like this!' while we just stood there amazed. Then he would watch us through this big squint of his. When you'd make a mistake, his eyes would suddenly go really big, and he'd say 'What was that? What was that you're doing?'" There was always the sense that if Johnson could have split himself in hundreds, he would've loved to dance the entire production himself.

BACK AT 152ND STREET, Mitchell struggled with the loss of his ballet mistress. He'd send up manufactured flares of need, then fume when McKinney-Griffith didn't heed his call. "He would tell me 'Well, you have to come in and rehearse *Forces of Rhythm* with the dancers,'" she says. "They've already done the ballet four thousand times, and now he wants me to come in and rehearse it? I'd tell him, 'These dancers already know this. They've performed it.' He'd say, 'Nope. You have to come in and rehearse this!' I would try to explain that I had a new contract I had to honor and couldn't just take the day off. But I know it infuriated him that I wouldn't come home."

And his losses were just beginning. Over seven hundred Black dancers were pouring into auditions for *The Wiz*, from New York, Los Angeles, Chicago, and Europe. Even Sheila Rohan, who'd officially been gone from the company for two years by then, wanted a shot at the movie. But by the time she called Johnson to see if he could use her, he was already drowning in dancers. "He told me 'No, darling, I have about two thousand dancers in here and I can't take another one,'" Rohan says with a laugh. "He was a wreck!"

Lydia Abarca, meanwhile, was twenty-seven years old and still getting by on her ten-thousand-dollar yearly salary when she asked McKinney-Griffith for Johnson's personal phone number. "Me in a dance movie?" says Abarca. "This is what I've been working toward my whole life! We had been with the company 24/7 for nine years. This was another pioneering moment for a Black dancer in New York City. I was going to meet every dancer in New York, from all genres of dance. Arthur's done Broadway; he's done movies. He knows! Come on, that's fair!" There was no review gushing enough, no part Mitchell could give her challenging enough, to convince her to stay. Her bank account was begging for her to make a break from ballet.

Her timing worked out well, sadly. At the end of the summer, Dance Theatre of Harlem had performances scheduled at Columbia University's Ferris Booth Hall, as part of a special community dance series. "This weekend may well be the last chance for New Yorkers to see the vibrant Dance Theater of Harlem in Manhattan for at least a year," wrote *The New York Times*. "The company has no plans to perform in the city outside its own school building until after September 1978. And it does not have any other bookings scheduled except August 19–20 at the American Dance Festival season in Newport, Rhode Island. Money, or the lack of it, is at the root of this sad state of affairs. The company has been experiencing financial crisis since last winter, when it canceled a season at the Uris Theater and went into a period of retrenchment."

And so whether they were simply avoiding the unemployment line or chasing Hollywood dreams like Abarca, that summer ten more dancers, many of them men, eased on down the yellow brick road to join McKinney-Griffith at the Kaufman Astoria Studios in Queens. Mitchell had lost nearly half of his company. Says De Rose, "Did it destroy him? No. But it did demoralize him, yes. He felt like we were a family. An army. 'We had gone on this mission together, and you desert me now?'" No matter how mad he got at them, though, how crudely he would demand them to return to him, those eleven dancers had signed contracts with the film. They weren't coming back until it was over, if ever.

MCKINNEY-GRIFFITH HEARD the rumors of Mitchell's fury but trusted in the end that he would remember their lunch in San Francisco. She wasn't a part of any mass exodus. If anything, he had encouraged her to join the production. "I would hear sometimes that he had put me in this group of people that he thought were trying to destroy the company. But we had already talked. We had an agreement. So all I could do was carry on with my work."

She helped corral the masses of dancers who had descended for pre-production rehearsals into smaller groups to start teaching them choreography. Younger-looking dancers and a pack of kid skateboarders were put in the Munchkins section. Professional models like Iman, Alva Chinn, Pat Cleveland, and Sterling St. Jacques, one of the first Black male supermodels, were herded into the large pool of the hundreds of dancers who would perform the glamorous Emerald City sequence. "In rehearsals, Louis would yell at us through his bullhorn," says Abarca. "'Bring your brains, people! Bring your brains!'"

The major stars of the movie were the last to report to set. To McKinney-Griffith's chagrin, Johnson tasked her with teaching a nineteen-year-old Michael Jackson, who would launch his solo career the following year, the buoyant steps to "Ease on Down the Road." She still groans at the memory. "Like you had to teach Michael anything," she says. "He knew those steps yesterday! I felt so stupid just doing these little 'Ease on down, ease on down' moves. How embarrassing! I remember that Michael was very shy, and he wouldn't really look at me. Then as soon as I went over the steps and the stage directions, his bodyguards swallowed him back up into the trailer."

The nearly seven-minute Emerald City sequence, in which Dorothy and her yearning friends finally reach Oz, was filmed on location at the World Trade Center. Twelve of the top fashion designers in the world, like Oscar de la Renta, Bill Blass, Halston, and Norma Kamali, contributed a whopping twelve hundred pieces to the number. The scene was shot over four freezing nights in November, and the cast of four hundred dancers and professional models made three costume changes throughout, shifting between glorious green, red, and gold outfits, as dictated by the Wiz's shifting sense of chic. While the wardrobe department rushed to make a hooded Calvin Klein cape lined in fox fur to keep the supermodel Iman cocooned from the night air, McKinney-Griffith and Abarca were left to battle the brittle temperatures in their diaphanous Norma Kamali numbers. "We had these little chiffon dresses on, and every time they said 'Cut!' we were like roaches, skittering to find little cracks to go into for warmth," remembers Abarca.

Luther Vandross wrote the film's triumphant finale, during which the once-captive Winkies celebrate Dorothy's defeat of Evillene, the Wicked Witch of the West. "Free at Last!" Nipsey Russell's Tin Man declares at the top of "A Brand New Day (Everybody Rejoice)." The camera lingers on a close-up of a grotesquely masked Winkie unzipping herself out of the leather covering, revealing Abarca's big daisy eyes and sunshine of a face alighting at the wonder of liberty.

When the movie was released, some critics roasted Diana Ross, who was thirty-three at the time of filming, for the sense of world-weariness she brought to an iconic character whom audiences associated with girlish innocence. And indeed, while they'd been filming, around the table during meal breaks, Abarca had heard some of the dancers, many of whom had come from the Broadway production, grumbling over Ross's casting, furious that Stephanie Mills had been denied the opportunity to recreate her iconic performance on film. But they applaud the way Ross had fearlessly thrown herself into the physical choreography of numbers like "A Brand New Day." "She was jumping off tables," recalls McKinney-Griffith. "All those men were so nervous that they were going to drop her. She'd just jump, and they'd flip her, saying 'We're not dropping Ms. Ross!'"

WHILE MCKINNEY-GRIFFITH AND Abarca worked on the film, Shelton remained in Harlem. She saw the thinning of company ranks as an opportunity for those left behind to make themselves more valuable in Mitchell's eyes. In the meantime, she grew familiar with the regular faces at the local unemployment office on West 90th Street, which the dancers referred to as Club 90.

Sells, who knew Louis Johnson from when they'd worked together on a ballet for the Cincinnati Ballet, remained in the company as well. "I'll admit, I was too afraid of Mr. Mitchell to leave," she says.

The following year, during a lecture-demonstration at Columbia University, both women were on stage with Mitchell when he spotted one of the dancers who'd left him for the movie in the back of the theater.

In front of the oblivious audience, Mitchell interrupted the proceedings to acknowledge the dancer trying to slip into his seat quietly. "Oh, here comes one of the Dumb Eleven," he spat, disdain thick in his voice.

"That was one of the times I really saw how ugly he could be," Shelton tells the Legacy Council. "I think he was just afraid of losing control, so he made himself the victim."

That same fall McKinney-Griffith dropped by Dance Theatre of Harlem to say hello and gather some of her things she'd left behind. As she was coming up the stairs, she spotted Mitchell coming out of his office above. "Mr. Mitchell!" she called out happily. He recoiled at the sight of her, raising his hands up into a defensive posture. "No, no, no, no, no!" he snapped. "Get back! Get outta here! Go home!"

McKinney-Griffith kept following him up the stairs, convinced he must have been talking to someone else. With mounting confusion, she reached out toward the man she'd worked tirelessly alongside for a decade. "I thought he was joking at first. I was still smiling because sometimes he could really clown around. And then he said, 'No! I don't want to speak to you. I don't even want to see you.' He put his hands up to block me from coming toward him."

Woozily, McKinney-Griffith made her way to the blue doors leading into Studio 3. "I was in a dream state because I didn't understand his rejection. I could not connect that this was Mr. Mitchell talking to me." Inside the studio, a room full of unfamiliar dancers stared uneasily back at her. She followed Mitchell's retreating back through the studio, mortified as he slipped out a second exit into the music room.

Looking wildly around what had for so long been her sanctuary, McKinney-Griffith spotted another dancer from *The Wiz* putting her shoes on in preparation for class. She cried out to her, a woman she'd considered a dear friend, begging her to make sense of the scene they had both just witnessed. "What is happening?" McKinney-Griffith begged. "Why is Mr. Mitchell screaming at me?" But the other dancer, likely terrified of being hit by the shrapnel of Mitchell's wrath, looked through her as if she weren't there. Humiliated, McKinney-Griffith fled the studio, leaving behind a decade of notebooks and files and old pointe shoes that would never be returned to her. Outside on the street, she let the tears she'd been holding back pour down her face.

· · ·

MCKINNEY-GRIFFITH CALLED HER parents that night, asking to speak to her father because she knew the story would upset her mother so much that Millicent would want to drive into Harlem to curse Mitchell out. "Whether Arthur is acting a fool," Harold counseled his daughter, "that's his thing, not yours."

McKinney-Griffith would later hear that Mitchell had condemned any dancer from *The Wiz* who hadn't returned to him tail tucked, begging for forgiveness and reentry into the company. He'd forgotten, or chosen to forget, the collegial lunch they'd had in San Francisco, his excitement over her fantasies of stage design, his delighting in her opportunity to work with Johnson.

Years later, when she shared the story of her departure from DTH with the Legacy Council, it was the first some heard of the messy details of her exit. "I had no idea it was so bad," says Abarca. "I mean, you must have been devastated. That was family. How could Arthur have done that to family?"

Rohan rolls her eyes at the question. "He was thinking *How could they do this to me?* Because we were his children. So *how dare they disobey me?* He took it as a personal insult, a betrayal. I can't say I was surprised, but Gayle had given this man her life. She really was the epitome of a ballet mistress. Bah! He lost a gem."

A couple of years after *The Wiz*, Mitchell would speak magnanimously about the eleven company members who left to do the movie, in an interview with *Ballet News* magazine. "I just couldn't compete with the salaries that Hollywood was offering my dancers. Anyway, for a lot of those kids, DTH was the only world they had ever known. They needed to branch out and experience new things. It's hard to lose dancers whom you've spent so much time training, but a good teacher doesn't try to hold his students to his breast and keep them at home. He encourages them to venture out and try new things. Sometimes it's the only way for them to grow."

Gayle

Walter Raines called me every day. He'd say, "Arthur's crazy. He's on his own planet." He would go on and on, trying to soothe my feelings. And my "Sheily." Sheila would talk to me for hours, just to give me strength and get me out of that funk I was in. Finally, I became defiant. I told myself, Arthur's not going to destroy me.

Sheila was making the rounds of the dance world, and sometimes when she couldn't teach at Ailey, she would ask me to substitute for her if I was in town. One of those times I was teaching a class, Alvin said, "Why don't you audition for the company?" I thought, Do I really want to be in a company again and deal with all the intrigue? I wanted to branch out.

I was always in the papers, looking for Broadway auditions. But every audition I would go to, there would be Debbie Allen and Mercedes Ellington, Duke Ellington's granddaughter. We all sort of looked alike, and we had the same style. After the four-hundredth time of being told "Thanks for coming in" and then hearing "Oh Debbie, dear!" I knew it was time to pack my bags whenever I saw either of them.

I did get to perform in several shows after Dance Theatre of Harlem with choreographers like Walter Raines [Almost Music], George Faison [Broadway Soul], and Louis Johnson [The Tale of Tremonisha, based on the Scott Joplin opera, and Miss Truth, a poetic piece about Sojourner Truth, starring Glory Van Scott].

In 1979 I had the papers to enroll in stage design courses when a friend called me out of the blue. Germany's Theater des Westens was inviting a group of dancers from the United States to be in different musical productions. They wanted three Black men and three Black women. My friend told me one of the dancers had dropped out. "You got to go see this man coming from Germany. You get paid!" It was going to be carte blanche. Beautiful hotels. Health insurance. Quadruple the salary of Dance Theatre of Harlem. They were talking thousands when I'd been getting hundreds.

In Berlin, we became a part of the German ensemble. A lot of the ticket sales were ambassadors and the military. They gave us the German text, and we learned everything phonetically. Our first musical was Showboat—that was horrible. I hated that show. I said, "Oh my god, we're back in slave times! Good thing this paycheck is hefty."

I always kept up my pointe work. There was one time when the Deutsche Oper, one of the hugest opera houses in Berlin, was creating a production about the life of Wagner. The choreographers, a Russian couple named Valerie and Galina Panov, had once been our teachers at Dance Theatre of Harlem. I ran across their minds because I was in Berlin, and they saw me at a performance. They told me, "Come in and audition. We're creating a piece about Wagner, with his music too." Oh, I thought, this is lovely, I'll get to dance on the Deutsche Oper stage on pointe again.

When I got there, we sat down at the table and we're going through the program, how it's going to be set up. They said, "You will be Wagner's mistress." They wanted me to be the whore. Well, I knew exactly how they were going to choregraph that. I was insulted that they would even think that I would go in that direction. Yes, you're a Black ballerina, but we can only think to cast you as a mistress. I said, "Oh no, if I'm going to do something it's going to have substance." They just looked at me like I was insane. I wanted to yell, "I'm from Dance Theatre of Harlem. Don't you remember?"

I thought I would stay in Berlin for six months, a year maybe. Then I married a man who went over with me for the Theater des Westens. My beautiful children, Don and Khadija, were born in Germany and attended the John F. Kennedy Schule, where I taught an after-school dance program for the students from kindergarten through high school in ballet, jazz, and modern movement. Khadija is a dancer too, so eventually she would teach classes there with me.

My husband and I wanted to create opportunities for dancers and artists *of diverse backgrounds. Unfortunately, my marriage was not always kind. If he was being horrendous, I told myself, that's just on him. I placed my energies and attention into my children and the projects that I was doing. If I didn't have a project, I would create one. I taught in several German cities as well as Italy, Switzerland, Liechtenstein, and Austria. I started the ballet department of what has become Tanzforum Wien. We started a youth dance program called Space and Time, working with social workers. Our goal was to keep at-risk kids off the streets and guide their energies into the theater and more creative outlets.*

NEJLA YATKIN, now an award-winning dancer and choreographer, first met McKinney-Griffith when she was an eighth grader, at a free class with Space and Time. Yatkin was a Turkish immigrant adrift in her Berlin school, the daughter of parents who didn't speak German and didn't approve of her love for dance. "But dancing was my place where I felt at home," says Yatkin. "From the moment I entered the studio and met Gayle, I fell in love. She was so kind and generous and loving. The way she enters a space, it's so very, very regal. I remember her coaching me one day, and she said, 'You have to extend and reach out in this direction.' And she extended her hand and her fingers, and it was like she went on forever. I was in awe of how one gesture could say so much." Yatkin studied under McKinney-Griffith throughout grade school, traveling with Space and Time on government-funded dance residencies to Holland and Italy. McKinney-Griffith became a kind of surrogate mother figure to her, a shoulder to lean on after Yatkin left home at sixteen and then again, when she was told by professional company directors in Berlin that she was talented but too dark-complected to hire. After moving to America, Yatkin joined Cleo Parker Robinson Dance, the Black modern dance company, explaining, "I always stayed connected in some distant way to Gayle, the woman who gave me a safe place to dance."

"My mom has always been so fluid in how she shared her wisdom," echoes her daughter, Khadija "Tariyan" Griffith, "so accessible and humble that I don't think growing up I understood all she'd accomplished in her life." Khadija liked to run around the apartment in her mother's pointe shoes as a child, but she wouldn't show any interest in lessons until she was ten. Even then McKinney-Griffith chose not to enroll her into a rigorous program. "She said, 'I wanted to protect your spirit,'" says Khadija. "I was a sensitive child, and she didn't want me in a strict space that would try to mold me. It was always, 'Look what I can do, Mom!' And she'd say, 'Beautiful!'" When she was twelve, Khadija happened upon a showing of *The Wiz* on TV, stunned to see her mother in a gold designer gown and planet-size hat dancing atop a grand piano with Quincy Jones on the keys. "I chased Mom around the house, like, 'What do you mean you were in this!?' The information of all my mother has done in her life has come in layers and bits like that. It was all there, in the pictures we had around the house, but I had to connect the dots."

In 2015 Khadija was in her Brooklyn apartment getting ready to audition for NBC's television production of *The Wiz Live!,* when her mother, as if feeling the tug of history, called her. "And Mom goes, 'I'm just thinking about you all the sudden. How are you?'" Khadija kept the audition a secret, not wanting to add pressure to the moment. After she got word that she'd been cast in the ensemble, she called her mother and her brother, Don, in a three-way call in which they joyfully celebrated the full-circle moment. "It was so powerful and surreal," says Don, a former semiprofessional basketball player and Connecticut attorney. "Whatever unfinished business Mom had, it felt like Dija was taking home." At the first table read, Khadija stood up and introduced herself as the daughter of one of the dancers in the original movie. A collective whoop rose from the cast, and the show's choreographer, Fatima Robinson, would later arrange for McKinney-Griffith to visit the top-secret set.

In 2016 McKinney-Griffith survived a final physical confrontation in her marriage. *It was spousal abuse. I had to leave Germany, my beautiful apartment, all my friends, the life I'd built there for over thirty-five years. I was devastated, but I just wanted to get out and be with my family and my children. I haven't spoken to him since.*

I've been surprised by how people can change. How they can turn on you. But I did feel like I got my apology from Arthur. I was at a book party for Alexis Wilson, the daughter of choreographer Billy Wilson. Arthur was ill at the time. He was walking with a cane and really struggling. I was there with my daughter, so I said, "Khadija, I want you to meet Mr. Mitchell." And he goes to her, "Oh my goodness, you are so beautiful." And then he said, "I would like to tell you that I'm very sorry that I hurt your mother." And she's just standing there because she didn't know our history. I never talked to my children about that because what would it get me, telling all my woes? I was shocked. He never really looked at me but just kept telling Khadija that he was sorry.

Then he said, "Come on, Gayle, come on and sit with me." I didn't want to, but he said, "No, no, no, come sit with me." We were right in the front. Alexis was telling the room all about the history of her book, and he's talking to me and laughing, disturbing me from listening. At the end, I got up and moved around, but then he was just there. He couldn't walk around. He just sat there for a while. So I said, "Arthur, do you need help?" He said, "I don't need any help!" I stood him up and said, "Well do you want me to go down with you in the elevator? Is your car there?" "No, I can do it! I can do it!" So I just said goodbye, and the doors closed.

Back in Connecticut, I went in for my annual mammogram, and they told me I had cancer. I couldn't believe it. I had just gone through that big blow-up in Germany. I was taking care of my mother. What was happening to me? My nerves were like razor blades. The doctors told me it was spreading into my lymph nodes, and it was going to be in my bloodstream. They wanted to operate right away. But because of what happened in Germany, my knee was injured, and I first had to have that surgery. Then I hobbled into the cancer center and had three operations in there. They put me on a cocktail of chemotherapy that just flattened me. I lost my hair, my eyelashes. I lost all my strength. I couldn't take care of my mother. It felt like all my walls had come crashing in and there was no floor. I just felt emotionally broken. I don't have any history of cancer in my family, but I'd been under so much stress and then my broken heart. Through all my upheavals, I would talk to Sheila. My friends. My mother. My children. When I wasn't strong enough to walk around, my son would carry me into my appointments.

"Talk about redefining strength," says Don. "I grew up with a different idea of what strength was. Now I realize that it's my mom who truly embodies strength. She has this quiet ability to weather any storm and come out the better for it. It's not loud and in your face. It's stay the course, stay disciplined, come out better. And that's what she's done. She doesn't break."

I decided I wasn't going to die because my mother still needed me. I got through it. Yoga and meditation helped. I don't have the energy and strength that I used to have, but I started teaching ballet again at the Dance Extension in Waterford [Connecticut]. *I'm a substitute ballet teacher at Connecticut College. I feel my peace returning. My son, Don, proposed to his girlfriend, Katy, who's going for her Ph.D. in education, on a beautiful beach here in Connecticut on the fiftieth anniversary of the* Loving v. Virginia *Supreme Court decision. They married a year later. At the reception, I heard Don say, "Mom, have I got a song for you!" It was "A Brand New Day."*

Tragically, in the years after the Legacy Council brought light again to McKinney-Griffith's storied past, her cancer returned, metastasizing in her spine. She spent weeks in a state of numbed paralysis, unable to speak the words aloud. *I was trying not to put the news in the air. If it goes in the air,* she told herself, *it'll get a power of its own. If I kept it contained, maybe I could squeeze it dead.*

When she finally found the words to share with the others, steady and wise Rohan surprised her by having the biggest emotional response, crying visibly on screen. McKinney-Griffith's eyes welled, remembering Rohan's tears. *She's my heart.*

I can't believe that this is happening again. I'm trying not to go down with depression. I don't like this at all. I feel vulnerable. When the group gets together, I'm always the one that's so quiet because I have no energy. I'm trying my best to keep present and to focus. I'm supposed to be the secretary of the council so I'm writing notes constantly. But I'm so tired. As a dancer, she knows what it means to work through the pain, cranking that smile on with a turnkey before taking the stage. But now she admits she is in a bad way. Sometimes it feels like the chemotherapy is draining her so completely of her life force that she'll have to lie down on the floor for hours. Her bones hurt. Everything tastes different. The neuropathy can get so bad she can't always feel her feet beneath her. She is going to lose her beautiful white hair again.

Not this fight. Not now, during this joyful time.

I've had to come to terms with, yes, I have this again. It does overwhelm you. Sometimes it's the physical pain where I'm just wiped out. But mostly it's emotional because I say, "Jeez, I've got to do this again?" I'm trying to hold on to the part of me that is still me and knows I can fight through this. But when a cancer metastasizes, where does it go? It can go anywhere.

I don't know how to fight it. So I'm relying on my meditation, breathing, yoga, movement, all these plant-based diets. My kids are focused on getting me through this. They're going to research and talk to the doctors and give me orders. I'm blessed. Coming from my marriage, I just know how to appreciate people. That taught me a big lesson. Never use anyone. Respect people. Understand that you're not the biggest fish in the sea. My work now is to hold on to some optimism. The treatments that I'm going through are supposed to keep me alive for a period of time. It might not kill the cancer forever, but I'm going to do everything I can to augment that thought process and keep it positive. Your body knows. Your soul knows.

She shakes her head, squeezing gently onto the tops of her arms. *If I had not danced, what kind of condition would I be in right now? All this pain. These pains let me know that my body is still trying, that it's still living. You live long enough to appreciate what you have and be thankful that you can still go for a walk outside. Every time I'm at the clinic, they ask me, "Do you need a cane or a wheelchair?" And I'm thanking myself constantly for being able to say "No, I'm okay." As a dancer I honed this body for so many years. When you're younger, a decade younger even, you think to yourself,* I don't like my hips. I don't like my legs. *I can't do an arabesque anymore. I can't lift my leg up. I get a cramp when I point my foot. But I'm okay. I'm okay. I'm okay. I wish there was something that we could say to people to remind them, "Your body is your house. Just be thankful for it and to it."*

But after months of treatment, McKinney-Griffith ultimately has to choose her words carefully to share news with the Legacy Council that she knows will be hard for them all to hear. *I'm at stage four. There are no more stages to go. They're trying to do as much as their knowledge allows. I'm still looking at other doctors and treatments, but my body is pretty fed up with all of this.*

Rohan leans closer into her camera, the power of her gaze tunneling through the screen. "Well, this is when your spirit takes over," she says. "And you're a very spirited person, Gayle. This is why you were always special to me. That's part of my attraction to you. You were the person that we all were drawn to. There you are. You have it in you."

It calls to mind a story Khadija shared about taking a vacation with her mother a few years earlier. She had just lost a job with a world-renowned company after questioning the racial stereotype of the character she'd been cast to play. Show business will try and try to break a Black woman's heart. Mother and daughter escaped to Miami for Christmas. "That time together has a taste and smell to it," says Khadija. "My mother just let me cry on her. We would go on walks together. We could see the water from our hotel room. I remember my mom saying, 'Do you see? We're connecting to sources. You have water. You have sun.' And I turned to her and said, 'And I have you. I have my source here.'"

I'm not going to give up, McKinney-Griffith tells her friends again, her voice taking on a reassuring heft of stubbornness. *I think about our group, and I think about our work. That's what keeps me going. At least they'll know I was here.*

McKinney-Griffith holds up a photo of her nineteen-month-old grandson, Emmitt, Don and Katy's child. He's wearing a black onesie with the words READ TO ME across his plump little chest. The brightness of his wide-open smile could power the sun. From the Tuesday when McKinney-Griffith first announced that she was going to be a grandma, to her announcement of Emmitt's first words, to his first steps, to his first face full of cake, the Legacy Council has celebrated each milestone right along with her. There is comfort in the knowledge that this child will grow up knowing everything his grandmother did as a girl, and then as a woman. McKinney-Griffith has put her story down on record. *It brings tears to my eyes when I think that I've done some work that he can be proud of one day.*

14

By the time Dance Theatre of Harlem went on hiatus in 1977, Marcia Sells had already deferred her college acceptance to Barnard. With the future of the company uncertain, she thought about trying out for Alvin Ailey in the meantime. But she knew she wasn't a modern dancer. She considered auditioning for Broadway or moving to Europe. "But at seventeen, I just didn't have that level of risk in me," she says. "I'd built this life for myself in New York around family, friends, and safety. All this thinking around auditioning made me realize I'd gotten spoiled. I'd always been good enough to just get asked to do the work. So when DTH stopped performing I had to really think, *How do I find a home?*"

After hearing that Marcia was considering pulling up stakes for Europe, Mamie reminded her daughter of a more practical next step. "Well, you already got into college," she said. "Why don't you call Barnard?"

And so in January 1978, Marcia Sells entered college as a midyear freshman. Eager to throw herself into the full college experience, she moved into a dorm for the semester, before transitioning to a two-bedroom first-floor apartment on West 110th Street that was a block away from Karlya Shelton's apartment building. That summer two new dancers—Judy Tyrus, who in 2022 published *Dance Theatre of Harlem: A History, A Movement, A Celebration* alongside Paul Novosel, and Melanie Person, who is currently the co-director of the Ailey School—moved in with Sells.

When the girls threw parties, they'd move all their furniture out into the hallway by the freight elevator to make room for dancing. Come fall, now a year since Dance Theatre of Harlem had been on tour, Sells signed up for another semester with a full courseload. She arranged her schedule with the precision of a surgeon so that she wouldn't miss Karel Shook's daily company class or Arthur Mitchell's evening rehearsals.

Mitchell had spent the last several months building back the company ranks with fresh young apprentices he called up from the school, some as young as fourteen. A couple of dancers returned from *The Wiz,* after he'd humbled them with a grueling reaudition process. The prevailing mood within the company, which had grown from thirteen to twenty-five members, with twelve apprentices on hand for larger works from their repertoire, was one of resilience. "After everyone left, it was just a reimagining and a regrouping," says Shelton. "It was a great opportunity for someone like me because I could step up. But it was strange not having our foundational rocks around."

OUT OF THE DUMB ELEVEN, it was only Lydia Abarca who Mitchell chased after to return. Before she left for *The Wiz,* her company salary had risen to $350 a week. Mitchell offered to make it $450 if she'd just come home. But her experience on the movie had reminded her of sneaking into that jazz class back when she was a teenager looking for magic. She wasn't ready to give it up.

It can be hard to shake the scarcity complex that comes from growing up sharing a bathroom with eight family members, always yelling at your siblings to leave the door open to keep the room from stinking, and to let the next person know when it was free. Abarca had spent ten years dancing for Mitchell. She'd had a decade of rave reviews and modeling jobs and the occasional magazine cover. Yet she was still broke. She had to share an apartment with her sister Celia and brother, Julio, to make rent. "What's recognition unless it brings a lot of money with it?" she once asked a reporter. "One day I'm going to make so much money, and then I'm going to buy my parents land and a house and everything they want."

Going home to Mitchell sounded like taking a step backward. She had to try something new. "I was this little mouse who knew what she wanted but had no idea how to get it," she says. Besides, she'd already helped build the company the first time around. She wasn't up for the rebuild, not when she finally had other opportunities to choose from.

During filming, Abarca had met a performer named Smokey who'd starred in the original Broadway production of *Bubbling Brown Sugar,* the great Billy Wilson musical revue about the Harlem Renaissance night-life scene, back when folks drank bathtub gin and scotch out of teacups. Smokey told her the show's producers were looking to launch a two-week engagement of *Bubbling* at the Paper Mill Playhouse in New Jersey, with the legendary bandleader Cab Calloway headlining. "Here was this jazz, this jazz in my life that I've always been missing," says Abarca. She took two days to cram in new tap-dancing skills and landed the role of Sophisticated Lady, the woman from the title of Duke Ellington's song whose elegant fur stole and opera-length gloves belie a broken heart.

After *Bubbling,* Abarca got word that Bob Fosse, the man who had literally brought jazz hands to the Broadway stage, was looking for dancers. The legendary choreographer and director of *Cabaret, Liza with a Z,* and *Pippin* was getting ready to make *All That Jazz,* his semi-autobiographical movie starring Roy Scheider and Jessica Lange. "There were about five hundred dancers in the theater," Abarca says of the audition. "The first routine that Bob Fosse always did is a ballet routine. I was in the front, and after my group finished, he said, 'Wait a minute, wait a minute. You. What's your name?'" After several more rounds of auditions, the casting director called her with good news. "Did you ever have any doubt?" the woman asked as Abarca squealed into the phone.

But Smokey, who'd been sweet on Abarca since *The Wiz* and finally won her heart on *Bubbling,* had been cut after the first round of the *All That Jazz* auditions. He had it in his head that his new girlfriend should follow him right out the door. He signed on to an international company of *Bubbling* that was heading to Europe for the summer, and he convinced Abarca to bail on the movie and join him abroad. "Smokey kept telling me, 'You're just going to be in the chorus,'" she says now. "'You got a chance to be the Sophisticated Lady in Europe. You know how they love Black dancers over there!'" When Fosse got word that she was turning down the movie, he called her personally to urge her to reconsider. Abarca can't help but cry when she recounts the brevity with which she told him no. She left for Europe, already worried that she was making the biggest mistake of her life, and all for the love of a man who liked her but loved cocaine more. "It will always be one of my biggest regrets. Sometimes I think *Wow, what a different life I might've had if I'd stayed.* I turned down the movie for all the wrong reasons. I just didn't know how to be a star."

Mitchell, aghast that she'd chosen Europe over Harlem, would've agreed with her. Whether he liked it or not, he'd have to rebuild without his muse.

THAT FALL Marcia Sells began dreading her time in the studio, knowing she'd have to deal with Mitchell's judgment. "I had gained the Freshman Ten. Which at my height is still the weight of a thin person but not ballet thin. I'd gone through puberty and filled out a bit. Honestly, it just made me look normal. I knew I was going to have to make some changes physically. I'd hit that point in my life where weight was suddenly going to be an issue." She never made herself throw up, like some of the other dancers, but she started skipping breakfast and lunch, relying on Tab soda for shots of energy, and experimenting with protein diets. But no matter what she tried, the fact was that she no longer had the body of a young girl.

"I think the piece that I still haven't fully come to grips with," she shares with the Legacy Council, "is that although we were a Black ballet company, we were still always confronted by the imagery of what white women dancers look like. I truly believe that Mr. Mitchell was still comparing some of us to that. It's why he'd choose girls I came up with who looked like a washboard over me, even though I would compare my pirouettes to any of theirs."

"He was mixed up," says Rohan. "In School of American Ballet, he was up against Louis Johnson. But Louis said Arthur got it because of his body and the way he looked. You see, Louis was manly looking. He had great feet, and he could jump and do fabulous things like Baryshnikov. But he was shorter and stockier. Whereas Arthur had that long look."

"And Mr. Balanchine was thinking who he could partner with someone like Tanaquil Le Clercq and Allegra Kent," adds Sells.

Rohan nods sadly. "Right, so Louis would've been a novelty, compared to where he was able to fit Arthur in. I think this is what Mr. Mitchell was doing with our company."

Sells was confused by Mitchell's seeming lack of faith in her. Occasionally in lecture-demonstrations, he let her get up on pointe. She got to perform the pas de neuf from *Holberg Suite* for an audience of children. She understudied for one of the eight corps de ballet roles in *Concerto Barocco*. But for the most part, Mitchell consigned her to soft-shoe ballets like *Caravanserai* and *Dougla*. She couldn't help but wonder if it was because of her body type and also the darkness of her complexion.

"Yes, there was colorism at Dance Theatre of Harlem," says Sells. "It was hard, and it was sad. I remember doing Skirt Girls in Louis Johnson's *Forces of Rhythm*." (In the ballet, the women cast in the role of Skirt Girls wear full-circle ankle-length skirts and kerchiefs and dance more modern choreography; Ballet Girls wear short ballet skirts and pointe shoes, dancing allegro variations with fast footwork, jumps, and pirouettes. Rohan, who started as a Skirt Girl but eventually was recast as a Ballet Girl, says the latter was the more coveted role.)

"I remember thinking *I'm really talented, why am I doing Skirt Girls and not Ballet Girls?*" says Sells. "But it was all the light-skinned girls in Ballet Girls and all the darker-skinned girls in Skirt Girls." She points out that her mother had been denied admission to Spelman College years earlier for failing to pass the paper bag test—the discriminatory practice within the Black community in which a person's skin tone was held up to a brown paper bag. "Colorism was not just a problem for Arthur Mitchell," says Sells. "This permeated Black life, period."

Years later Marcia Sells would write a letter to her mother describing how her passion for ballet faded under Mitchell's care. "Somehow my growth as a dancer regressed once I joined the company," she wrote. "I think my emotional and mental growth started exceeding my growth as a dancer and affected my dancing. As my emotional attitude toward dancing changed, my satisfaction with DTH decreased. My weight then proceeded to increase. This combination of events had a profound effect on how I saw DTH, and they saw me."

That fall Mitchell called Sells into his office, informing her once again that she needed to drop weight if she was going to stay in the company.

She remembers feeling bruised and angry but not ashamed. "I'm deep into feminist literature at Barnard by this point, and I had this amazing professor Cate Stimpson, who is one of the leading feminist scholars, teaching me in a class. So I'm rethinking everything and asking myself, *Do I have it in me to still listen to him talk about my weight?*" She laughs, remembering the time she responded to one of his lectures by saying, "You know, you're not really being helpful to my emotional health right now." Mitchell was so unused to being talked back to that all he could do in response was sputter for her to get out of his office. Years later he would tell people of Sells, "Oh yeah, she used to be my smarty-pants."

Eventually Mitchell made the mistake of trying to form an alliance with Mamie Sells. He called her behind Marcia's back, looking to tag-team the girl to lose weight. "Like what did he think was going to happen?" says Sells. "She's not going to beat me. I'm certain she did not let him bad-mouth me. She had my back. As much as she loved ballet and was overjoyed that I'd found this thing that I loved, she was not a dance mom in any sense of the word. She wasn't living through me. She was appreciative of the talent, and she loved the art form and she loved classical music. But she never made me feel like I had to look a certain way or do a certain thing. I think the call really worried her. *My baby is there, and you're saying what to her?*"

Mitchell remained obstinate that Sells couldn't balance college life with the task of getting back into performing shape. Dance Theatre of Harlem was getting ready to embark on a West Coast tour. One morning Sells rushed up the stairs, knowing that she'd overslept after staying up late the night before studying and had missed the start of rehearsal. She stood against the wall leading into Studio 3, waiting for a chance to slip in among the dancers. When Mitchell noticed her standing there on the landing, he shook his head in exasperation. "What is that girl going to do?" he demanded of the studio. "Would that girl just make up her mind?" Sells felt her face go hot but forced herself not to cry or flee in embarrassment. "I would've walked out of class, but I didn't want to give him the satisfaction."

In Legacy Council meetings, she shares for the first time the heart-break of his ultimatum. "As much as I loved college, my whole life existence has been ballet. I'm a ballerina. I'm going to be in a ballet company.

I'm in a ballet company. The hardest part was then it didn't match all my dreams. The artistic director from the Cincinnati Ballet, which I left at sixteen, once told my mom, 'Well, we got her best years.' And that's sad to me. Because I know what I was able to do."

After rehearsal, Mitchell called her into his office. The two sat looking at each other, each painfully disappointed in the other. "I was just so sad and angry that he was making me make this decision to quit dance that I didn't think was actually necessary," she says. "I could've just taken a deferral from school and stayed. But at that point I was just so mad at him. I remember saying to him, 'You have psychological problems,'" she says, amused by her younger self's boldness. "I was eighteen years old. Disappointed, disillusioned, and feeling my oats of what I was learning in school. So yeah, '*Mr. Mitchell, you have psychological problems, and this is just ridiculous.*'"

Then she walked away from the life she'd dreamed about since she was a child, without the comfort of knowing she'd reached her potential. Besides the death of her mother, it would be the great loss of her life.

While setting the ballet *Ancient Voices of Children,* choreographer Manuel Alum practices a lift with Sheila Rohan in 152nd Street's Studio 3. *(Photo by Martha Swope © The New York Public Library for the Performing Arts)*

Lydia Abarca, still in pink tights, and Derek Williams perform a section of George Balanchine's *Agon* for a 1974 open-house crowd that includes *(from left to right, beginning with Abarca's extended leg)* Margaret Thatcher, Arthur Mitchell, Princess Margaret, Lord Snowdon, and Karel Shook. *(Photo by Martha Swope © The New York Public Library for the Performing Arts)*

Gayle McKinney-Griffith and Derek Williams take their final bows after dancing the pas de quatre in Arthur Mitchell's *Fête Noire*. *(Photo by Martha Swope © The New York Public Library for the Performing Arts)*

Lord Snowdon captured this image of Jerome Robbins with Lydia Abarca during rehearsals of Robbins's ballet *Afternoon of a Faun*, in which a young male dance student becomes romantically obsessed with a ballerina. *(Photograph by Snowdon / Trunk Archive)*

Gayle McKinney-Griffith, after the transition to brown tights and shoes, is finally chosen by Mitchell to don the purple tutu and dance the pas de deux with Paul Russell in *Le Corsaire*. *(Photo by Martha Swope © The New York Public Library for the Performing Arts)*

At the age of ten, Marcia Sells traveled to New York City to attend Dance Theatre of Harlem's first summer intensive program. Here she is practicing her sautés à la seconde in a studio full of older teenagers. *(Photograph by Mamie Earl Sells, courtesy of Marcia Sells, private collection)*

Gayle McKinney-Griffith performing with Roman Brooks in DTH's adaptation of Lester Horton's *The Beloved,* in which McKinney-Griffith plays a doomed wife wrongly accused of adultery. *(Photo by Martha Swope © The New York Public Library for the Performing Arts)*

may 1975
$1.50
calendar
of
summer
dance
events
equus

the
ravel
festival

cologne
dance
forum

dance
theatre
of
harlem

lydia
abarca
in ·
"bugaku"

Lydia Abarca appears on *Dance Magazine*'s May 1975 issue in *Bugaku* costume, making history as the first Black ballerina from a traditional company to land the cover. *(Studio portrait of Lydia Abarca photographed by Kenn Duncan. Reprinted with permission from Dance Magazine)*

While sightseeing on a day off in San Francisco, Arthur Mitchell spontaneously struck a pose in front of the Golden Gate Bridge for Karlya Shelton. "He was just being silly, and the performer in him came out," says Shelton. "Arthur Mitchell was not one to want to take a bad shot." *(Courtesy of Karlya Shelton-Benjamin, private collection)*

When the dancers were told their Chicago hotel rooms weren't yet ready for check-in, the women opted for a lovely afternoon at the park across the street. Lydia Abarca set her camera on a timer, and they crowded in for a photo. *From left to right:* Virginia Johnson, Karen Brown, Gayle McKinney-Griffith, Karlya Shelton, and Lydia Abarca. *(Courtesy of Lydia Abarca-Mitchell, private collection)*

Sheila Rohan in the majestic principal role of the Bride in Geoffrey Holder's *Dougla,* which became one of DTH's signature ballets. *(Photo by Martha Swope © The New York Public Library for the Performing Arts)*

From left to right: Ronda Sampson, Karen Brown, and Marcia Sells perform as Skirt Girls in another of DTH's early signature ballets, *Forces of Rhythm,* during a Nashville taping for the 1977 *Dance in America* television special *(Courtesy of Karlya Shelton-Benjamin, private collection)*

In 1979, DTH added Balanchine's *Serenade* to its repertoire. Audiences were treated to the glorious sight of seventeen Black ballerinas standing in a state of luscious anticipation as the curtain rose on the first movement. Here we see Karlya Shelton front and center. *(© Jack Vartoogian / Front Row Photos)*

In an artful twist on the traditional ballet blanc, Arthur Mitchell wanted his *Swan Lake* dancers swathed in shades of blue: the deeper the dancer's skin tone, the darker the blue. From left to right at the point of the V are the four cygnets, Yvonne Hall, Terri Tompkins, Karlya Shelton, and Judy Tyrus. *(© Sharon W. Birthwright-Greco)*

Members of DTH performed at the White House during the Reagans' first State Dinner on February 26, 1981. Afterward, they were thanked by President Reagan and First Lady Nancy Reagan. *From left to right:* Donald Williams; Theara Ward and Lorraine Graves in Skirt Girl costumes from *Forces of Rhythm;* Karlya Shelton, who performed an excerpt from *Allegro Brillante;* and Mel Tomlinson. *(Courtesy of Ronald Reagan Presidential Library and Museum / NARA)*

In 1979, as the company reimagined itself after so many of its dancers left to perform in *The Wiz,* Karlya Shelton danced in the principal role in Choo San Goh's *Introducing. From left to right:* Shelton, Stephanie Dabney, Ronald Perry, Melva (China) Murray-White, Hinton Battle, and Karen Brown. *(© Jack Vartoogian / Front Row Photos)*

Marcia

Who was I going to be in this world now? I've invested all this time into ballet, and who was I without that? After college I went to Columbia Law School, where I started my switch into what my other life was going to be. At the time I'm thinking, Oh, I'll be an entertainment lawyer. That's how I stay in dance and the art world. But then I intern at the NAACP Legal Defense Fund, the Cincinnati Institute of Justice, the NOW Legal Defense Fund. I turn in some ways to the social justice issues that my parents have always focused on and find my identity there instead.

I become an assistant district attorney trying rape and child abuse cases for the Kings County District Attorney's Office. I have to say my mom was really quite proud of me. I used to talk to her on the phone and run through my summations with her, and she would give me pointers. The biggest case I won was helping to convict the Flatbush rapist who had committed four rapes. I was twenty-seven years old, with three years of experience under my belt. A win like that gives you a mixture of feelings. It's sad to see people go to jail. For me, it's still sad. But it is also important that people believed the women, one of whom was maybe just eighteen or nineteen years old, who got up to testify.

When I went to the DA's office, I knew that I'd found my purpose. Not just because of those cases. I knew I could develop the tools and the language of law. But the reality of being a trial lawyer is also having the ability to communicate with people who are not trial lawyers. The performance part *made me comfortable. I knew how to connect with an audience, a jury, on things I felt righteous about. It goes back to Mr. Mitchell's training. His core thing was you had to move. If you're a tall person, you couldn't shrivel. You couldn't look like you were static. "Shit or get off the pot," he'd tell us. Commit to the movement. You had to expand your arms. Take up space. That idea of taking up space has stuck with me my entire life. I try to walk into a space feeling like I know I'm going to own the room. Not from the standpoint of I want everyone to know me, but I'm here to learn something about people. Around this time, there was a story in* Smithsonian Magazine *about Dance Theatre of Harlem. I remember reading it at my mother's house. In it, Arthur Mitchell mentions, "Yes, one of our former dancers is a prosecutor in the Brooklyn DA's office." Like, wow, I thought this man who had once been a father figure to me had no idea what I was doing, nor cared. When I read that he actually claims me as one of his own, it warmed my heart.*

After my parents divorced, my mother started her own human resources consulting business to push matters of diversity, equity, inclusion, although the work wasn't called that then. She worked with companies like Procter & Gamble and the University of Cincinnati to recruit and keep minority hires. But when her health started really failing, her health insurance plan was expensive. I left the DA's office for a corporate job that paid triple my salary because the bills were just too high. It was the hardest job I ever left. Even with all the craziness and the sadness of the work, I saw myself becoming the bureau chief there. I was already a supervisor in the bureau. I was trying big cases. I loved the work. My mother was furious. I told her I was going to leave New York altogether to come live with her, and she said, "No, you are not. You're not leaving."

I was blessed with this huge apartment, so as my mother's health failed, she used to come and live with me for four months out of the year. I was in my twenties, and I had to get an oxygen tank, and we had the emergency numbers for all the doctors. Even toward the end when she was on oxygen 24/7, literally rolling an oxygen tank, she was determined to live. Her doctor inserted in her one of the early stents of a trachea and told me, "She's not eligible for a lung transplant. This is the last thing I can do for her." She made me move her back to my grandmother's house in Ohio because she wouldn't let me live with her as her health was really declining.

At the end of my first year as dean of students at Columbia Law School, I remember coming back to Ohio for a visit. Friends of my mom greeted me at the airport. They told me she was in the hospital, and they needed to take me directly there. And that was it. She was in the ICU for three weeks, and she died in July 1992. I now realize just how young my sixty-two was compared to hers. She was robbed. Although she wasn't expected to ever have children, and she did that.

A lot of people don't acknowledge how much of life is about grace. When my daughter, Alix, was born in 2001, I went into the hospital a little earlier than we needed. The next evening my roommate woke up and started screaming, "I need more drugs! I need more drugs!" She was completely alone and had just given birth, and she really needed to get high. And I thought about my daughter and how whatever mother we get as a child is completely random. My husband is a molecular biologist. My father was in the hospital visiting me with my stepmother, who also has a Ph.D. All these other family members were coming in, and I'm thinking, Here are the people that are going to surround my daughter's life. *I didn't know whether this woman sharing my room had a boy or girl, but I know we both had babies born days apart. And that is why I've spent my career looking for opportunities to create spaces of equity—so that life isn't just about grace and what families you are born into.*

When your child is born and you experience all this new emotion and vulnerability, you see the world differently. I remember looking at Alix thinking, Holy shit. How did my mother let me go and move to New York City? New York City! *When my daughter went to kindergarten, I remember thinking,* Somebody else is going to be in control of Alix's life now. How can I do this?

I started bringing Alix as a baby around Dance Theatre of Harlem because I was helping the company out with some neighborhood grants. Mr. Mitchell was so sweet with Alix and used to massage her six-month-old feet so they'd be pointy and she'd have good turnout when she got older. We enrolled Alix in classes at DTH when she was a little girl. Mr. Mitchell taught her a few times. That was weird. It was almost like seeing your dad when he's with your children. On the one hand, you recognize that he's not being as hard as he was on you, but on the other, you're like, I'm not putting up with any nonsense. "I remember him trying to get us to listen and use his technique," says Alix. "He was getting really frustrated with us and my mom had to be like, 'Mr. Mitchell, they're five.'"

Alix wanted to be an athlete, not a dancer. She played T-ball, baseball, hockey all through high school and into her first year at Barnard. Oh god, she used to always ask me, "Would your mom have liked watching me play hockey?" Well, my mom would've loved watching her play. She would have absolutely loved everything about it, except for the cold. My mother was still around when Grant Fuhr was the first Black player to win the Stanley Cup.

MARCIA SELLS'S DAUGHTER graduated from her alma mater, Barnard, in 2023. "I want to work in sports and community outreach," says Alix, who was her mother's date at the world premiere of *Fire Shut Up in My Bones* at the Met. "I want to help grow the game of hockey in terms of including women and more people of color. It's one of the fastest-growing sports in the United States but still demographically doesn't reflect what it could. There's a lot of work to be done there. I think a lot more people could appreciate the sport if they had access to it. And, yes, I'm very aware that I sound like my mother's mini-me."

At the Legacy Council gathering when Lydia Abarca shared the story of her abortion, Sells surprised the group by sharing that she had had an abortion too, when she was a teenager. She was a college student at Barnard, and *Roe v. Wade* was the law of the land by then. Her abortion was legal, and it was safe. "I did not have to go through what you did, Lydia," she says, her face full of compassion. "And I had no shame. My mother always said, 'Try doing pirouettes with a baby on your hip.'"

"Wow," gasps Abarca, stunned. And then later: "But what other choice did I have? I was only seventeen. Every year I say what age they would've been if they were alive today. But do you know what I still pray every night? That that spirit I denied was able to be born into a loving family. That its soul found its way to a mother and father ready to give it the life it deserves. I ask for forgiveness. It was a hard choice, but it was also the only choice I had if I wanted to pursue my dream."

If I had to carry a child for forty weeks when I was in college, I don't think I would've been able to become the person I became. There are lots and lots and lots of women who raise kids and do a marvelous and amazing job as single parents. I don't know that I would've been that person. When I was at the DA's office, I handled so many cases of young people who sadly had children way too early and were in courts because they committed crimes against those children. Those are the saddest cases I worked.

There's that grace again. Sells was able to build a life of her own making, a career that ended up being modeled after her parents', who worked so hard to create spaces that were safe and inclusive to all. But it took joining the Legacy Council to realize she never really left ballet, and it didn't leave her.

For most of my career, I didn't put my performing background on my résumé. I thought it might make me sound unserious, to be frank. I thought people might think it was silly. But then when people did find out, they'd be like Oh my god, you were an actual ballerina! *I realize now that the discipline of ballet—every single day you go to the barre, and you start all over again, and you keep repeating the movements—gives you a real grounding in terms of how you tackle life. Music will come on, and parts of the steps will come up for me, even whole sections of the ballet. You have an emotional and physical body memory of that time, even though you can't do it anymore. American Ballet Theatre is doing* Swan Lake *at the Met right now, and the music is piped into my office speakers. "Oh, there's the dance of the four swans, the échappés." You remember it, always.*

15

In 1978, just four months after leaving New York for the European tour of *Bubbling Brown Sugar,* Lydia Abarca was on a plane back home, crying into her tray table. It had been sweet for a while. Escargots and champagne during rehearsal weeks in London. A show opening in Amsterdam, before moving on to the Théâtre de Paris. Then she says her boyfriend had convinced her that they should call in sick from a performance and take a day trip to England to hang out with the London cast. When they returned to Paris, they discovered that the show's producers had ordered all their belongings packed up. Their ruse of illness had earned them an immediate dismissal from the show. Abarca, who'd never been fired in her life, was humiliated, furious at herself for listening to her boyfriend again. They'd stay together for a while longer, but the honeymoon was over. Upon their arrival back in New York, her boyfriend immediately returned to Paris to retrieve a wolf-fur coat he'd left behind on layaway at a store. Abarca went to 152nd Street, begging for her old job back.

Arthur Mitchell gave her a hard time, but for better or for worse, Abarca could always count on him to take her back. "Lydia wanted so much more for herself," her husband of forty years, Al Mitchell, surmises, "and Arthur held on tight to her and acted like a tyrant. But no matter how crazy he acted, he would always have open arms for her when she would come back. She'd leave and come back, leave and come back, and he would always take her, which he didn't do for everyone." But when she asked if the offer to pay her $450 a week still stood, Arthur laughed in her face. She'd come back at $350, as punishment for choosing Europe over him.

"Arthur could've destroyed Lydia," says Sheila Rohan. "He could've used her up. You know how they make you a star and the next day they throw you away? She was always under so much pressure at DTH. He could've gotten mad at her at any time and pushed her aside."

"I think the one thing everyone at the company knew is that nothing bad was ever going to happen to Lydia," agrees Karlya Shelton. "Arthur was not going to ever be truly mean or ugly to her because she was his prized person. That's who he always wanted at the top of the Christmas tree for the company."

SINCE ABARCA HAD LEFT, Dance Theatre of Harlem had added another Balanchine ballet, *Serenade,* to its repertoire. Mitchell immediately recast her in the principal role of the Dark Angel. He divided his ballerinas into a tall cast and a short cast, with the latter always relegated to second cast and understudy roles. Abarca, Virginia Johnson, and Lorraine Graves— five-six, five-eight, and five-ten, respectively—danced the principal roles of the Dark Angel, the Waltz Girl, and the Russian Girl. At five-three, Shelton was assigned to the second cast, understudying Graves.

Serenade opens on the transcendent scene of seventeen women on stage, swathed in the palest and pearliest of blues, the tulle of their long skirts dusting the tops of their ankles. The soft blue lighting hits the women like moonlight. They stand with their right arms raised; their palms extended as if to gently hold back the weight of the stars. The Tchaikovsky score is luscious, feminine, a hymn to all things lovely and romantic. "As soon as the curtain went up, and the audience saw us all standing there, there would always be an immediate applause," says Shelton. "Your skirt would softly blow because the curtain produces a little bit of wind. You're stand- ing in that opening position, and then there's that first move with your hand, that break of your wrist as you bring it to your temple. It's all so lovely and indulgent. Every night you felt beautiful."

Shelton says there was something magical about their corps de ballet. It wasn't just the depth of talent on stage, the mastery of technique and precision. "We just loved dancing with each other so much," she says. "'Oh, what is your arm doing? I'm going to put my arm just like that. Let's make sure we match. Let's make sure we're all together.' In *Serenade,* we had a little competition. 'I'm going to do a triple pirouette here. We should all do triples here!'"

Privately, though, Shelton yearned for a chance to step out from the corps into principal roles. If only Mitchell would see in her what she knew she had to give! On tour in Dublin that fall, she finally got a chance to shine.

A few hours before showtime, Mitchell got word that Lorraine Graves, whose career as a principal ballerina and ballet mistress at Dance Theatre of Harlem would span eighteen years, was down with a bad case of food poisoning. Shelton was out on her dinner break when Mitchell made the cast change. When she returned to the theater, the stage manager met her at the door with her marching orders. She had two hours to get ready to go on stage in the technically challenging role that's full of multiple pirouettes and quick footwork. She rushed out of her street clothes and rehearsed some of the passage's spacing with Abarca and Johnson and practiced the lifts with her partner. To add to the challenge, the Dublin theater had a raked stage typical of European venues. In America, the house of a theater is on an incline and the stage is flat. Across Europe, it's the opposite, which left company members fearing "the rake monster." Explains Shelton, "The closer you danced toward the mouth by the pit, the more it felt like the monster would swallow you." Turns suddenly felt more treacherous. A dancer would have to adjust her spotting, raising her head and upper body slightly so as not to go tumbling down.

But that night on stage, Shelton remembers feeling so focused, so alive and in flow. "I wasn't going to let the rake freak me out," she says. Afterward all the dancers clapped for her backstage. "You did it! You did it!" If Mitchell approved of her performance, he didn't tell her. But she didn't care. Shelton had danced in a role that she'd coveted since she was a child, and she knew she'd done it justice.

JUST AS SHELTON'S AMBITION was peaking, so was Abarca's sense of restlessness. In a profile that winter, *People* magazine bemoaned the fact that "time is about to catch up with Abarca, 28. For almost a decade she has been a prima but little-celebrated performer." In a *Washington Post* feature titled "On the Brink of Stardom," Abarca gave voice to her growing impatience: "Time is short. Ballet is like athletics; there aren't that many years to get what you want." When the reporter asked what exactly she wanted from the world, Abarca was charmingly blunt: "I'm just ambitious. I want to be a star."

The day after the *Post* story ran, Mitchell, likely still smarting over the Dumb Eleven and Abarca leaving him for Europe, called her in for a meeting. He brandished the newspaper like a weapon. "You don't want to be a star!" he yelled, stabbing at her words on the page with his finger. "You want to be an artist!" Abarca couldn't believe his outrage. "An artist? A starving artist, I guess. All I did was share my childhood dream. I wanted to be a star, and I didn't know how or when it was going to happen doing *Concerto Barocco* for him."

Dance Theatre of Harlem had always billed itself as an ensemble company, without the traditional stated hierarchy of principals, soloists, demi-soloists, and corps. Mitchell wanted the only star to be the institution itself and thus, by extension, its creator. "He saw himself as God-appointed," says Charles De Rose. "Arthur was narcissistic in a way. He didn't like others getting any undue recognition. He thought everything should be about Dance Theatre of Harlem. As a dancer, you were part and parcel of the package. This wasn't a star system like at American Ballet Theatre. You weren't supposed to stand out as a star like Misty Copeland. The more people who came to see Lydia, the more asses we put in the seats. But he never allowed anyone to get a big head."

In that same *Washington Post* interview, Abarca crosses her fingers for the role that would change her whole trajectory. "Hopefully one of these days I'll be getting that one ballet that will knock everyone down. And then everyone will have to say wow!"

Mitchell too was looking for an iconic piece. With the company's ten-year anniversary behind them, he felt that DTH was at a crossroads. "I want to make this a great company," he told *The New York Times* before the start of their new season at City Center. "Although we have lots of fans, I know we're still not a truly great company. To say that we are is like comparing a sapling to a mighty oak. Yet I think we can be a great company one day." Becoming one meant swinging for the fences with the same spirit of gusto and fearlessness with which he had started the company. "The time was right for us to do the classics," said Mitchell later, reflecting back on that moment. "We had to do them."

And so in January of 1980, Dance Theatre of Harlem gave its first two performances of nineteenth-century Russian classics: a divertissement from *Paquita,* staged by former Ballet Russe de Monte Carlo stars Alexandra Danilova and Frederic Franklin, and the drama-packed second act of *Swan Lake.* Franklin had been in the process of staging the suite of dances from *Paquita* when Mitchell first broached the idea of attempting the famous ballet blanc. A *New York Times* article described the brevity of their exchange: "I went home one night, and the phone rang. 'Freddie,' Arthur said. 'What do you think about *Swan Lake*?' 'What am I supposed to think?' Mr. Franklin countered. 'Good,' Mr. Mitchell said. 'We'll start it Monday.'"

The decision was a bit of an about-face for Mitchell, who had long said he had no interest in the company ever attempting one of the Romantic-era ballets where the female corps were costumed in white tutus, their limbs powdered white to heighten the dreamlike atmosphere. Now he'd decided audiences were ready to have their preconceptions of the ballet blanc aesthetic expanded. To help ease them out of tradition, DTH's *Swan Lake* would not be tied to the specific time or setting of the original German fairy tale. The program would be changed to identify the villain as "the Sorcerer," rather than "Von Rothbart," and the leads as "Swan Queen" and "Prince," rather than "Odette" and "Prince Siegfried." Finally, it was decided that white tutus against the Black skin of the sixteen swan maidens would appear glaring under the stage lights. So Mitchell and his costume designer settled on tutus in gradations of blue. The darker the woman's skin tone, the deeper her blue.

"I got tapped for the Swan Queen," recalls Abarca with a groan. "And that's when I realized, this is not what I want." Mitchell paired Abarca with Ronald Perry for the grand pas de deux, making them the first Black couple ever to dance in the ballet's leading roles. Says Abarca, "I remember Geoffrey Holder coming up to me saying, 'You look like an exotic bird.' I wasn't trying to be a bird. I was trying to be a swan!" Abarca felt like an imposter in a role she neither desired nor trusted that the world would let a Black woman claim as her own. "The Russians start learning this role in their bassinets," she tells the Legacy Council. "I didn't want to be held up against those dancers. Why were we doing this? It felt like *Oh we'll do* Swan Lake, *and then we'll be considered a real company.* Like, come on! How many years have we been trying to prove ourselves? We're Dance Theatre of Harlem. We do our own thing. This is stupid. Don't compare us to American Ballet Theatre."

On opening night, just before curtain, Abarca found herself surrounded by some of the most powerful men in ballet crowding her head with a flurry of last-minute instructions. George Balanchine, who was there for moral support, wanted her to make the dance brighter somehow and pick up the tempo. Mitchell was after her to find a place to add the Zah! moment. Franklin told her to go out on stage and melt like butter. "When the curtain went up, I didn't know what the hell to do," she says. "I was lost. I heard the overture, and somebody had the nerve to come over and say, 'Good luck Lydia!' I'm not Lydia! I'm trying to be the Swan."

But after their grand pas de deux in the first performance, the applause lasted for so long that it interrupted the ballet. Mitchell had so drilled into his dancers' heads never to make a move without his consent, they remained paralyzed in the wings, unsure if they should return to the stage to acknowledge the crowd. "If we hadn't practiced a bow, we didn't do one," she says. "We didn't know what to do because they would not stop clapping."

However much the audience loved it, critics were decidedly muted in their appreciation. "Although Lydia Abarca has a beautiful body, she doesn't so much dance as enact a ritual learned second-hand," said *The Christian Science Monitor.* "Abarca looked like a beautiful Swan Queen, and caught in isolated movements, that is what she was. But neither she, nor her prince, Ronald Perry, tried to link those moments," wrote *The New York Times.*

Mitchell worried over Abarca's response to her uncharacteristically damp reviews. The normally poised prima waved him off, declaring in front of the entire company, "Opinions are like assholes, and everybody's got one. I'm going to kill myself over one bad review?"

Rohan winces as she talks about being in the audience on the night of the premiere. "From the moment I heard that Dance Theatre was doing *Swan Lake*, I thought it was ridiculous," she says. "And then I saw it, and I was embarrassed. I'm sorry Lyd, this is nothing personal against you. The production was weak. The older ballerinas and us that came were like *Oh well, he had to try*. But I left there feeling a little embarrassed that Arthur had felt the need in the first place." She pauses to check in with Abarca, to make sure she hasn't hurt her friend's feelings.

"I love your honesty," promises Abarca. "I have absolutely no ego around this. You do certain ballets, and you feel great about them. That one, my heart wasn't in it."

Shelton, though, appears briefly stung. "I'm surprised to hear that you were embarrassed," she says, her voice tender. *The New York Times* had taken special note in a review that "the four cygnets—Judy Tyrus, Karlya Shelton, Yvonne Hall, Terri Tompkins—utterly wowed the audience. One has never seen pas de chat jumps performed with such precision at the same level in the air."

ABARCA DANCED IN just two performances of *Swan Lake* before being taken down by a flu that was sweeping through the company. Her illness gave her a few quiet days away from the bustle of the theater to confront an irrefutable truth—she was finished with ballet.

On the morning she was due to return to class, Abarca remembers crying into her breakfast sandwich, pacing between the bodega across the street from her apartment on Riverside Drive and the stoplight on 157th Street. Avon Long, a famous vaudeville performer who lived in her building, stopped her on the sidewalk on his way to the subway to make sure she was okay. "I think I'm going to quit Dance Theatre today," she cried to him, the words gathering force as she let them tumble out of her mouth. Long gave her shoulders an encouraging squeeze. "Good for you!" he said. "We need to see more of you."

That afternoon she knocked on Mitchell's office door and started crying before she'd even taken a seat. She told him that after all this time in the company, she could still barely make her rent, forget about her dreams of buying her mom a house. She was getting ready to turn thirty. She had to do something else while she was still young enough to try. "And he just started screaming at me," she says. "'You're just lazy! You've got to work harder is all, and you don't want to!' But everything he was saying was exactly why I was leaving. I'd had a chance to work with people who didn't abuse me like that for $350 a week. Every time it seemed like the door was going to crack open a little bit wider, it never happened. So why was I working, working, working to do this bird ballet that I couldn't find the jazz in anywhere?"

She left him fuming in his office. Out on the street, the air had a sudden freshness to it, the promise of possibility. "I had given Dance Theatre of Harlem everything I had," she says, "and now it felt like the rest of my life was about to begin."

ABARCA HAD HEARD that Bob Fosse was looking to replace dancers in his Broadway musical revue *Dancin'*, which had cleaned up at the Tony Awards when it premiered in 1978. After blowing her first chance to work with him, she wasn't going to let such an opportunity pass her by again. He'd come to represent the pinnacle of everything that that little girl who grew up on *Million Dollar Movies*, who read *Variety* and sneaked out to audition for *Hair*, who sobbed over *West Side Story*, who'd wanted to be a star since she was in the fourth grade, and who still believed in happy endings, wanted from the world.

Abarca joined the show in an ensemble position, but not long afterward Fosse needed to find a permanent replacement for the Trumpet Solo, which he'd originally choreographed on Ann Reinking. The great smoky-voiced singer with Trans Ams for legs had made famous the two-minute dance number, a riotous, hair-whipping, high-kicking explosion set to Benny Goodman's "Sing Sing Sing." Abarca auditioned and won the coveted part. Fosse called her into the rehearsal studio to see how he might tailor the choreography to best suit her style. He encouraged her to tone down the sharpness of some moves, leaning instead into her slinky sex appeal. "When I was done rehearsing," says Abarca, "I overheard him say to the drummer, 'Wow, she's beautiful.'"

Abarca was dancing in the part of her dreams—and suddenly pulling in a five-hundred-dollar weekly paycheck. "They had a chair in the wing when I came off because I had to catch my breath. There was a part where I had to run and slide on the floor next to the trumpet player. I kept banging my knee, and the dance captain said, 'Well, we can modify it,' and I said, 'No, no, I'll be okay.'" When City Ballet's Jacques d'Amboise greeted Abarca backstage at the Ambassador Theatre after her first show, he exclaimed, "I didn't know you could do jazz!" "I told him, 'I could always do jazz. Arthur just never let me.'" After being kicked out of jazz class all those years ago for taking advantage of her ballet scholarship, she was finally in the center of the action.

AS ABARCA KICKED her way across the stage at the Ambassador, David Bowie was in the theater next door, starring in a production of *The Elephant Man*. Word got to Abarca that he wanted to take her to dinner, but she declined. She'd recently fallen in love.

"I was definitely dating up," says her husband, Al. "She was riding high. When we'd go out, she'd be turning heads everywhere we went. We were walking down the street past a newsstand one day, and she goes, 'Hey, look, that's me on the cover of that magazine!'"

Al, who worked for IBM and acted on the side, grew up on 152nd Street, around the corner from Dance Theatre of Harlem. He was a regular on the Battlegrounds courts and one of his buddies worked as a custodian at DTH. He even came to the rescue of one of its ballerinas once, during a wintry blizzard, before he'd started dating Abarca. "I was driving around my IBM service territory in Harlem," he explains. "I'm going down 110th Street, and I see this woman shaking on the corner, snow blustering all around her. I felt sorry for her, so I decide I'm going to go around the block. If she's still there I'm going to offer her a ride. Sure enough, there she was. I stopped in front of her, rolled down my window, and said 'Hey, I'm no weirdo, but I noticed you standing out here in the cold. I'd be willing to give you a ride?' And she looked at my three-piece suit, white shirt, and tie and finally said, 'Okay, I'm going up to Dance Theatre of Harlem.'"

Karlya Shelton got to work safely that day, neither of them the wiser that her hero was Abarca's future husband.

Still at DTH after Abarca's departure, Shelton was missing her friend. Abarca may have been Arthur Mitchell's muse, but she was also the type of girl who would paint the relaxer onto your head and then wash it out for you in the bathroom sink after the chemicals set. She'd play dress-up in your closet with you and sing into hairbrushes while you both pretended to be pop stars. One afternoon when Abarca was still in the company, she and Shelton dressed up in leather mini-skirts and burst in on Mitchell at the studio, demanding of his impatient self in unison to "Stop . . . In the Name of Love."

On a night off, Shelton bought herself a ticket to go see Abarca on Broadway. She sat by herself in the audience and marveled at the electric sparks shooting off her friend on stage. "Oh, she was just so, so good," she says. "I never knew Lydia wanted to be a star so badly. How could I have when I thought she already was one?" Shelton didn't know the bigger dreams her friend had for herself, or that she danced with a fear that somehow, just as she was getting close, all those dreams would get snatched away from her.

SIX MONTHS INTO her Broadway run, Abarca found herself increasingly unable to put weight on her right leg. When she could no longer dance through the pain, she went to see a doctor. Tests revealed torn cartilage around her right knee. The repetitive slamming down on the boards at the end of the Trumpet Solo had steadily chipped away at her bone. On the operating table before the anesthesia fully kicked in, she heard one of New York City's top arthroscopic surgeons mutter to his nurse. "Well, what does she want me to do with this? She's too old anyway." When a tearful Abarca returned to the Ambassador on crutches to pack up her things, the wardrobe mistress hugged her tight. "Oh Lydia," the woman sighed. "I'm so sorry."

Her knee was busted. "She knew she was never really going to be able to dance again," says her sister Celia. "That was heartbreaking. All she knew was pointing that foot, that toe. Dancing was her whole world. We knew she was smart, but she wasn't prepared for anything else."

Abarca spent eight weeks on crutches in the first stretch of her recovery. Every afternoon she'd take a cab to her cousin Iris's brownstone, where she'd watch hours of soap operas with her grandmother in the basement. During a commercial break one day, Goldie, who'd been in the library audience for Lydia's first performance in pointe shoes, looked at her granddaughter with worry in her eyes. "Oh Lydia, how are you going to get along without the applause?"

Lydia

I didn't dance for a while. I met Ms. Frances Rhymes, a former dancer with the Katherine Dunham Dance Company who founded the St. Benedict School of Dance in Jamaica, Queens. She told me, "You have all this knowledge, you have to come teach class and share it with my kids!" I was so grateful that she gave me a new focus. My knee was just starting to get better after two years when Arthur called and asked me to come back for Scheherazade. The part was in heels so I wouldn't be on pointe. I happily accepted, but warm-up classes were a cruel reminder of what I could no longer do without pain. The New York Times did a story, "Lydia Abarca is back!" No, I wanted to tell them. I'm not.

I got a job on the movie The Cotton Club [directed by Francis Ford Coppola], but it took forever to shoot because the script kept changing. We still hadn't shot anything yet, and I was pregnant with Daniella. I'll never forget when I finally had to say to Mr. Coppola, "I'm sorry, I just cannot dance the fast numbers anymore." I remember Gregory Hines was like, "Good for you. You have that baby and take care of it." The cast threw Al and me a surprise baby shower with gifts of a crib, all the linen, even savings bonds. I got a credit for the movie, but you can't really find me on the screen because I'm hiding in the back. Darn!

My parents finally got out of the projects. They ended up getting a house in Paterson, New Jersey. But I had nothing to do with it. They had to put their pennies together. That was a huge disappointment for me.

202 · THE SWANS OF HARLEM

Al and I got a little starter house five blocks from them. I opened a dance school at Daniella's Catholic school. It started out with me just doing talent shows with the kids. I'd spoken to the principal and said, "If you let me use the cafeteria, I'll only charge the kids five dollars a class and give the school a dollar for each one." At the end-of-the-year recital, there were so many people who wanted to see it we had to do it two nights in a row.

When I was forty, Geoffrey Holder called and put me in his production of House of Flowers. *By that time, I had two kids, and it was nice to do something. My kids came with me to rehearsals. Walter Raines, my former partner, called me one night to say, "I wanted you to know that Arthur and I came to see the show. He didn't want me to say anything to you, but he told me, 'She's still got it.'" Of course, Arthur didn't say anything to me, so it meant the world that Walter shared that.*

I wasn't really dancing anymore, but I had my brain. I'd taken Latin for one year in high school. I taught myself medical transcription. Al tapped me around this time and said, "We're moving to Atlanta," because his job got transferred. My New York life was over. I got a job as a medical transcriptionist at a doctor's office down here. It was fine. I can always find something to enjoy where I am. People ask me "What'd you do before this?" And I'd kind of mumble, "I was a ballerina." "Yeah, well, can you type?" I thought office work was the easiest thing in the world after dancing. Everyone would complain, "Oh, I can't wait for five o'clock!" Please, you don't know what hard work is.

I missed my family so much that every year I'd drive up, just me and the kids because Al had to work. Each trip I made a point to go by Dance Theatre of Harlem. There used to be a big framed picture of me in Carmen *on the staircase up to Studio 3. One time after the building had been renovated, Arthur was like, "Oh, let me show you around." And everyone we passed, he'd be like, "Oh, this is my first ballerina, everybody. This is Lydia Abarca." Well, okay, I guess he's not mad at me anymore. One time I went up there, and of course I had the kids with me. While we were in there, someone took a picture of the four of us. I remember standing there with Mr. Mitchell and my kids, and he says, "Look, this could have been us." I didn't know what to make of that, so I just blocked it out.*

I started coaching for Ballethnic Dance Company here in Atlanta in 1993, which was started by two former Dance Theatre of Harlem dancers, Nena

Gilreath and Waverly Lucas. Since then I've helped run the rehearsals for their productions of The Urban Nutcracker *and* The Leopard Tale. *Coaching for them has made me feel like I've kept a toe in ballet. It taught me a whole new skill of how to try to get results like Arthur did, but without being mean. He was always that third eye for us. Now I'm trying to see the dancers from the eye of the audience that paid money for tickets. This past year I caught myself in rehearsal sounding like Louis Johnson on* The Wiz: *"Bring your brains, people. Bring your brains!"*

When I first started reading about Misty Copeland, I was like, "Wait a minute . . ." I did the ballets. I did Broadway. I did movies. I did everything except stand on my head. And it all just went away? I guess it was my mistake and vanity to think history would remember the first prima ballerina and all the other beautiful ballerinas and fabulous male dancers of Dance Theatre of Harlem. It doesn't feel as good when you have to toot your own horn. Humility was just so drilled into us. Even our bows were very much like Oh, me? Thank you. *I just think it's sort of sad that because we were so quiet and so humble that nobody knows about us or can appreciate what we did and how hard it all was.*

"We all felt that Lydia could've been Misty Copeland," says her sister Celia. "And, you know, Misty was doing On the Town *on Broadway back in 2015. My cousin bought me a ticket. I really didn't want to go, because of that jealousy that I had. That could've been Lydia up there. But then again, it's a whole different time. Fifty years have gone by!"*

LYDIA STRUGGLED WITH an emptiness she'd felt since she'd had to stop dancing. The joys of her family helped fill it. So did working with the dancers at Ballethnic. Even though her office job was tedious, she took pride in a job well done. But as her kids got older, and she crept up in years, she found herself self-medicating more and more with alcohol. She'd put in her eight hours typing away at the office, then come home and watch TV alone upstairs with glasses of rum and Coke for company. Al, who'd lost his father to the bottle, didn't know how to reach her.

One morning Abarca, before her yearly mammogram, took a couple of shots to calm her nerves. On the way to her appointment, she noticed a red light too late and clipped a police car. *These four men get out with guns around their waists. I was afraid to talk too much out of fear they'd smell it on me.*

It got to the point that Daniella would borrow her mother's car and find a half-empty Coke bottle filled with rum instead of soda in the driver's side door. And empty liquor bottles stashed underneath the spare tire in the trunk and hidden behind Abarca's hair products under her bathroom sink.

Everything came to a head when Abarca discovered that a younger woman she'd been tasked with training at the office had been hired to replace her. It felt as if the world was getting ready to dispose of her again, shoving her aside for someone younger who could do the work because she showed her how first. They'd forget she had ever been there, while she floundered without a Plan B. All that anger and helplessness she'd been stuffing down for so long came roaring to the surface. She screamed at her manager and left the office in a blind rage.

Earlier in the day, in a terrible confluence of events, Al had been admitted to the hospital with heart palpitations. Lydia and her son, Eric, went to visit him in the emergency room where they were told he needed to spend the night for observation. She went home bereft. She took a full bottle of Bacardi out of the closet and locked herself in the guest room. *I was drinking and feeling so bad for myself, you know? This girl stole my job. What the hell am I going to do? Al's in the hospital. I just started talking crazy.* She drank and she drank. She smashed a lamp across the wall, shattering the base. A terrified Eric, knowing that his mother had pills in the room with her as well as alcohol, pounded on the door, begging her to come out and talk to him. She just kept screaming and sobbing that she wanted to die. Eric called his aunt Celia, who told him to call 911 immediately.

At the hospital, Daniella spent the night going back and forth between floors to visit both of her parents. It took Lydia several hours to sober up. When Eric first came to visit her, she'd looked at him meanly from her bed. "What are you doing here?" she teased. She says now that she meant it as a joke, though to him it came out like an accusation. Unwilling to be cast as the bad guy after the ordeal she'd put him through, Eric turned around and left the room without a word. Later that night Lydia called him and sobbed that she was sorry, that she loved him, and then she thanked him for saving her life. Around four in the morning, she was transferred in her nightgown and flip-flops from suicide watch to a nearby rehab facility, where she stayed for eight days. She started going to AA meetings. She hasn't had a drink since, hasn't even wanted one.

That's it. That's how I got my act together. I'm pretty proud of what I've accomplished. I realized the reason I was drinking so heavily was because I had never really mourned the loss of my dancing career. Then after twenty years as a self-taught transcriptionist, my job was being taken away from me. I was feeling like Now what am I going to do with my life?

"My mom went through all that hell," says Daniella. "She had all those demons she needed to deal with. This has just been a whole journey of awakening. All this had to happen to get her clean, to get her sober so that when it's time for her light to shine, there are no hidden skeletons in her closet. She's free."

In 2017, after Daniella blasted me for keeping all my history packed away, we took a road trip as a family up to New York. We went to Dance Theatre of Harlem. There's no more pictures of me anywhere, but I got to see my four-year-old granddaughter running around Studio 3. Afterward we went to the library at Lincoln Center, and I showed my kids an old black-and-white recording of my pas de deux in Combat. *They lasted about two minutes because you could barely see me. It's just little figures on a stage.*

Then Al said, "Call Arthur." Arthur answered the phone, and I said, "Mr. Mitchell, hi, it's Lydia. Can we come by?"

I'd only seen Arthur here and there. We never talked on the phone. Never went for a meal or anything. But now we're in his apartment. He'd just gotten out of the hospital. I think he was on dialysis. Both hips had been replaced. One of the first things he said was "Who's that?" about my granddaughter. And he said to her, "Come here, let me see your foot! Stand up straight!" I heard how terse he was: "No, the foot! Turn this way!" Then he told my family all these nice things about me, and that I had been his star student. "All the ballerinas still ask, 'Where is Lydia?'"

I don't know why I'm crying. It's funny, because I think of myself as the kind of person who when I leave a situation, I just wipe the dust off my hands and move on. But I guess all those feelings were still trapped inside me. I was just so glad we got to meet with him. That was closure. For my family to meet him, and to hear him talk like that, was so special. I guess there really was a love for each other there.

I've been blessed in my life, I know that. Broke, but blessed. You have to understand, I had such big dreams for myself. So much emotion came up for me when Misty Copeland started getting all the stuff I wish I had gotten. I wish her the best. It's her time. But damn, I wish I'd had a publicist back then. Somebody who could argue with Arthur and tell him, "She's going to Hollywood to do this quick movie. She'll be right back."

I do extra work on movies sometimes, which is so tedious. Long hours, and you're not ever sure if you're going to get any face time in the finished product. But I've never given up. I've never given up. That's why I've stayed a size eight all these years. Recently I got an agent and started taking some acting classes. Who knows? Maybe one day somebody will say "Oh! Lydia. Let's have her come in."

16

~

Come 1981, the wolf was once more at the door. The Ford Foundation wanted to pull its support for Dance Theatre of Harlem. At Arthur Mitchell's request, Charles De Rose rushed to the studio to meet with representatives of the foundation, pleading with them to reconsider. But they told De Rose they'd continue supporting DTH financially only if Mitchell agreed to step down as its leader. "If you don't think that cut his heart out," says De Rose. "I told them he couldn't step down. He can't."

Mitchell was growing more ornery and arbitrary with age. He frequented psychics and told De Rose they'd warned him that people would try to take the company away from him. "He had such an insecurity about losing control," says De Rose. "So when people tried to help him take it to the next level, he couldn't let go. When there were ways to make Dance Theatre's administration more sophisticated, with computers and technology, Arthur wouldn't let anybody do anything he couldn't understand. He'd chase good board members away. If they felt personally insulted by him, they didn't care what the reviews were from Barcelona Opera House. It's a complicated story, but he didn't want to ever feel that this beautiful, noble thing he had built was being taken away from him."

He fought and he fought and he fought to stay alive. Even as the debt accumulated, Dance Theatre of Harlem was performing at the Kennedy Center in front of President Ronald Reagan and First Lady Nancy, and

Vice President George H. W. Bush and Mrs. Bush, in the presidential box. And a few weeks later, in February 1981, Karlya Shelton was one of a handful of dancers chosen to perform at the White House during the Reagans' First State Dinner welcoming British prime minister Margaret Thatcher.

A limousine picked up Shelton and the other dancers at their hotel in Washington, D.C. She danced in Balanchine's *Allegro Brillante* in front of an audience that included politicians, dignitaries, and celebrities like Charlton Heston and Bob Hope. At the reception afterward, she changed into a black sequinned gown designed by Hutaff Lennon. Years later, while going through photographs, Shelton realized with chagrin that the top of the dress—under which she'd opted not to wear a bra—was sheer.

THAT SUMMER Dance Theatre of Harlem returned to London, where it became the first Black dance company to perform at the Royal Opera House. The thirty-eight dancers performed fifteen ballets over their two-week engagement.

But just a few months later, *The New York Times* ran a story under the headline "Dance Theatre of Harlem Cuts Back." Classes for as many as one thousand students a year had been dropped, along with the sewing and tailoring classes, the percussion ensemble, and the choral ensemble. A company statement declared that over the year, "The Dance Theatre of Harlem experienced a thirty percent drop in private support and a twenty percent increase in expenses." It needed to raise $200,000 by the end of the year "to maintain its current level of operations." Says De Rose of their hustle to raise the needed funds, "We fought like hell."

Everywhere they traveled—Australia, Japan, Italy—they broke box office records. But the stress of money always kept Mitchell dangerously on edge. Shelton, never one to back down from a fight back then, had a limit to how much abuse she was willing to take. "All the dancers would tell me, 'Don't take it personally,'" she says. "But to me it was personal. I would always try not to cry in front of him, because sometimes it felt like tears gave him power. 'See, I can break her down.'"

Mitchell believed deeply in astrology and was known to ask dancers to reveal their sign upon first meeting. He was an Aries, like Shelton, who would get a tattoo of the zodiac constellation on her right arm when she turned sixty. "We were similar personalities in a way," she says. "When something happens that makes an Aries mad, you snap and slash. If I was like a bonfire on the beach, he was that blazing fire that ate up all the trees."

Shelton remembers taking a day off in Israel, where the company had performed at the Tel Aviv Opera House. "I wasn't dancing that day, so one of the ladies cornrowed my hair into a low bun in the back," she says. "Arthur Mitchell came up to me and said, 'Why do you have your hair like that?' And I said, 'Well, it's my day off and it's hot.' And he said, 'Well, you'll find out when you get your pink slip.'" Shelton refused to budge. "I said, 'You're going to give me a pink slip, because I'm wearing my hair the way I want to on my day off?'

"After he made that scene, I went back to the dressing room, and I was so mad that I actually hit a dressing room mirror and broke it," she says. The other women on the Legacy Council gasp at her revelation. "I know it pissed you off but it's a good thing you didn't get fined for that," says Marcia Sells. Shelton shakes her head as if to clear Mitchell's voice reverberating inside. "I was so angry that my face was paralyzed."

A great dancer rises to the level of expectation set for her and the quality of the roles she's given. On a transcontinental tour that would include a stop in Denver, Shelton pleaded with Mitchell to let her dance a principal role in Balanchine's *The Four Temperaments* in front of her hometown crowd. He let her go on as Choleric, a role that suited her fiery temperament. "The movements are sharp during the solo, and there are lots of turns," says Shelton. "Her movements are slightly sensual." She and her partner, Eddie Shellman, who had come up as apprentices together, had practiced a series of lifts on their own when the ballet was first being set. "We had worked it out so that he would throw me and let go of me, and I'd freeze in the air," she says. "Then I'd descend, and on the way down, he'd catch me, and we'd go on to the next and do it again. We never tried it again until that Denver performance. At the top of the lift, Eddie took his hands away so that it looked like I was suspended in air, and I could hear the audience gasping. It was a perfect performance. Afterward Arthur Mitchell said, 'Very good. I didn't know you could do that.' And I remember saying, 'Just let me out there. I can do a lot more than that!'"

But Shelton felt forever resigned, in Mitchell's eyes, to the second cast, the short cast. "I wanted to do *Allegro Brillante*. I would've loved to do the second pas de trois in *Agon*. But I don't think he ever saw me as a 'leotard and tights' dancer. I never felt he was comfortable with my body shape. I'm five foot three. Even though it wasn't big, I had a shapely butt." She was envious of dancers who could eat anything they wanted without gaining weight. So she dieted and experimented with laxatives. "I told myself I would get really thin and maybe he'd let me do *Firebird*." But he remained a withholding force, never giving her the opportunities she craved.

After *Swan Lake,* Mitchell reversed course once more and ushered in a new era of American story ballets at DTH. The company's revival of Valerie Bettis's *A Streetcar Named Desire* premiered during its season at City Center in 1982. The repertory shift scraped at Lydia Abarca's heart when she heard the news, as Mitchell publicly explained that story ballets "would serve as major vehicles for our dancers. . . . It is time to establish our dancers as individual artists, and we've provided them with roles of star caliber." He declared that Dance Theatre of Harlem had long since proved that Black dancers can do classical ballet, so it was time to shift the narrative from social to artistic resonance.

The following year the company premiered *Fall River Legend,* Agnes de Mille's devastating take on Lizzie Borden and the 1892 Massachusetts murder. "Ms. de Mille was a hoot," says Shelton. "One time in rehearsal she got coffee on her glasses. When she realized, she said, 'Oh my God! No wonder you all look darker.' "

By then the company had a new teacher and coach, William Griffith, or "Mr. Bill" as he was known, a trained concert pianist turned ballet dancer who'd previously taught company classes at American Ballet Theatre and Joffrey Ballet. He came to Dance Theatre of Harlem in the early 1980s as Karel Shook's health deteriorated. Mr. Bill had the body of a football player, all broad shoulders and narrow hips, and a commanding, deep voice. "He could say two words to you, and you knew what he meant," says Shelton. "He would say 'something here' and point to a part of your body. And you would just know. Or there'd be something in the music, and he'd tell you, 'Change the accent.' He could unlock the mystery. I felt like he saw me." It was ultimately he, not Mitchell, who would help push her dancing to the next level.

And it was Mr. Bill who bore gentle witness on 152nd Street when Shelton's heart was broken. Her boyfriend, who was also her frequent dance partner, had arrived late to company class, entering Studio 3 with a new girl in the corps. Shelton was in conversation with Virginia Johnson when she clocked the way her boyfriend smiled at the woman, touching her back before they parted to prepare for rehearsal. A chill of intuition went through her body. Later when she confronted him, he admitted that he'd been seeing the other woman behind her back. Worse, everybody but her seemed in on his betrayal. "I remember asking one of the other male dancers if he knew, and he goes 'Yeahhhhhh?' I just lost my footing. Here are these people I'm with all the time, and no one said anything? This thing I thought was secure was not secure. Now I still have to dance with this person."

The next week, still raw from the breakup, she had a private rehearsal for her variation in Balanchine's *Pas de Dix* with Mr. Bill. At the end, he shared some advice she's never forgotten. "You need to develop a sense of loneliness," he told her in his dry tone of voice. "You have to learn to be alone and pull from that to develop your artistry." At first, she was insulted. Mr. Bill was well versed in the company drama and knew what had happened to her. But she let his words marinate before coming back to him a few days later, eager for his approval. She pretended that she'd understood what he'd been trying to tell her. "No, you don't," said Mr. Bill with a patient smile. "If you knew what I meant, you wouldn't have to come and tell me."

With time, Mr. Bill's message took root within her. She realized how much she'd loved dancing with her boyfriend, working on their variations together. He was one of her favorite partners. He had made her feel special, chosen. She realized she'd given over her power to him, on stage and off. "It felt like Mr. Bill was telling me, *You have to find you. And you have to develop you. Without this one or that one. It's just you,*" she says. "I became more gathered after that and started to find my footing again. All the noise that was out there, I didn't have to hear it. Mr. Bill handed me this big nugget of gold that became a part of who I grew into as an artist. I took that mental shift with me everywhere—in class, in rehearsal, outside rehearsal. I could've just stayed floundering, but he reminded me I needed to find me. That's when I truly became a ballerina, I think. She was always in there. I just found her and let her go. My dancing did change after that. And then one afternoon in class, Mr. Bill just looked at me and nodded. He recognized it too."

She started getting more principal roles in the new ballets. "Though every larger role I ever got was because of someone who saw me in class other than Arthur Mitchell," she says. She calls out choreographers Choo San Goh (*Introducing . . .*), Terry Orr (*Graduation Ball*), John Butler (*Othello*), and Domy Reiter-Soffer (*Equus*), all of whom successfully lobbied Mitchell to cast her in their ballet's principal roles.

Shelton danced brilliantly in the New York premiere of *Equus,* in what she calls one of those flawless performances a ballerina doesn't take for granted. Afterward she was celebrating with her partner outside the theater, the two of them basking in the knowledge of a job well done. Later she was told that after their final bows, Mitchell had searched for her in the dressing room. "He was looking for you," a dancer told her. "He had tears in his eyes he was so moved." Recently, the choreographer Reiter-Soffer praised anew the perfection of Shelton's performance in the role of *Equus*'s stable girl. "By the way," he added, "Arthur Mitchell thought the same."

In the May 1983 issue of *Dance Magazine,* she got one of the best reviews of her career. "Karlya Shelton is the most sweetly, lightly authoritative junior Mistress of Ceremonies one could imagine," praising her work in the *Graduation Ball* ballet. "Her variation, with its jumps, pirouettes, and extended hopping on pointe is so beautifully, unaffectedly phrased that it registers not as the usual display number but as part of this girl's special, mischievous nature." And later, singling out her "piquant" performance in a *Pas de Dix* solo, *Dance* described her as an "extraordinary performer." The ballerina who for so long had felt trapped within was now getting the chance to exalt on stage.

THAT FALL there was another fallow patch on the company calendar. The dancers were again placed on hiatus, which meant a return to Club 90. During the month-long break, Shelton fell in love with a dashing man who worked in finance and wined and dined her at the finest restaurants in town. By the time Mitchell called the company back into the studio, she'd put on ten pounds of courting weight. Mitchell was disgusted. He banned her from traveling with the company for dates in Arizona, benching her until he deemed her body acceptable to go in front of an audience.

By the time the company returned to New York, Frederic Franklin had begun casting a production of the full-length version of the classic Romantic-era ballet *Giselle*. The story of love and betrayal was originally set in Germany, but Mitchell ingeniously reimagined it in the bayous of Louisiana, set among a community of free Black people. Virginia Johnson, as gifted a dramatic actress as she was a ballerina, was cast as the titular peasant girl who's driven mad by deceit and then haunts the man who broke her heart from beyond the grave.

Karlya Shelton returned to the studio on the day Franklin was casting dancers as the friends of Johnson's peasant girl. Her mother, Jean, happened to be visiting New York at the time and was sitting quietly in Studio 3's observation gallery. As Franklin eyed the line of dancers, he called Shelton's name, beckoning her from where she stood at the barre to the center. "And that's when Arthur Mitchell went off," says Shelton. "He started yelling in front of the whole room, in front of my mother, 'Oh no, I don't even know where you've been! You haven't come up here once for class. You're not doing this ballet!' " She stood there stunned, as all the air went out of the room. Franklin looked down at the floor, aghast at the scene playing out before him. The other dancers grimaced and bowed their heads. Jean rose from her chair, unwilling to sit and watch her daughter being berated.

Mitchell stormed out of the studio, and Shelton snapped out of her paralysis. She followed him, but he shut his office door in her face. "I remember sitting outside in the hall hearing his voice get louder and louder," says Jean. "I'm just throbbing mad, but Karlya told me to let her handle it."

After years of holding her temper, Shelton entered his office and let it rip. "There weren't many opportunities at Dance Theatre of Harlem to say what you wanted to say. I was finally going to take my opportunity." She stood over his desk, forcing him to pay her mind. "How dare you do that to me!" she snapped. "You put me on hiatus! You never told me I had to report here for class!" The more she spoke up for herself, the angrier it made him.

"I want you bone thin!" he finally yelled. "Don't come back until you're bone thin!"

Shelton looked coolly at Mitchell's midsection, which by that time was no longer the washboard of his youth, thanks to his love of ice cream. "It's not that easy to be bone thin," she reminded him. "You should know that, right?" Desperately trying to hold back her tears, she turned to leave the room. "I will not be back," she said, her hand on the doorknob, "because I won't be treated this way ever again."

"Kar comes out of the office," says Jean, "and she's crying. I said, 'I can go talk to him. When I get through with him—'"

But Karlya shook her head no. "This is my fight," she said. "I'm done."

Jean followed her daughter downstairs to the locker room, where Karlya packed up all her things, her power notes and gifts from the dancers, the company photographs taped to the front of her locker. She stopped at Zelda Wynn's costuming room, telling the older woman, who had kept her looking so beautiful, that she was leaving and never coming back. Wynn enveloped her in a hug, promising the weeping girl that she would be okay.

Outside on the corner, Jean held her daughter's hand and suggested the two go for a drink. "She knew this was my whole world," says Karlya. "And Arthur Mitchell had just crashed it with a hammer."

The only relief was in the clarity of her decision. She vowed that from that day on she would never again call him Mr. Mitchell.

Karlya

'd been dancing since I was four years old. And I didn't get all the dancing out of me at the company of my dreams. I was lost. But when you
live in New York City, you've got to do something quick. I auditioned for
Alvin Ailey. Mr. Ailey was there and said he liked me, but I had very, very
little modern training. I joined a contemporary company that was just starting up. Mel Tomlinson and Charles De Rose came to see me dance there.
Afterward Charles said, "You shouldn't be here. You're much too good for
this company." Well, what am I supposed to do then? Where am I supposed
to go?

Bob Fosse called me once. He left a message on my answering machine—I
saved that cassette for a long time. "This is Bob Fosse and I'd like you to
come down and sing for me." He was getting ready to set a revival of Sweet
Charity on Broadway. I got a personal one-on-one audition with him. I
sang that Stevie Wonder song, "Come Back as a Flower." He wanted me to
sing something upbeat, so he had me sing "Isn't She Lovely" instead, which is
not an easy song! I told him on the way out, "You know, I can sing, but I'm
actually a really good dancer." Oh well. Debbie Allen got the lead.

I had a job as a coat check girl at the Fifth Avenue Grill. That gave me
a little pocket money, but it wasn't sustainable. Two French girls danced at
the company with me, and we would look through The New York Times
for bilingual jobs at beautiful places like fashion houses and perfumeries.
There's a flow to the French language that takes you right into the world of

glamour and beauty and fashion. Ballet is in French! I decided to go to the Berlitz School in New York. Then my aunt, who is fluent in French, convinced me to go to Paris instead to immerse myself in the language and the culture. I took my savings of a couple thousand dollars, packed up all my belongings, and moved there without knowing anybody. I was still so heartbroken, I had to leave New York. If I could've gone to the moon, I would've.

I was just trying to start anew. Leave it all behind. There was a point where I wouldn't even let people know I was a dancer. It was painful to talk about, and I told myself that that life was over. Now I was a student at the Alliance Française, living in the Latin Quarter. I'd been in Paris about a month when I met these cabaret entertainers. Every night I would go to this jazz club at the Hollywood Savoy to see them perform, and that's where I met the fashion photographer Richard Allen, who was the first Black friend I made in Paris. He asked me, "Do you need a job?" There was a part-time opening at this company owned by Saudi Arabian sheikhs. The job was administration. One day the COO, Omar, suggested that the staff all go shopping. I thought it was going to be a group outing with everyone in the office, but when I got to the place where we were supposed to meet, it was just Omar. He had called everyone else and canceled. He and I went all over Paris. We rode the Ferris wheel at the Tuileries. He walked me back to my apartment, and there was a protest on Boulevard St. Jacques, with a fire burning in the middle of the street. You couldn't ask for more on a first date. I quit the job once we became an item.

Marcia came to Paris for a visit when she was at Columbia Law School. Omar took the two of us out to dinner at L'Arpège. There was a wistfulness for me in seeing her because I could tell she had really found her niche with law. I was still missing the DTH family that we had.

Learning French opened a whole other world to me. I stayed in Paris for three years, then came home to New York fluent. The story of the Central Park jogger had just hit the news, and Donald Trump was calling for the boys' deaths. I got a place downtown where a group of boisterous drag queens would gather outside my window every night. First I got a temp job at Balenciaga, but the thought of being around jewels was much more inviting. I joined Van Cleef & Arpels, working upstairs in their office. One night Dance Theatre of Harlem performed at City Center, which was right around *the corner from the store. How did it feel to see them dance? It was different than the old days. It hurt.*

Omar was living in Los Angeles then, and we were going back and forth. One Saturday Philippe Arpels called me over and teased; "I am tired of seeing your long face. I have a position that's open in the Beverly Hills store. Are you interested?" Marcia rented the truck and helped me move out of my apartment in Brooklyn. She took my record collection. My Diana Ross, my L.T.D., my Earth, Wind & Fire. She also took my bed. I lived on the fourth floor, so instead of walking the queen-size mattress down the steps, the DTH dancer Tyrone Brooks, who's now the artistic director of the Tallahassee Ballet, just pushed it over the railing and let it drop through the stairwell.

I moved into a higher role in the Van Cleef Beverly Hills office. I loved working there and learning the world of haute joaillerie. I was the only Black person in both the New York and Beverly Hills stores besides the security guards. I was the executive assistant to the vice president. Nancy Reagan used to visit him. One day she was waiting with her Secret Service. I told her, "I danced at the White House when you were the first lady." My clients included everyone from Brad Pitt to Alfre Woodard. I remember one afternoon driving to Arnold Schwarzenegger's house, which was my first opportunity to present jewelry outside of the store, and on the way over I was so nervous that I repeated the Dougla prayer in my car.

The West Coast was so different. There's a closeness of people in New York, but everything in L.A. is so spread out. It was harder to make friends. Everyone's first question is, "What do you do? How can you help me?" I didn't have very many friends. I missed my Dance Theatre of Harlem family, and thought I'd never have those types of relationships again. I think I felt lost.

WHEN LYDIA ABARCA first opened up to the Legacy Council about her struggles with alcoholism, Shelton had a visceral reaction. She cried silently through Abarca's initial confession, and then called her friend afterward to tell her how grateful she was to her for once more leading the way.

During the next Legacy Council meeting Shelton took a shaky breath and released herself from her own secret shame. "It got ugly there for a minute," she began.

She'd always liked to drink socially. Champagne after performances, wine in Paris. In Los Angeles, she turned to vodka. She started a Friday tradition of having one-hundred-proof martinis at the Grill in Beverly Hills, which was around the corner from the Van Cleef & Arpels store. Her habit escalated to the point that she'd need a drink first thing in the morning so she could function. Eventually she went to rehab. She tried going to AA meetings, but sharing her lowest moments there only left her feeling more isolated. She waited a year to get pregnant with her son. The family moved to Oakland. It was a good life, and a full one.

Then in 2019 Karlya's beloved father, Lloyd Shelton, died. *To this day, I'll just be in the car and memories of him will cause me to burst into tears.* She and her husband, Omar Benjamin, moved to Denver to be closer to her mother, staying with Jean in the family home until they found a place of their own. *Being in the house was so strange without my dad there. There were so many memories and smells.* Her parents had a fully stocked bar in the basement, and she started sneaking a glass for herself down there. One January afternoon Omar came downstairs and saw her tipping the whole bottle into her mouth. She ended up having to go to the hospital, she was so dehydrated. When the Legacy Council gathered for the first time five months later, she never thought she'd tell any of the women that she was an alcoholic, or that the pain of losing her father had caused her to relapse. *It takes time to let go of the shame. Society has always told you to be ashamed of addiction. That it's a weakness. I had shame from when my son saw me at my worst. When I apologized, he told me "You should have no shame. It's a part of what made you who you are—strong."*

Watching my son, Chè, grow up was my best thing in life. He's an old soul. I had a full-circle moment when he was a freshman in high school. He was a huskier guy at the time because he had to take steroids for his asthma. He was very good at tennis, but the gym teacher told him, "You're too over- weight to play tennis. Someone your size needs to go out for football." It just hurt him to the core. He came home and told us about it, and I was like, "I'm going up there! I want a piece of him." And Chè told me, "No, Mom, I'm doing this." And he went up there and told the guy, "You can't write my future. Only I can control that." That's my boy. So wise beyond his years.

When he was little, we got him a keyboard for Christmas. He works in the music business now as a copyright and royalties manager. He's put out three EPs and is working on his first full album. It's amazing when I think about when he first started playing the piano as a little kid. I remember when we played a duet of "Hey Jude" in a Halloween recital together, and we both dressed up like Beatles. I tell him to follow his gift. "That's what God gave you. God expresses itself through you, and that's your way of expressing God."

"My mother has always trusted me to figure out my own life," says her twenty-five-year-old son, Chè Benjamin. "When my mom was growing up, my grandma saw her discipline and her determination for excellence. I like to think my mom sees that in me too. She knows that the path of an artist is never linear and straightforward, but she trusts and believes in the process. There might be heartbreak, but you have to let people do what they feel called to do."

I'm an artist. That's who I am. Music. Jewelry. Photography. But I was always missing dance. A few years ago I snapped at my husband about something, and he said to me, "Hey, I'm not Arthur Mitchell. You're driving yourself crazy, and you're going to drive me crazy. Please do something, or you're just going to stay unhappy."

So in 2011, on the advice of a life coach, Shelton sent Mitchell a one-page typed letter in which she expressed a desire to "let go of baggage." *Sitting down to write it was hard. But what did I have to lose? I had to get right with me and let him go. I just couldn't carry him around anymore. I wrote him a letter and said that I'd been angry at him for a long time, but that I could never know how hard it was to be him during that time. Starting a Black ballet company at the end of the civil rights era. I didn't know what he went through, but I thanked him for creating the company and giving us a place to dance. "I want you to know that I honor you for the person that you are and thank you for your role in shaping me into the artist and the woman that I am."*

He called me and said, "I really liked your letter." And he started to tell me about how hard it had been to be both the artistic and the executive director. He talked about going downtown to try to raise money from donors, and they'd all say yes, yes, yes, but then they'd have changed their minds by the time he got back uptown. He said, "A lot of times I would come into the studio, and I would just see an arabesque. I wouldn't even see a person. I would just start yelling at a body." We talked for about an hour and a half. Well, he did most of the talking. You don't really talk that much with Arthur Mitchell. I did tell him I'd been angry at him for all these years. I don't think he ever said, "I'm sorry." But it allowed me to let my anger go and be at peace. It was like shedding a heavy coat. Finally I've set this baggage down. And he did tell me during that conversation, "You were a beautiful dancer."

As you get older, you have the desire to pay it forward. Share with people what you've learned. A few years ago I started coaching and mentoring a young Black ballerina named Angela Watson when she was with the San Francisco Ballet Academy. I helped her with her audition for the Paris Opéra Ballet summer intensive, which she got, and then multiple variations for her company auditions. She's now a full company member with the San Francisco Ballet.

"I met Karlya when I was fifteen," says Watson. "It was the first time I'd met a Black ballerina who actually felt what I felt in the ballet world. I carry her advice and lessons with me throughout every space I'm in. I tend to overthink in company spaces. Every time I dance, I feel that it is extremely important to be perfect or better than perfect and that I always have something to prove. She let me know how important it is to let myself exist and that 'letting myself just be' is one of the most powerful and important things that I can do. I carry this piece of advice with me everywhere, and I feel so much more gratitude now as I dance. Karlya always reminds me that I am standing on the shoulders of so many Black ballerinas before me, and we are always here to support one another, and that each step I take catapults the next generation of Black dancers into even more excellence."

I tell Angela not to worry about what other people think about her or what she thinks they think about her. Mr. Bill once told me, as I told her, "You have to develop this sense of loneliness where nothing comes between you and your artistry." Block out everything and just be present in that moment as that character or doing that step or with that piece of music. If you're going to be the violin, you have to be the violin.

Some wisdom comes with age—like the knowledge that artistry comes from within. It has nothing to do with ego or audience or approval. It is a person's most authentic expression of self, and thus it can never be taken away.

17

⌒

G rowing up can sometimes feel like a long series of goodbyes and chapters ending. By the end of 1983, the five women had all left or lost the company. The luxury of a long life is the chance to make peace with those parts of ourselves that we leave behind along the way. But time is a gift that many of the women's partners did not receive.

The AIDS crisis ripped through the dance world like a tornado in the 1980s and '90s. Decades later the women still tremble when talking about the dawn of the epidemic: friends complaining of nodes in their throats, shortness of breath, and descriptions of the worst flu imaginable, while the medical community and the media labeled it with the castigating moniker G.R.I.D. (gay related immune deficiency). The vitality of a generation of artists had begun spilling out across stages and studios onto city streets, and the powers that be were busy blaming the victims.

"We were seeing dying, and dying quickly," says Marcia Sells. "It was a vanishing, literally. So many loved ones here one minute, and then gone the next. Talk to anyone from Dance Theatre of Harlem, and they will tell you how much loss we felt."

President Reagan waited until 1985, four entire years after the first AIDS case was reported in San Francisco, to publicly mention the disease. Five thousand people, most of them gay men, died during those years of refusal to acknowledge and respond. And even when the media started reporting in earnest on what was fast becoming a public health crisis, the press coverage focused on the plight of white gay men, even though Black people, who made up 12 percent of the U.S. population, accounted for 26 percent of the nation's first three thousand cases. (And almost two decades later, in 2020, Black people accounted for 43 percent of HIV diagnoses and 44 percent of HIV-related deaths, according to the CDC and the Kaiser Family Foundation.)

Throughout the AIDS crisis, Black gay men were routinely excluded from high-profile activist groups. Such an intersectional failure—like the one the feminist movement has still not honestly reckoned with—had lethal consequences. "While we were living in the early days of the eighties and our friends were dying, dying, dying, nobody was doing crap," says Sells. "Only when Larry Kramer and the others started ACT UP and the Gay Men's Health Crisis, all from fairly well-off white families with access to resources, only then did it become a thing."

"The lack of leadership and compassion was a slap in the face to all those who had to watch helplessly as their loved ones died," says Lydia Abarca. Such a profound sense of abandonment led to conspiracy rumors of a strategically targeted attack. "I was one of those with the people who said it was the government," says Sheila Rohan, as the others nod in agreement. "This was a genocide of gay people, Black people."

That hurricane of loss still overwhelms thirty years later, as the women live through another pandemic that's hit underresourced and undervalued Black and brown communities especially hard. Their Tuesday gatherings provide them with the space to grieve the present losses, as well as the boys of their youth. "These beautiful men who threw you up in the air and caught you," says Gayle McKinney-Griffith. "You would run and jump, knowing they wouldn't let you fall. And suddenly you can't see them. You can't hear them. I think of what those beautiful, creative minds could have done. And you'll never know what their lives could have been. It leaves you speechless. I'm stuttering."

She remembers when Paul Russell, who'd staunchly fought alongside her to unionize the company, surprised her in Germany with a phone call out of the blue in 1991. "I was like, 'Paul! You're calling me. It's so great to hear from you.' We talked for a long time, and then his voice started crackling and he sounded very weak. I said, 'Paul, are you okay?' And then he said, 'I'm going to say goodbye now and I love you.' 'Well, I love you too, Paul.' I didn't know what was happening. Then he said 'Goodbye.' I said, "Bye Paul.'"

Paul Russell was the first Black man to dance Siegfried in a full production of *Swan Lake*. He once danced Romeo to Abarca's Juliet in the balcony scene pas de deux at the New York Dance Festival. He died in San Francisco at the age of forty-three, a week after his phone call with McKinney-Griffith.

Tragically, he was one of many from the Dance Theatre of Harlem family to die of AIDS. Karlya Shelton remembers when she first realized that Roman Brooks, whom *The New York Times* once hailed as a "dancer with a long, lyrical ballet line and quiet inborn grandeur," was sick. They'd spent an afternoon with other dancers lolling on the grass in Central Park's Sheep Meadow, but it was impossible to ignore how thin he'd gotten, how withdrawn. A grayness seemed to have taken up residence beneath his once-radiant skin. "I remember asking him how he was doing. And he said, so softly, 'Yeah, I'm not well.'"

Brooks was born in Millington, Tennessee, where his path to ballet began in a social dancing class during college. He went on to perform with Eugene Loring's Los Angeles Dance Theater before Dance Theatre of Harlem rolled into town and recalibrated his ambitions. He and Abarca, who had been his partner in *Holberg Suite*, kept in regular touch long after they'd both left the company. One afternoon she called him and was surprised when his mother picked up the line. "Oh baby," the older woman sighed through a heavy voice. "He passed." Abarca remembers hanging up the phone, flattened by the drumbeat of losses. "Oh my god, they really are all dying."

And beautiful, genteel Walter Raines. As his health deteriorated, he'd ask his circle for reassurances that his skin hadn't yet taken on the orange tint of the dying. "Do I have it now? Have I changed?" he'd ask. And they'd promise him, "No, no, no, you don't have that." Shelton and another DTH dancer, Melanie Person, paid a visit to Raines in the hospital, their heads filled with terrifying headlines instead of facts. "We didn't know what to expect so we stopped at the nurses' station to ask, 'Can we touch him? Can we hug him?' And they told us not to kiss him."

Toward the end, Raines raged against both the physical torment of the virus and society's disregard for those in its terrible grip. "He was very angry," says McKinney-Griffith. "Virginia used to tell me 'You can't talk to Walter. You can't reach him. He's screaming. He doesn't like anyone. He's mad with the world.' And it broke my heart to hear all that. The disease pained not just his body but his soul."

Walter Raines died in 1994 at the age of fifty-four. He created ballets for Dance Theatre of Harlem and the Capitol Ballet of Washington and was the first Black choreographer to work at the Royal Opera in London. After chairing the ballet department at Alvin Ailey, Raines returned to DTH in 1989 to serve as director of the school. He once told a reporter that in his obituary, "I'd just like to be called 'a man of the theater.'"

"My memories of Walter are good," says McKinney-Griffith. "He is robust and alive, and I can hear his voice and his laughter. He had a silly laugh. Ahhh. All of them had silly laughs." The women sigh in unison, pained half-smiles on their faces. They pause to let their bodies remember the sensation of their partners' hands on their backs, forever guiding them and keeping them safe.

Mel Tomlinson first tested positive for HIV after collapsing at a dance conference in 1995. He went on to survive three harrowing hospitalizations, each time stunning his doctors when he'd emerge back into the bright of day. Lydia Abarca and Karen Brown, another former DTH dancer, drove together to visit him during one of those fraught hospital stays. "The nurse told us Mel didn't want anyone to see him in his condition," says Abarca. "Excuse me? This is family. I just wanted to kiss him goodbye."

Tomlinson is one of the few people with the select honor of having danced with three major companies during his illustrious career—Dance Theatre of Harlem, Alvin Ailey American Dance Theater, and New York City Ballet. His defining performance was arguably that of the serpent in Arthur Mitchell's *Manifestations,* a ballet based on the story of Adam and Eve. Tomlinson took the role so seriously he toured with a pet snake he named Martine for inspiration. Each night the tall and rangy Tomlinson would make his acrobatic descent onto the stage from a lowered vine. He was a master of slink and breathtaking contortion. From the wings, his fellow dancers would watch in awe, as rapt as the mesmerized audience in their seats. "Ooh, that long leg of his looking almost like a clock handle," remembers Sells. "That arabesque!"

"I witnessed an entire male ensemble pass away," Sheila Rohan says of the epidemic. She was working at Alvin Ailey in those years. "These were our Black gods. Prima donnas of the dance world. And then you had to see them decline. At least twenty-five, thirty of them, one right after another dropped. I often cried and asked my spirit why this had to be and why to these friends who expressed only love. There was a big poster of them as you enter the hall of the school. Finally, we asked them to take it down because there was maybe one person, Dudley Williams I think, left out of the whole picture. It made your heart sick."

They are still furious at how their brothers were abandoned by a cruel and callous government. They never once believed their partners brought their fate down upon themselves, no matter what public opinion would have preferred them to think. They were neither scared of their friends nor ashamed of them. They held their brothers' hands. They cried with and over them. They sat bedside with them. To this day their muscle memory aches with longing for these essential young men who deserved the luxury of full lives.

And so they lift up the memory of Mel Tomlinson. Allen Sampson. Walter Raines. Roman Brooks. Samuel Smalls. Gary DeLoatch. Paul Russell. James Exxum. Woody Louden. Hutaff Lennon. D'artagnan Petty, who after a performance at the Kennedy Center danced with Shelton and Donald Williams around a gazebo while listening to Prokofiev's "Montagues and Capulets" from *Romeo and Juliet* on a boom box. "Okay, you run over here to this column and penché!" they'd call out choreography to each other.

"Each name broke off a piece of you," says McKinney-Griffith. "You lost parts of your heart."

ONE MORE PRECIOUS PIECE in 2022: their sister Stephanie Dabney, who leaped into history in Dance Theatre of Harlem's Caribbean-themed production of *Firebird,* died of cardiopulmonary arrest after living with HIV for over thirty years.

Abarca remembers when the younger dancer first called her back in 1990 with the news. "She said 'Lydia, I have AIDS.' I thought she said 'Eggs.' So I said, 'What, Stephanie? What?' She said, 'AIDS, Lydia. I have AIDS.' And my legs just gave out on me."

Dabney lived for years in the Dorothy Ross Friedman Residence, an affordable haven for artists living with HIV just a few blocks south of Lincoln Center. Rohan and other former DTH dancers, including Yvonne Hall and Ronald Perry, took shifts caring for her, tidying up her apartment, and making sure she ate food and took her pills. Friends would occasionally run into Dabney on 57th Street heading off for errands in her motorized wheelchair. "Hey Stephanie!" they'd call out. "I can't talk right now, I'm busy!" she'd say, waving behind her as she went on about her day. She remained a treasured audience member at DTH's Sunday Open Houses, an enduring gift to the public that now happens four times a year.

"Stephanie was just a little sprite," says McKinney-Griffith, remembering the sixteen-year-old girl who first joined Dance Theatre of Harlem in 1975. "She was always here and there. I remember when I would rehearse her in *Adagietto #5*, and she would go over and over it until even I was tired. She had this tremendous backbend in *Adagietto* where she would come up almost at a right angle." Swooning, Abarca says, "And she would make it look so flawless."

In 1982, Dabney danced the lead in choreographer John Taras's *Firebird*, set to the original Igor Stravinsky score. The genius Geoffrey Holder was tasked with transposing the Russian folktale to a tropical Caribbean setting. His sets and costumes were lush and luxurious, with Dabney swathed in crimson feathered plumes and a magnificent headdress. The miracle of DTH's *Firebird* wasn't just the fact of a Black Firebird finally taking flight in this world. It was how Dabney's fluttering energy, her speed, and her impeccable technique elevated the role to new heights. Jack Anderson in *The New York Times* would declare her "the most incandescent Firebird imaginable."

Dabney would go on to perform *Firebird* at the opening ceremonies of the 1984 Olympics in Los Angeles. Four years later, she led Dance Theatre of Harlem's triumphant performance in the Kremlin's Palace of Congresses. "In Russia kids climbed through the bathroom windows to get in!" says Charles De Rose. "They had never seen Black classical dancers on pointe."

·　　·　　·

AFTER HER DIAGNOSIS, Dabney spent much of her time confined to a wheelchair. She survived four bouts of severe pneumonia in one vulnerable year alone. A lung collapsed. Toward the end of her life, a leg was amputated. Throughout, her DTH family stayed in faithful touch, reminding her that the people who knew her when she flew still had her back. Every time someone called, Dabney would answer the phone herself. Energetic and bubbly, flitting from one subject to another, she did most of the talking in the conversation. A sprite until the end.

Karlya Shelton spoke to Dabney in the final weeks before her death. The two had started together at Dance Theatre of Harlem as teenage apprentices in 1975. As girls, they called each other "Pal" and would help each other get into character before curtain. On the phone, Shelton reminded Dabney of how she used to wait in the wings for her during *Firebird*. There's a section in the ballet called the Berceuse, when the firebird lulls the monsters to sleep. Dabney would dance a series of bourrées to Stravinsky's soft and haunting music until she contorted her body into a magnificent backbend and floated off stage.

"I would wait for Stephanie to get as close as she could to the edge of the wing," says Shelton, "and then I'd pull her in because she couldn't see with her head looking up at the lights in her backbend. I remember one time when she came off stage, I grabbed her by her rib cage and she just held on to me for a while. Her shoes were so soft, probably because Mitchell notoriously hated the sound of hard shoes on stage. 'My god,' I told her. 'I can see your bunions through the fabric.'"

The firebird just clung to her friend, holding on to Shelton to help take the weight off her screaming toes. Shelton remembers asking her if she needed help crossing to the other side, where the crew would hook Dabney up to fly in the finale's joyful celebration of love's triumph. But she shook her head no. All she needed was to hold on to her sister for a few seconds longer, while she gathered some strength for the end.

"Do you remember that?" Shelton asked.

The two women spent a moment in silence, lost in their shared memories of youth. "Live your life as best you can," Dabney told Shelton before saying goodbye.

Act Three

18

In 2004, Dance Theatre of Harlem disbanded its forty-four-member company for what was originally supposed to be the remainder of its season. The company went on hiatus in order to pay down a $2.3 million deficit, incurred because fundraising couldn't keep pace with Arthur Mitchell's grandiose artistic vision. He had shot for the moon with the production of *St. Louis Woman*, an hour-long blues ballet with a million-dollar production budget that had opened at Lincoln Center the previous year. "Arthur said, 'Come on, let's put it all in here,'" says Charles De Rose. "I remember him calling me, 'I need $100,000 right away. The orchestra is going to walk out of Lincoln Center if they don't get paid.'" Mitchell was betting everything on the hope that *St. Louis Woman* would transition to a long-running Broadway production, whose box office would nicely fill DTH's coffers. "There were a couple of Broadway producers that met with him after the premiere," says De Rose. "But Arthur wouldn't let anyone in the meetings with him. And then nothing happened."

What was supposed to be a temporary hiatus stretched on for a devastating eight years. Most of the dancers failed to get jobs in other companies, or when they did, they were brought in at positions beneath their experience and talent level.

In 2010, Virginia Johnson returned to the company following Mitchell's personal request that she take over his role as artistic director. "It was a bitter pill for him," says De Rose. "Very difficult. He was eating pounds of ice cream, which eventually killed him."

During the void left by Dance Theatre of Harlem's absence in the landscape, the legend of Misty Copeland was born, and the culture at large embraced her as the first Black ballerina. Her anointing was pushed by the American Ballet Theatre, whose ticket sales soared. "Misty is an extraordinarily beautiful dancer and deserves everything that she's gotten," says Johnson. "But she also had a machine behind her that very carefully strategized that moment and that position. I felt like Misty went out of her way to bring up DTH when she could. But the thing that hurts me more when I hear that statement about her being the first is that in 2004 the DTH touring company closed. And for all those years, we stopped being a presence in the dance world and in the world at large. The human mind is very fickle. Not having the constant reminder that we are in this art form, and we have made magic here, we were forgotten. Yes, it did get forgotten. That's where the tragedy is."

Under Johnson's direction, Dance Theatre of Harlem began auditioning dancers for a revived troupe in 2011, then embarked on a string of performances with its new training ensemble the following year. In 2013 a lean company of eighteen members performed at the Rose Theater at Lincoln Center.

In the spring of 2016, Johnson extended an invitation to all the women who'd graced the company throughout history, as well other Black women who'd made their mark on ballet, to join in a celebration of "Black Ballerina Magic." All that talent who'd worked so hard to make ballet more beautiful and expansive so that a woman like Misty Copeland could rise. Together they would gather on stage, during the intermission of DTH's final performance of the season at New York's City Center, for the first time in history.

We were there. We were there. We were there.

SINCE THEY LEFT the company, Lydia Abarca, Gayle McKinney-Griffith, Sheila Rohan, Marcia Sells, and Karlya Shelton had all stayed in sporadic touch. There were Christmas cards and phone calls and letters. One of McKinney-Griffith's first stops every time she visited the States was to see her Sheily. Then she'd bring her children up to visit Sells when she was the dean of students at Columbia Law School, or to the NBA offices, during her brief stint working as vice president of HR and organizational development. ("Marcia would spoil us," says Khadija. "We thought she worked at the NBA store.") Sells served for a period on the board of the Nanette Bearden Contemporary Dance Theater. She became close with Rohan's niece Diedra Harris-Kelley, who is the co-director of the Romare Bearden Foundation. Abarca kept in touch with Shelton, who traveled with her family to visit her in Georgia once. And all five of the women attended *The Gathering,* an alumni event in 2005 hosted at Dance Theatre of Harlem. "It was like a family reunion," says Abarca. As soon as she embraced Rohan, Abarca started weeping: "I'm always just a big crybaby with her."

But the Black Ballerina Magic event was a rare opportunity to gather en masse and remind an audience of living history. McKinney-Griffith originally wasn't planning on attending. She felt weak, tired, and overwhelmed. Though it wouldn't be diagnosed for a couple of months, the cancer was already growing. "I wasn't doing well at all," she says of the time. "I was taking care of my mother, which was nonstop 24/7. That was a stress. But then I went anyway because I wanted to see Karlya, and Lydia, and Marcia, and Sheila."

The ballerinas gathered backstage before intermission. Debra Austin was there. Joan Myers Brown. Lauren Anderson. Delores Browne. Carmen de Lavallade, who was also there on behalf of her cousin, the ballerina Janet Collins, who broke the color line with the Metropolitan Opera in 1951 and died in 2003. Rohan introduced herself to Raven Wilkinson, who would die just two years later at the age of eighty-three. "I only knew about Raven from reading about her in books," says Rohan. "Raven and I embraced. I felt like I was meeting one of my idols."

Johnson and DTH's rehearsal director, Kelley A. Saunders, began calling the dancers to the stage, in rows from youngest to oldest. All that power and legacy, the breathtaking visual of community. "Then one by one they read each person's name, and we each had an opportunity to take a bow," says Sells. "Row by row, we would go off into the wings. The next generation would then come out to the middle and bow. By the end it was Raven Wilkinson and Delores Browne."

The following day the women who are indeed Black Ballerina Magic

reunited in Studio 3 for brunch. The fire escape was gone. The large indus-
trial fans that used to whir in the corners had been replaced by central air.
Rohan couldn't attend, but Shelton sat next to Abarca. McKinney-Griffith
sat at a table next to Sells. "Debbie Austin brought us all to tears," says
Sells. "She spoke about her time at the School of American Ballet and
then in City Ballet."

"I don't personally know why anybody would want to stay somewhere
that's not going to boost you up," says Abarca. "This is a short career.
And you're just hanging in there, wasting your professional years, hoping
someone takes you seriously."

Lauren Anderson, the first Black principal ballerina with the Houston
Ballet and the first Black woman to perform the lead in a full production
of *Swan Lake,* also gave a stirring speech. "She spoke about seeing Dance
Theatre of Harlem perform when she was a girl," says Shelton. "How
much we impacted her."

The final speaker of the afternoon was Dr. Joselli Audain Deans, a
dance scholar and educator who'd prepared a speech celebrating all that
Dance Theatre of Harlem had done for the art form. "I grew up at DTH
hearing about how it was the first permanent Black ballet company," she
tells me. "I never questioned what that meant. I didn't realize there were
other Black ballet companies that existed before DTH until I went and
did the research."

Deans had started taking classes at the DTH school when she was ten
years old. She'd sit on the little step at the entrance of Studio 3, taking in
the beauty of the older dancers. Her parents took her to all the company's
performances. She'd been in the audience when McKinney-Griffith did
the iconic sit lift in *Forces of Rhythm.* When Rohan commanded the stage
as the Bride in *Douglas.* When Abarca premiered ballets like *Carmen,
Combat,* and *Afternoon of a Faun.* Deans watched Shelton's debut performance in the corps in *Bugaku.* And when Shelton had the opportunity to
go on in a principal role in Dublin in *Serenade,* it was Deans who stepped
into her position in the corps.

"I grew up watching these women and witnessing not just their incredible talent," says Deans, "but their devotion to each other. Their camara-
derie. The way they took care of the younger dancers." When Deans was
little, Abarca taught some of her classes. "She was so intimidating to me,"

she says. "Like as much as Arthur Mitchell, that's how much I admired her. But oh my god, she was a wonderful teacher. Patient, gentle, and of course, gorgeous to look at. Everybody wanted to dance like Lydia." Then when Deans joined the company as an apprentice, it was Shelton who would take her under her wing. The Brooklyn girl didn't have a clue when it came to stage makeup. "Karlya took me aside one day and said, 'Okay, let me show you how to do this,'" says Deans. Which is exactly what McKinney-Griffith had done for Shelton when she first joined the company.

Deans stood up to speak at brunch that day back in Studio 3, and Christina Johnson, who during her thirteen years at DTH danced in the principal roles in everything from *Swan Lake* to *Giselle,* called out to her friend proudly: "Dr. Deans!"

"And I sort of did what I always do," says Deans. "I said nah, nah, nah, you know, downplaying my title. And then something overtook me. I'm a very spiritual person so I say it was probably the Holy Spirit. My speech went in another direction. I said, 'You know, I was just about to say, let's not talk about me being a doctor. But we Black women have to stop doing that. We have to stop downplaying all that we have done.' I told them that I knew the stories of most everyone in the room. Women in general in ballet suffer because it's a man's world. The danseurs are coddled. But Black women? And then dark Black women? And I just went on from there."

"I remember her telling us we need to be proud of all we had done and to start speaking up about it," says Abarca. "But we were always taught to be humble. I'm guilty of always downplaying what I've done." The other women nod. "I think we all were," says Shelton.

Back in Denver, Shelton sent Deans a letter thanking her for her urgent plea. "I wrote to her that I had known Joselli for a long time. But this was the first time I saw Dr. Deans." Deans keeps Shelton's letter as a kind of power note, even bringing it with her when she left the East Coast for a faculty job in the dance department at the University of Utah, where she's continuing her research. "I look at Karlya's card for inspiration when I'm feeling tired," she says. "Delving back into history as a Black person is draining."

Before she started taking classes at Dance Theatre of Harlem, Deans used to go to the library to search through dance books for anybody who looked like her. Then when she began at the school, she used to do class projects centered on the feats of the company. She's saved a report she wrote in markers about Arthur Mitchell. She also has a seventh grade art project about the importance of seeing oneself, in which she cut out the back of a child looking in the mirror. In the reflection of the glass, she pasted a picture of Gayle McKinney-Griffith and Derek Williams from the pas de trois in *Forces of Rhythm.* "What do you want to be when you grow up?" a young Deans wrote at the top of the page in cursive script. "A dancer."

The vanished legacy of Dance Theatre of Harlem astounds. "The little girl in me is really, really angry at a world that wants to deny and destroy my incredible experiences growing up admiring all these women," says Deans. "The dancer in me who danced with all these incredible people says, *How dare you forget what we did?* I danced in twenty-some odd countries, okay? Then there's me the historian. And that's the one that is truly outraged."

It's not just Black women who get forgotten in ballet, though, as in most matters of justice and parity, they fare the worst. "It's the nature sadly of this art form too," says Sells. "Singers and musicians get to perform farther in their lives. The Met just celebrated a woman who's been sixty years in the orchestra. There's no ballerina who is sixty years old anywhere, unless she's teaching or working in a school. It ends so quickly. If you make it to your forties, you have another half of your life to live. We don't do enough to remember our history. I used to have this conversation with Arthur Mitchell over and over. He spent so much time trying to rev up and keep viable Dance Theatre of Harlem that he could forget about preserving its legacy."

Looking around Studio 3 that morning at all the women who had done so much for ballet, Shelton remembers feeling the stirring of power. *We just can't let this die,* she told herself in the most important room of her life. *There's too many of us. Everybody deserves their flowers.*

19

In 2018 Arthur Mitchell died from complications of heart failure in a New York hospital. A few weeks before his passing, Tania León visited him in his apartment. He'd agreed to speak with Alejandro J. Madrid, the author of her 2022 biography *Tania León's Stride: A Polyrhythmic Life,* on the condition that she be present for the conversation. In his apartment, he told Madrid about his great affection for his Taniacita. She couldn't believe her ears. "Arthur was always very reserved," says León. "He would let you know that he loved you because of his gestures. Flying Lydia's brother, Julio, over to Italy. Giving Sheila a raise because she had children. My grandmother died four years after my arrival in this country, and when Arthur found out, he left his office and sat with me for an entire day. He wouldn't tell you that he loved you. He would show it. We were his family. We were his artistic family and the ones who realized his dream. He drove everybody crazy. I'm telling you! I don't know when he slept! He had the energy of someone who was always in a hurry."

Mitchell later called León to let her know he was on his way to the hospital. "And of course, he likes to boss me around, to boss everyone around, so he told me 'But don't come visit me!'" she says. "He liked to think that he was very strong, and he didn't need anybody. A few days after, I get this call that he's dead."

A pall fell over the dance world at the loss of such a giant. Sheila Rohan called Gayle McKinney-Griffith with the news. "I was speechless, it hit me so hard," says McKinney-Griffith. "It was like losing a parent. You just felt so lost."

Karlya Shelton was driving when she first heard. She had to pull over her car to catch her breath on the shoulder of the road.

Lydia Abarca happened to be on hold with Dance Theatre of Harlem, trying to get information about discounted tickets for the Fiftieth Anniversary Gala, when a cousin texted her: *Arthur Mitchell is dead.* Right then DTH's director of individual giving, Sharon Duncan, came on the line. "And she said, 'I want to be the first person to tell you that Mr. Mitchell has passed. I remember saying to her, 'This can't be. He doesn't have our permission to go.'"

Marcia Sells was in her office at Harvard Law School when the news alert came up on her cellphone. She Googled for details. She called Dance Theatre of Harlem. Friends reached out to her, saying they wanted to tell her themselves. "And then I just wept in my office," she says. "I couldn't work. I had to leave. Like Gayle said, it was like a parent going. My father died in 2005. My mom died in 1992. At this point, Arthur was one of the few people of that generation who'd seen me as a little ballet student trying to be a dancer. Now this person who knew I had been a ballerina and that I'd had skill and talent was gone."

Sells had begun encouraging Mitchell in 2014 to preserve his archives. "I used to talk to him about this. 'You want the legacy of DTH to go on after you've gone.' But sometimes he was like, 'Well, not if they're not going to do it the way that I want.'" Appealing to the importance of history, she successfully spearheaded the sale of Mitchell's archives to Columbia's Rare Book and Manuscript Library.

In the windup to the illustrious 2015 symposium celebrating both Mitchell's career and the acquisition of Columbia's first major dance collection, he would call Sells in fits of pique. He argued that Columbia was being cheap after it balked at paying for an evening of performances. "He goes, 'Well, I think we're just going to have to cancel,'" says Sells. "I said, 'Well that's not up to you. This is happening, and it will be a shame if you're not there.' He was used to being the person in charge. I called him Mr. Mitchell to the end and had always been very respectful, but at some point, I had to tell myself, *You're a grown-ass woman.*"

At the symposium, he went to greet Sells, then paused. "He said, 'Well,

I don't know if I can hug you, you're so big.' I was like, 'I'm not dancing anymore. I'm not even worried about that. Please, don't even try.'"

"He didn't have any filter at all," says Abarca. "I made a point to go see his Columbia archive exhibit too. I was hiding in the crowd. When I came out from behind somebody, he goes, 'Oh, there's my first ballerina! Come here! Are you pregnant again?' Come on man, I was sixty-seven."

The women can't help but laugh at the man's nerve. "We all have good things to say about him, but he could be a pain in the butt," says McKinney-Griffith.

"We're old enough to say exactly how we feel, but the love has never gone away," says Abarca. "He could beat us down in a second, but he also built us up."

Says Sells, "Nobody knew how ill he was. The hip surgery and his kidneys and dialysis."

Until the very end, he remained a force as complicated as he was pure, as maddening as he was noble. As a young man, he'd forced the world to bend to meet him, and he never stopped.

What icons like Arthur Mitchell must have encountered on their willful rise to the top, the women muse. "I was talking with some of my older friends who came up through the theater," says Rohan. "We were talking about how people must have spoken to this group of men—Arthur, Alvin Ailey, Louis Johnson, and them. They must have been treated really badly coming up as they found a way to stay on stage and have a career. So maybe it was unconscious that they all did the same thing to us, you see? Arthur made history. And he probably took whatever they gave him."

"He birthed all of us," says Abarca. "From the ground up. He was our chaperone. He was our spokesperson. He was our protector. He was who made us feel worthy of the big stage."

"We adored him because of his stature," says McKinney-Griffith. "What he taught us. The opportunity he gave us to be the best in the world. We were encompassed into his life, and he didn't let us go."

Shelton has a picture of Mitchell she took in San Francisco. The company was out on a sightseeing tour, which Mitchell liked to organize at every major destination. Shelton was snapping pictures for her personal collection, as she always did, when Mitchell started striking poses. She captured a moment of him being beautiful, which he always was, and silly, which he didn't always have the luxury to be. He's standing in front of the Golden Gate Bridge in fourth position croisé relevé. His arms are extended, the left stretching high toward the sun, the right behind him in noble counterbalance. His fingers are long and elegant, suspended in the flirtatious flick of ballet dancers. His whole body is reaching, reaching toward something unattainable and out of view. The sunlight catches the sharp planes of his exquisite profile, bouncing off his forehead and cheekbones, the white of his teeth. He's shot from the hips up, giving him the appearance of a phoenix in a silk-blend shirt with a wide collar, rising from waters pulled in from the Pacific Ocean. "I loved him and what he did for us," says Shelton, studying the photo. "I did. I really did. I know he loved me too. He loved all of us."

The 152nd Street Black Ballet Legacy Council exists in part because of Mitchell's passing. Some stories can be shared only when the giant living in them is gone. "I do believe that he would've tried to control us," says Rohan. *"What are you doing now? Why are you doing that? Let me suggest this."* It would have become the Arthur Mitchell story. Or the story of Dance Theatre of Harlem. The women would have remained in the background, interchangeable, replaceable.

ON DECEMBER 3, 2018, mourners gathered for Mitchell's memorial service at Harlem's Riverside Church. The founding dancers—or the Grandparents, as they called themselves—gathered in a room before the service, minus Rohan, who was still recovering from hip surgery. There was a comfort in that private time beforehand, just for those who were there first.

During the grand service, one of Mitchell's younger relatives stood up to thank the overflow crowd of over 2,500 mourners for gathering to honor "Uncle Junior . . . who loved Thanksgiving and made sure that there was enough ham and turkey." Remy Martin sang Frank Sinatra's "I Did It My Way." Alicia Graf Mack, orphaned after Dance Theatre of Harlem's 2004 shuttering, unable to find work in another classical dance company, performed Mitchell's solo "Balm in Gilead." Cicely Tyson delivered a twenty-three-minute eulogy to her best friend, recalling the days of their youth, when Mitchell used to walk her home at night from the subway station.

Sells, sitting in the church she'd belonged to since 1984, mourned an essential member of her childhood. She cried and laughed at the wonder of Mitchell's life, comforted by the knowledge that his archives were in good hands and that his legacy would endure.

It was an evening of song and dance and the balm of remembrance. But for the founding dancers, there was also injury. They had been told that the first three pews of the church would be reserved for alumni. The organizers had them enter in a processional behind percussionist Baba Don Eaton Babatunde and his band, and once they got to the altar, the founders were supposed to peel off into their reserved seats. "They started playing the drums," says McKinney-Griffith. "But when we came in, there were people already in our reserved pews. Misty Copeland was up there sitting in our seats! There was no space for us. Lydia and I were looking at each other like *'What is this?'* And she said, 'Come with me, we'll walk down together.' We just walked in a circle around the church looking stupid, saying 'Excuse me, excuse me,' as we tried to find whatever seat we could."

The men and women who built Dance Theatre of Harlem belonged in those front few pews together, mourning the man who had brought them all together in the first place. "That was our daddy that we lost," says Abarca. Blame it on the chaos of grief, but during the service, the organizers of the event failed to acknowledge them. McKinney-Griffith sat in the back between strangers. Abarca found a seat next to Shelton. Before the reception that followed, Abarca tugged on Shelton's arms, as she would throughout the rest of the evening, saying, "Don't leave me. Don't leave me." She felt unmoored, not just from this great father figure in her life, but from her younger self, who had given everything to make his vision real. If her friend abandoned her now, she worried she might evaporate, and nobody would even notice.

Throughout the evening, the women kept finding each other in the sea of mourners, grounding each other with the salve of touch and shared memory. The tender circle of them, bound by a poignant truth.

We were there too.

20

These are women well familiar with the kinetic passage of time leading up to a performance. When they were in the company, there was always a warm-up class at the theater. Then a retreat to the dressing rooms, where they'd do their own makeup and get into costumes. They'd listen for the half-hour call. Then at fifteen minutes the butterflies would start. The stage manager would yell "Places!" The dancers would gather in the wings looking down at their ballet shoes one last time, praying to God not to see any ribbons sticking out. A last trip to the rosin box. Their superstitious rituals. Gayle McKinney-Griffith would knock three times on every stage floor. Before *Serenade*, Karlya Shelton and another dancer would put their right index fingers to their left ears. Before *Afternoon of a Faun*, Lydia Abarca and her partner, Ronald Perry, liked to whisper to each other "1, 2, 3, go!" Then they'd release their pent-up tension in a full-bodied shake. You never wished another dancer good luck. *"Merde!"* they'd cry to one another instead. *"Toi, toi, toi!"* Take their places on stage. Center themselves with a slow breath in and a long exhale out through pursed lips. Wait for the music. *It will take you over. There. You're free now.*

"Ahh, there's nothing like it," says Abarca. "That was our world."

ON DECEMBER 1, 2021, six months after *The New York Times* article about the 152nd Street Black Ballet Legacy Council, it's almost showtime in Boston. A young person dressed in stage blacks tells the women they have thirty minutes to go before they will join Misty Copeland on stage at a sold-out WBUR CitySpace event.

Copeland is promoting *Black Ballerinas: My Journey to Our Legacy,* her latest nonfiction book aimed at children, which offers a brief window into the lives of twenty-seven dancers who came before her. None of the Legacy Council members are in the book, because she never heard of them before reading the *Times* article. She learned about Lydia Abarca reading the Sunday paper on a park bench in Oakland, where she was filming a short film about intergenerational equity told through dance.

The Legacy Council passes the thirty minutes in a spartan conference room, with a table full of catered food sitting untouched. They'd had their hair and makeup done in a shared hotel room that afternoon. Everybody wears sparkly new outfits from TJ Maxx and Nordstrom's. They look beautiful and nervous, unsure what to expect from an evening they've long hoped for but never truly expected. They form a circle together, clasping hands and bowing their heads, thanking God for all that has brought them to this moment. "Our ancestors are rejoicing," says Abarca.

When Copeland enters the room, dressed in an oversize black sweatshirt and black sweatpants from her train ride up from New York, it takes the women a second to recognize her. Rohan is the first to stand, holding herself erect as she gazes on the younger dancer. Whatever hesitation hangs between the generations evaporates immediately as Copeland bursts into tears.

"Thank you all so much for being here," she says to the women, and they all rise to their feet. "I can't wait. It's so important to tell your story." She envelops Rohan in a warm hug, then goes down the line embracing each of the others.

"And I thought I was the crybaby!" laughs Abarca.

Before Copeland changes out of her traveling clothes into a black blazer and crisp white blouse over a pair of tight black jeans and heels, she reveals to the women that she is five and a half months pregnant with her first child. Everybody cheers.

WHEN THE AUDIENCE LIGHTS dim for WBUR's first in-person CitySpace event since the start of the pandemic, Lydia Abarca is introduced as the world's first Black prima ballerina. Copeland claps the loudest of all for her and angles her chair so that she can face the other women more directly. She knows who the real stars of the evening are and seems grateful just to be in their presence.

"We've wanted to meet Misty for the longest time," Abarca tells the crowd. The first Black prima ballerina sitting next to the world's most famous Black ballerina. Their feet still arch to the gods, though tonight they're both wearing four-inch heels. ("Between the two of us, I don't know whose foot was pointed harder," Abarca laughs later to her friends.)

"It's long overdue," says Shelton. "Long overdue."

"It's so emotional," says Copeland. "We've already cried."

The audience audibly sighs at the beauty of black-and-white photographs blown up on the screen behind the women during the conversation. A young McKinney-Griffith looks every bit the Disney princess in a black leotard and skirt, tiara resting atop her ballet bun. A joyful Shelton kicks her leg to the heavens while dancing the principal role of *Introducing* . . . Copeland pauses at a shot of Rohan, Yvonne Hall, Melva Murray-White, and McKinney-Griffith in Walter Raines's ballet *Haiku*. She says she can't tell from the black-and-white photo if they're wearing pink shoes. She asks the women to tell the audience how they started dyeing their own tights and shoes to match their skin tones.

Given McKinney-Griffith's poise on stage, nobody in the audience would ever have guessed how nervous she was beforehand. Only her sisters see the twitching beneath her eye. But whatever stage fright she has vanishes as soon as she starts speaking. When the evening's moderator, WBUR culture and arts reporter Cristela Guerra, asks the members of the Legacy Council to discuss the importance of telling their stories now at this moment in history, McKinney-Griffith responds with terrific gravity. "Because we all have a voice," she says, looking intently around the room. "And we all need to project that out into the world. Otherwise someone else is going to write our history. Or not."

Shelton nods somberly, before acknowledging a cultural landscape finally reckoning with the idea that Black Lives Matter: "People are listening. People are hearing. We have to take this moment to preserve our history."

FOR ALL THE WARMTH on stage that evening, there is a nod at the inciting elephant in the room. Guerra asks Copeland how it could possibly be that she'd only just learned of the women up on stage with her. A cloud of regret passes over the younger dancer's face. The book she is here to sell, about Black ballerinas throughout history, stays largely tucked beneath her seat. "It's just—it's so frustrating," she says. "In writing this book, I felt so proud with being able to share so many stories of women that we should know about, but we don't. And then hearing about your stories and legacies. . . ." She looks crestfallen as she makes eye contact with each woman. "It just keeps coming. Every day I learn about an incredible new part of our legacy. You've all contributed to getting me to where I am. I wouldn't be a principal dancer with ABT without all of your efforts. They deserve to be told and acknowledged."

Rohan interrupts Copeland, her voice full of authority. "But you should also know how proud we are of you. Not just us. The whole dance community."

"And we're always here for you," says McKinney-Griffith. "We're always here for you."

Copeland clasps her hands over her heart, as she takes in the power of her community expanding in real time. "Thank you, thank you," she says, before turning to Abarca. "I wish I would've seen that *Dance Magazine* cover."

Abarca smiles graciously, with a modest little shrug.

"The first person of color I saw on a *Dance Magazine* cover was Lauren Anderson, and I was stunned," says Copeland. "I couldn't identify or recognize what it was that hit me to my core because I was so young still at the time. But it was that recognition of yourself. *Oh, I do belong here.*"

Abarca reminds the younger woman about the value of sisterhood in their lives. "We had to have each other," she says, smiling at her friends on stage before shining her light on Copeland. "It was too hard to do it by yourself. And we're here for you. We have to be here for each other. You've got people who love you."

Guerra shares that it's Rohan's eightieth birthday. The audience erupts into a spontaneous round of "Happy Birthday," which makes Rohan cover her face in shy delight. "Oh no," she laughs, bowing her forehead in gratitude to her prayer hands.

At the end of the event, the audience rises in a standing ovation. "Would you all take a bow?" Guerra asks the ballerinas. Copeland stands up first and grabs ahold of Abarca's hand. Then all the women rise and join hands at the front of the stage. As the audience claps, the generations hold on to each other, bowing in unison. At the end of the row, Shelton's loose arm rises gracefully. Her ballet fingers are exquisite, from her gently tucked thumb to her slightly lowered middle finger.

AFTER A FLURRY of hugs and photos and goodbyes, the older women pile into a shuttle bus back to the hotel. The mood is boisterous. As the women replay their favorite moments of the evening, laughing and complimenting one another, they pass a roll of candy from the front to back seats. Back when they were girls, there were hundreds of bus rides just like this one after jobs well done.

Meanwhile Copeland is on a train back to New York City with her longtime friend and manager for company. She was the only Black woman at the American Ballet Theatre for the first ten years of her career. These women on the bus never had to experience being in a company without a sense of community. They always had the gift of each other—on stage, in the wings, in the dressing room, in the studio, out in a world that didn't always know how to love them or take care of them. They danced with the core knowledge that no matter what, they were not alone.

Back at the hotel, they decide to keep the celebration going. After wiping off their makeup and changing out of their sparkly outfits, they reunite in Shelton's room in their pajamas and bathrobes. There are complaints of cramping ankles and arches and toes from an evening in high heels. McKinney-Griffith sighs that when she removed her false eyelashes, she lost some of her own, which she'd been so patiently growing back since her cancer. Shelton examines her face. "No, you still have lashes left, I can see them," she assures her friend.

They are already fielding calls from family. Everyone is so proud of them. *It's a Wonderful Life* is playing on the television. Shelton passes around pieces of Rohan's birthday cake.

The 152nd Street Black Ballet Legacy Council came together to write themselves back into history. In doing so, they've written themselves back into each other's lives. It's remarkable how intimacy builds when given the constancy of time and routine. "We're still learning from each other, still growing," says McKinney-Griffith. "Our sisterhood is present. It's active. It's a blessing."

"Well, this is our third act, isn't it?" says Shelton. "A proper teaching of history seems to be a problem in this country. There's a stubbornness there. Or an unwillingness. There's been so much African American history that's been denied its proper place in the annals of our country. It's really important that while we have the opportunity and a platform, we set the record straight. There have been Black ballerinas for a long time, and the fact of that takes away from no one."

THAT EVENING in Boston offered a chance to examine the real problem of the narrative of Misty Copeland's singularity. It tries to keep her isolated in a way she never asked to be, and it leaves all those who came before her stranded on the outside of history, feeling suspicious and neglected. The enemy has never been Copeland's success or her popularity. It's a culture whose narrow, cloudy, distractible eyes refused to see beyond her.

Perhaps there were people in the largely white WBUR audience who'd never heard of Dance Theatre of Harlem before that evening. Who didn't know that Black ballerinas thrived on international stages decades before Misty Copeland was born. It is a good thing when people can recognize how very little they know about the world, then wrestle with the idea of what they haven't been taught. May they follow a spark of curiosity to resources like MoBBallet.org, where the writer and consultant (and Dance Theatre of Harlem alum!) Theresa Ruth Howard has been curating and preserving the lesser-known histories of Black classical dance artists since 2015. Or the work of dance historians like Dr. Deans or Dr. Brenda

Dixon Gottschild, who teach us that the story of Black people and ballet can't be summed up by a passing mention of Arthur Mitchell making history at City Ballet back in the 1950s.

When the women first reunited, so much of what they hoped to accomplish was linking the generations as they did that night with Copeland. The visual of them on stage together called to mind Copeland's 2015 debut in *Swan Lake,* when she was presented with bouquets from Raven Wilkinson and Lauren Anderson during her final bows, the latter hoisting the younger dancer onto her toes in a fierce embrace.

"To me, we're just the tip of the iceberg," says Abarca. "I think everyone from Dance Theatre of Harlem deserves a chance to tell their story." They want to pass the microphone to all the other dancers who blew past the gatekeepers. Who expanded the definition of "flesh tone" tights and ballet shoes. Who thrived not just because of their fearless leader but also because of the sturdy scaffolding of backstage departments whose lifework enabled and enhanced their art. We need all our heroes, and they in turn deserve our humility and curiosity and respect.

As Rohan said on stage with Copeland, "We're all creative artists who they tried to stifle, you see, for whatever reason. But we have to go on and build with that creative spirit that's in us. This is what makes our sisterhood so wonderful. We all care for each other, support each other. And this is what we want for the world. Not just ballet arts. This is what we want for everyone, and for that next generation. We're not on an ego trip, where we want people to see us or know us. No, no. We have something to say and something to do."

There's a young dancer out there who needs to hear Rohan's words right now as she works toward making her own dreams come true. Maybe she'll write them down on a piece of paper and tape them on her bedroom wall, as Sells did with the poster of Dance Theatre of Harlem's founding company so many years ago. If Arthur Mitchell was once a lighthouse, may new generations of dancers look to the women in the Legacy Council as lanterns. The path is long and uncertain, but it has been traveled before. Trust in the light and the promise of a long table up ahead. A Black child twirling in front of a mirror deserves to know that being the only one in a room doesn't mean that they're alone. The elders, even the ones who have passed on, wait with arms outstretched.

Révérence

During Black History Month in 2022, the 152nd Street Black Ballet Legacy Council were the honored guests at a benefit gala for the Philadelphia Ballet. The five women spent the afternoon together getting their hair and makeup done upstairs at the venue in a hotel suite. Lydia Abarca wondered if the slit in her floor-length cranberry sequin gown was too much. (It was perfect.) Sheila Rohan pleaded affectionately with the makeup artist to be able to recognize herself in the mirror at the end of her time in the chair. Karlya Shelton regaled the hair stylist with the story of how she and her husband, Omar, first fell in love during a shopping trip while living in Paris. Marcia Sells arrived late because of Met obligations but entered the suite with a flurry of stories of people she'd run into recently. As her daughter, Alix, attests, Marcia is somehow connected to just about every person in New York City. The room was awash with laughter and excitement and sequins and the smells of lotions and perfumes. Gayle McKinney-Griffith sat quietly and gracefully on the sofa, her legs crossed delicately at the ankles, holding on to her bottle of water. She was tired but insisted that the pleasure of being reunited in one space with her sisters overrode any discomfort.

At the VIP cocktail reception before the dinner, members of Philadelphia's Chocolate Ballerina Company introduce themselves, bowing before the women with their palms pressed together in gratitude. Afterward Rohan, wearing an embellished chartreuse floor-length caftan with a matching ribbon holding her locs in a bun, marvels at the young people's awe. "They were hanging on my every word," she tells the others. "'Oh Ms. Sheila! Ms. Sheila!' They must think we're goddesses."

The women take their assigned seats in the ballroom, split up at different round tables. I sit at a table with Nardia Boodoo, a former apprentice with the Philadelphia Ballet who later joins five other Black alums from the company on stage for bows and bouquets. The twenty-eight-year-old ballerina is dressed in an elegant black cocktail dress with little black jewels affixed to the corners of her eyes. She says she considered Arthur Mitchell a mentor from her own summers in Harlem. Before his passing, he'd encouraged Boodoo to join Dance Theatre of Harlem, but she'd turned him down. In her years since, at predominantly white companies, she's stood up to various microaggressions and awareness gaps. After George Floyd's murder, Boodoo helped organize a discussion, among her colleagues at the Washington Ballet, of Michelle Alexander's book *The New Jim Crow*. With nearly fifty thousand Instagram followers and a Wilhelmina modeling contract, she has smartly parlayed her success on the classical stage into other areas of activism and opportunity. At the end of the event, she gravitates naturally toward Lydia Abarca, the two lingering over a warm embrace. It's haunting to see them both together, as if Abarca were meeting her younger self and urging her forward.

LATER, after the women change out of their formal wear into bathrobes and soft pajamas, they comment on the *Swan Lake* pas de deux that was performed as part of the evening's entertainment. "I was doing the choreography with her in my head," says Shelton. "Wasn't everybody?" The women all raise their hands, with dreamy looks in their eyes.

The body remembers. "Music will come on, and parts of the steps or whole sections of the ballet will come up for you," says Sells. "When I hear *Holberg* on the radio, and they play the Grieg suite all the time on WQXR, I'll start moving and doing the combination, and my daughter will roll her eyes. "

"Wait a minute, what about *Concerto Barocco*?" asks Abarca. "It came on the radio the other day, and I had to jump up even though every bone in my body was cracking."

"*Barocco* and *Serenade*," offers Shelton.

"You know what else?" says Rohan. "Gayle in *Forces of Rhythm*. That pas de trois to 'He Ain't Heavy.' Whenever I hear that, wherever I am, I go straight to Gayle and that lift."

"If you put on any music that we've ever danced to, we're definitely going to move," says Shelton. "It may not look the same, but we'll stand up."

"And you know what?" says Sells with a laugh. "You can do *Serenade* sitting in a chair."

The next morning Sells returns to New York City, back to Lincoln Center, where she greets everyone from the general manager to the security guards with the same level of familiarity and respect. "Well yeah, I'm interested in them as human beings. Some of the people of color who've worked around here have felt like, *There's nobody here for me. There's nobody who'll understand. I would never go to HR. I don't trust HR.* I think we have begun to move that needle. If that is a piece of what I can do, then okay, I'll be happy."

The remaining women pile into a van, bound for the Philadelphia Ballet, where they're scheduled to lead a company class. Dressed in dance shoes and leggings and gray long-sleeve T-shirts, they seem slightly tired from the night before, a little anxious about whether they still have the chops and energy for the task ahead.

When they enter the studio, forty-two dancers stop in midconversation and immediately start applauding. All these young people, their bodies strung like tight ropes, not a line on their faces. Their still-cold muscles are swathed in layers of thin, brightly colored fabrics, leg warmers on top of tights. Some wear booties over their ballet shoes and have wrapped their pining ankles and calves in tape.

McKinney-Griffith, her voice somewhat tremulous at first, introduces herself to the dancers. As soon as she begins leading the class through barre exercises, her soft power casts a spell over the room. Everything in the noisy, tedious outside world melts away. There is just the quiet firmness of her directions and the pianist's melodies.

After running the dancers through their first series of ronds de jambe, McKinney-Griffith trades off with one of her sisters. Now Abarca demonstrates a series of barre combinations to get the dancers on their legs and centered, her limbs endless and graceful.

The dancers start shedding their layers. Hairlines dampen. An air of humidity rises in the room, released by bodies at work.

Shelton takes over from Abarca, guiding the dancers through center combinations of adagio movements, phrases of pliés and tendus and battements, finishing with small warm-up jumps. She demonstrates her requested foot and leg work mostly using her hands and arms. The elegance of her fingers and wrists is almost startling. A ballerina's grace forever flows throughout her body, a little Zah! beaming out of a sixty-six-year-old's extended pinky finger.

She tags off again with Abarca, who leads the dancers through their petit allegros to their grand allegros across the floor on a diagonal. The piano melds with the steady alighting of dancers' feet on the floor, the whuffs of their breath, the rhythmic call of Abarca's voice as she urges them higher and stronger. The other women observe from their folding chairs at the front of the room, admiring the movements with an occasional sigh of empathy or affection.

EVERY BALLET CLASS ends the same way: with a révérence, a brief combination in the center of class, offered up as a thank you. Much like a bow at the end of a performance, this final section is an expression of gratitude—for the pianist, for the teacher, for each other. It also allows for a structured moment of personal exhale, a chance to go inward and honor one's own effort and exertion.

Rohan takes her place in the center of the room. "So now we're doing révérence," she says. "Very simple, old school. We'll start in fifth position." She asks the pianist to play something slow. Abarca and McKinney-Griffith, who she first met all those years ago in a church basement, flank her on either side. Rohan floats both of her arms into demi-second position, a bird gently flexing her wings, then lifts them in tandem toward the sky, as the dancers behind her follow along. There is something almost spiritual about the generational energies during these sacred final minutes. At the front of the room is a line of calm majesty, women who know their own value, no longer fighting for the attention and respect of their teachers or critics. Behind them are rows and rows of dancers in leotards soaked with sweat, their faces flush with vigor and ambition, all their sinew and muscle, their striving and hunger. How vulnerable it is to be young. How easy it is to get lost in the tunnel of self.

After Rohan guides the dancers to a final bow, the room takes a few beats to emerge from her spell. Jermel Johnson, Philadelphia Ballet's first Black male principal danseur, and one of a handful of dancers of color in class that day, approaches the women with tears in his eyes. "Thank you, thank you, thank you," he murmurs, holding his hand over his heart.

Later, he'll try to explain the power of being in the Legacy Council's presence in the studio that morning. "I still can't really put the experience of them into words," he says. "It was more of a feeling. I don't get starstruck often, usually because people are so full of themselves. These women weren't about that. It was like they brought this soft, regal, sincere feeling into the room. They were there for us. They had achieved something great in their lives, and now we're getting to see that it wasn't the end of what they had to offer."

"MY MOTHER'S FLAME has been reignited," says Lydia Abarca's daughter, Daniella. "I see that she finally understands that it's okay for her light to shine and she doesn't have to stay hidden."

A few months have passed since Philadelphia. The Legacy Council gathers over weak coffee and dry muffins in a hotel lobby, waiting on a van to drive them into Harlem. "Isn't this all a fairy tale?" says Abarca, who recently celebrated five years of sobriety.

"We've given each other back that connection to that piece of our lives," says Sells. "So much of the past informs who we are today. When we first started getting together and sharing stories it was like, 'Oh yeah, that was real. I'm not just remembering some fantasy in my head.'"

"It's been invaluable to be able to verbalize, release, reaffirm," says Shelton.

"Even if we didn't have cellphones and Instagram and tons of pictures all over the place," says Sells. "There are other people who were physically there and remember it all. It's like *Brigadoon,* that moment in the mist. It wasn't fake. It actually happened. Oh yeah, I did do that. I did see that. We did know that. It existed in this amazing moment in time, and now we've confirmed it to each other. We were physically together in that space dancing and trying to achieve some perfection."

"You know how they say dancers are instruments?" says Rohan. "We didn't realize all those years that we were allowing Arthur to use us. He used us to build that wonderful place."

"We worked so damn hard," says Abarca.

"Otherwise, we would have been fired," says McKinney-Griffith. "Remember, he was always saying 'You're replaceable!'"

"He didn't realize himself what he had in us," says Rohan. "That first group. Those first ten years. We were like disciples. Not of him, but of the mission."

"Of each other," says Abarca.

Shelton pulls a manila folder out of her bag, stuffed with archival research. "I have something that I wanted to show you all," she says. "I found another Black ballerina in an old magazine that I'd never heard of before." She passes around the August 1968 issue of *Sepia*, a national photojournalistic magazine dedicated to the celebration of Black excellence that went out of circulation in 1983. The issue is from the same month four members of the future Dance Theatre of Harlem company performed in an upstate New York library. The article inside, "Girl on Her Toes," features photos of an elegant woman wearing what looks like the Swan Queen's costume of an ornate white leotard, white tutu, and pale pink tights and shoes.

"Oh yeah," says Rohan, studying the picture. "I know Cleo Quitman. Oh sure. Oh yay!"

The story describes how a seventeen-year-old modern dance student came under ballet's spell after watching the Russian ballerina Alexandra Danilova perform on a Detroit stage. "I was perfectly unaware of this incredibly gracious, light, and beautiful art form—ballet—with that soft, dream-like quality," Quitman told the interviewer. "I was just sitting there with my heart throbbing in my throat and tears of joy running down my cheeks!" Later rejected from the School of American Ballet, she'd go on to train for two years at the Metropolitan School of Ballet alongside four other Black students, including Thelma Hill. Quitman joined Hill as one of the six founding members of the New York Negro Ballet Company, touring extensively in Europe in the late 1950s. After the company ran out of money, Quitman eventually returned to the States and started Dance General, an eight-member group that toured the South in two station wagons crammed with tape recorders, theatrical props, and costumes. In 1965, Quitman appeared as a guest artist in the American Ballet Theatre's staging of Agnes de Mille's *The Four Marys* alongside Judith Jamison, Glory Van Scott, and Carmen de Lavallade. The four women were cast as maids, dancing on a set that included five white columns representing the antebellum South of de Mille's vision.

At the end of the article, the writer projects an airy optimism onto the dancer. "Miss Quitman feels that the world of ballet and dance is now open to the Black man and woman." Even though on the very same page, Quitman describes how she and her dancer husband couldn't book work when they returned from Europe to America because nightclubs didn't think a "Negro dance-couple" was good for business.

Don't you dare tell a woman a problem is fixed when its lack of resolution is still staring at her in the face.

"Remember, Cleo was married to that eccentric dancer and costume designer," says Rohan.

"Bernard Johnson!" says Abarca.

"Oh my god, really?" says Sells. "Louis Johnson choreographed for her too."

Shelton shakes her head in frustration. "Now see, I don't know why I'd never seen or heard of her before. You all knew of Cleo Quitman, but somehow I didn't. It's a reminder that history isn't a one-person thing, or a one-group thing. It's going to take all of us."

People will forget a Black woman's work. Strip it of its magnitude and joy. Deny she was ever there in the first place. Rob the next generation of her example. The women order more coffee, their suitcases at their feet. There are so many stories still to tell.

Bis, bis, bis!

Acknowledgments

When you are the mother of a Black child, you look for representation in every room, on every screen, in every book, on every stage. You want your daughter to be so surrounded by the power of example that when she looks in the mirror at her own beautiful self, she can imagine herself as anyone and anything. It has been the gift of my professional life to be let into the worlds of Lydia Abarca-Mitchell, Sheila Rohan, Gayle McKinney-Griffith, Karlya Shelton-Benjamin, and Marcia Sells. I thank them for their substance, their vulnerability, their generosity, and their courage. My daughters are so lucky to have more lanterns in their lives.

Thank you to the Swans' families, who always made me feel at home. Al Mitchell. Daniella Mitchell Hampton, whose powerful prayer is at the heart of this book. Hannah Daniella Hampton. Eric Mitchell. Katie Mitchell. Delores Rohan. J. Ellsworth Mitchell. Gary Mitchell. Charlene Muhammad. Sheila Mitchell (aka Little Sheila; aka Freshie). Hope Clarke. Don Griffith. Khadija "Tariyan" Griffith. Katy Griffith. Emmitt Griffith, whose beauty and goodness lightened his grandmother's spirit. Maxine Hunter. Victoria Hale. Todd Hunter. Kevin Hunter. Luanne Benshimol. Omar Benjamin. Chè Benjamin. Jean Shelton. Kyle Shelton. Alix Kruta. I wasn't lucky enough to meet Mamie Earl Sells, but the elegance of her archives, including copies of handwritten thank-you notes from P.S. 161 students, made me feel in some way as if I'd had the pleasure.

I am grateful for the conversations with Dance Theatre of Harlem family who helped widen my window into the early years of the company. Tania León. Charles De Rose. Virginia Johnson. Aminah Ahmad. Nena Gilreath. Pamela Jones. Dr. Joselli Audain Deans, who repeatedly asked me to call her Joselli, but will always be "Dr. Deans!" to me.

And thank you to Misty Copeland. Gabri Christa. Nejla Yatkin. Angela Watson. Nardia Boodoo. Jermel Johnson. It was my luck to witness them falling in love with the Swans, or to hear how the women had brought grace into their lives.

All my love to Barbara Jones, the formidable captain of our large and hopeful ship. And to my agent, Betsy Lerner, who's been the wind at my back for well over a decade now. We all had the luck to work with Naomi Gibbs, who is brilliant and devoted and kind and also a fantastic walking partner on the beach. (Hi, Bina!) Thank you to Natalia Berry, Julianne Clancy, Michiko Clark, Cat Courtade, Altie Karper, Lisa Lucas, and the rest of the team at Pantheon Books who have rallied around us with so much enthusiasm. Thank you as well to Rachel Saltz, who first green-lit this story at *The New York Times,* Chloe Knapp, Ali Lefkowitz, Soleil McGhee, Howie Sanders, Nina Shaw, Nancy Utley, and everyone else who's had the best and purest interest in this project from start to finish.

So many kind friends gave me a quiet room in which to work along the way. Thank you to my beloved Kalimba Bennett Tuck. Sallie Patrick. Lizzie Dulien. Amber Williard and Tim Merrifield. Anna Krachey, Jen Cavner, Becky Tenney, and my favorite lover of words, Katy Chrisler, who doesn't dance but wants to.

I'm grateful for the love and support of my family, especially my dad, Gary Valby, who I know is looking forward to asking each of the Swans for a little dance; my stepmother, Kathy Awkard; and my aunt and god-mother, Elaine Valby.

I forever am trying to make my daughters proud. Ava, when you walk into a room, the lights turn on, and Zinnia, you are the precious breeze. Maybe you girls will grow up to be dancers, or Broadway stars, or paint-ers, or community activists, or musicians, or lawyers, or social justice warriors, or teachers. Whatever your callings, may you meet them with a sense of possibility and passion. Trust in your sisterhood.

My family wouldn't be as healthy and whole as it is without the love and support of China Smith in our lives, and the vision she fights so hard to manifest at Ballet Afrique Contemporary Dance. Thank you, China, for your commitment to all of Austin's Black girls and boys looking at themselves in the mirror.

Writing is hard, tedious, lucky work. So is mothering. This book wouldn't have been possible without the constancy of my husband, Tim Dallesandro. He packed the school lunches, drove the kids to dance and gymnastics and soccer, read all the drafts, and turned down jobs so that I could do mine. Oh, Tim! Look what we made.

Acknowledgments
from the Swans of Harlem

Lydia Abarca, Gayle McKinney-Griffith,
Sheila Rohan, Marcia Sells,
and Karlya Shelton

We offer our deepest, heartfelt gratitude to our families for their never-ending love and support.

We are forever indebted to Arthur Mitchell for his creation of Dance Theatre of Harlem, which initiated the sisterhood of the 152nd Street Black Ballet Legacy. We'd like to acknowledge Karel Shook, Cicely Tyson, Brock Peters, and Charles De Rose for laying the foundation of DTH; Zelda Wynn, our wardrobe mistress; Tania León, our first musical director, conductor, and composer; and *each and every dancer,* along with stage crew, musicians, teachers, choreographers, and administrative staff, whose blood, sweat, and tears transformed Mr. Mitchell's ambitious vision of a Black ballet company into reality. You are loved and not forgotten.

We owe tremendous debts of gratitude to Barbara Jones, our literary agent, who introduced Karen Valby to us and was instrumental in getting our stories published; Karen Valby, our author, whose *New York Times* article about the Legacy Council ignited the spark of public interest that resulted in the creation of this book; and Nina Shaw, our lawyer, who has looked out for us from the day we met. These ladies have all shown genuine interest in our well-being and have become good friends and invaluable assets in our lives.

We wish to thank Lisa Lucas and Naomi Gibbs of Pantheon Books for their outstanding dedication and professionalism in producing this awesome publication, and we acknowledge the Lenape and Wappinger peoples and their ancestral lands, which include Harlem, where so much of our story took place. Thank you to our readers!

We are blessed and eternally grateful for this publication, which is only the beginning of our Act Three. Act One brought us together as pioneers in the world of ballet, and Act Two was going our separate ways to explore what else life had to offer. Throughout it all, our sisterhood stayed very much alive. Thank you all, and thank you, Heavenly Spirit and Creator.

Selected Sources

PROLOGUE

Akinleye, Adesola, ed. *(Re) Claiming Ballet*. Intellect, 2021.

Allen, Zita. *Arthur Mitchell's Dance Theatre of Harlem: The Early Years*. Columbia University Libraries Online Exhibitions, 2018. https://exhibitions.library.columbia.edu/exhibits/show/mitchell/dance-theatre-of-harlem--compa/zita-allen.

Collins, Karyn D. "Does Classicism Have a Color?" *Dance Magazine*, June 2005.

Gottlieb, Robert. *George Balanchine, The Ballet Maker*. HarperPerennial, 2004.

Gottschild, Brenda Dixon. *Joan Myers Brown and the Audacious Hope of the Black Ballerina*. Palgrave Macmillan, 2012.

———. *The Black Dancing Body: A Geography from Coon to Cool*. Palgrave Macmillan, 2005.

Gratz, Roberta Brandes. "A Talk With: Arthur Mitchell." *New York Post*, January 2, 1971.

Hughes, Catharine. "Poet in Motion: Arthur Mitchell Continues Premier Role in Dance World." *Ebony*, October 1968.

Kourlas, Gia. "Jacques d'Amboise: Apollo at 83." *New York Times*, February 2, 2018.

Maynard, Olga. "Arthur Mitchell and the Dance Theater of Harlem." *Dance Magazine*, March 1970.

Slater, Jack. " 'They Told Us Our Bodies Were Wrong for Ballet.' " *New York Times*, April 27, 1975.

Sulcas, Roslyn. "Black Ballerina, Playing a Swan, Says She Was Told to Color Her Skin." *New York Times*, December 11, 2020.

Valby, Karen. "Five Pioneering Black Ballerinas: 'We Have to Have a Voice.'" *New York Times,* June 21, 2021.

· 1 ·

Ahmad-Crosby, Mina. *The Story of Black Ballerina Llanchie Stevenson.* Landa & Wildan, 2021.

Barthel, Joan. "When You Dream, Dream Big." *New York Times,* August 18, 1968.

Estrada, Ric. "3 Leading Negro Artists, and How They Feel About Dance in the Community: Eleo Pomare, Arthur Mitchell, Pearl Primus." *Dance Magazine,* November 1968.

Latham, Jacqueline Quinn Moore. "A Biographical Study of the Lives and Contributions of Two Selected Contemporary Black Male Dance Artists—Arthur Mitchell and Alvin Ailey—in the Idioms of Ballet and Modern Dance, Respectively." Ph.D. diss., Texas Women's University, 1973, https://twu-ir.tdl.org/handle/11274/7752.

Mitchell, Arthur, interviewed by Julieanna L. Richardson, October 5, 2016. No. A2016.034, HistoryMakers Digital Archive, https://www.thehistorymakers.org/biography/arthur-mitchell.

Sandomir, Richard. "Baseball: League's Founders Draw Wide Praise." *New York Times,* August 16, 2002.

Taylor, Savannah. "Women's History Month: Harlem School of the Arts Founder Dorothy Maynor Is Peak #BlackGirlMagic." *Ebony,* March 7, 2022.

Tobias, Tobi. *Arthur Mitchell.* New York: Thomas Y. Crowell, 1975.

· 2 ·

Aldred, Lennox. "Better Late Than Never—Patsy Ricketts Follows Her Dream." *Gleaner,* May 2, 2021.

Copeland, Misty. *The Wind at My Back: Resilience, Grace, and Other Gifts from My Mentor, Raven Wilkinson.* Grand Central Publishing, 2022.

Estrada, Ric. "3 Leading Negro Artists, and How They Feel About Dance in the Community: Eleo Pomare, Arthur Mitchell, Pearl Primus." *Dance Magazine,* November 1968.

Harss, Marina. "Virginia Johnson: An American Ballerina." DanceTabs, September 17, 2013, https://dancetabs.com/2013/09/virginia-johnson-artistic-director-dance-theatre-of-harlem/.

O'Meally, Robert G. *The Romare Bearden Reader.* Duke University Press, 2019.

· 3 ·

Latham, Jacqueline Quinn Moore. "A Biographical Study of the Lives and Contributions of Two Selected Contemporary Black Male Dance Artists—Arthur Mitchell and Alvin Ailey—in the Idioms of Ballet and Modern Dance,

Respectively." Ph.D. diss., Texas Women's University, 1973, https://twu-ir.tdl
.org/handle/11274/7752.

Madrid, Alejandro L. *Tania León's Stride: A Polyrhythmic Life.* University of Illi-
nois Press, 2021.

Shook, Karel. *Elements of Classical Ballet Technique as Practiced in the School of
the Dance Theatre of Harlem.* Dance Horizons, 1977.

Tobias, Tobi. "Talking With Karel Shook." *Dance Magazine,* January 1973.

· 4 ·

Fruchtman, Milton, dir. *Rhythmetron.* PBS, McGraw Hill Films, March 26, 1973.

Latham, Jacqueline Quinn Moore. "A Biographical Study of the Lives and Contributions of Two Selected Contemporary Black Male Dance Artists—Arthur
Mitchell and Alvin Ailey—in the Idioms of Ballet and Modern Dance,
Respectively." Ph.D. diss., Texas Women's University, 1973. https://twu-ir.tdl
.org/handle/11274/7752.

Morton, Carol A. "The Dance Theatre of Harlem: An Experience in Blackness."
Essence, May 1972.

Mitchell, Arthur. "Ethnicity and Classicism: A Beautiful Connection." *Journal of Education* 6, no. 2 (July 1984): 144–49. https://www.jstor.org/stable
/42742050?read-now-1&seq-1#page_scan_tab_contents.

Ribowsky, Mark. "The Black Invasion of Ballet." *Sepia,* April 1976.

· 5 ·

"Arthur Mitchell and the Dance Theatre of Harlem." *Harper's Bazaar,* December
1970.

Barone, Joshua. "The Metropolitan Opera Hires Its First Chief Diversity Officer."
New York Times, January 25, 2021.

Dunning, Jennifer. "A Dancer Who Had a Dream." *New York Times,* April 14, 1974.

McDonagh, Don. "Thelma 'Mother' Hill Dies at 53: Noted Teacher of Black
Dancers." *New York Times,* November 23, 1977.

Tommasini, Anthony. "Review: 'Fire' Brings a Black Composer to the Met,
Finally." *New York Times,* September 28, 2021.

Voigts, Madelyn. "There Is But One Miss Jones Who Has Only Time for Dancing." *Kansas City Star,* January 2, 1972.

· 6 ·

Barnes, Clive. "Ballet: Mitchell's Troupe." *New York Times,* March 9, 1971.

———. "Harlem Dance Theater Comes of Age." *New York Times,* December 14,
1971.

———. "Lovely Dancers—Black, White, or Green." *New York Times,* January 24,
1971.

Buirski, Nancy, dir. *Afternoon of a Faun: Tanaquil Le Clercq.* American Masters, 2014.

"A Dance Debut Set by Harlem Troupe." *New York Times,* January 5, 1971.

Dowling, Collette. "Birth of a Black Ballet Company: Dance Theatre of Harlem." New York State Theater edition, *Playbill* Magazine, May 1971.

Elson, John. "Music: Doing the Thing You Do Best." *Time,* March 22, 1971.

Kent, Allegra. "My Surprising Duet with Arthur Mitchell in Cold War Moscow." *New York Times,* September 25, 2018.

Kisselgoff, Anna. "Harlem Dance Theater Shows High Promise at Jacob's Pillow." *New York Times,* August 21, 1970.

———. "Harlem Dancers Excel at Guggenheim." *New York Times,* January 10, 1971.

Kratovil, Dee. "Harlem Dance Theatre Performance Dazzling." *Daily News,* St. Thomas, V.I., December 1, 1971.

Mazo, Joseph H. "The Dance: Dance Theatre of Harlem." *Women's Wear Daily,* January 11, 1971.

Morin, Raymond. "Harlem Classical Ballet Group Does Balanchine." *Worcester Telegram,* December 4, 1971.

Shaw, Ellen. "Dance Theatre of Harlem." *Evening Bulletin.* November 3, 1971.

Shertzer, Jim. "Black Dancers Seem to Electrify City Audience." *Winston-Salem Journal,* April 24, 1971.

Takiff, Jonathan. "Harlem Ballet—A Sensation in Sepia." *Philadelphia Daily News,* November 3, 1971.

Warren, Virginia Lee. "Alva Gimbel: Gives Helping Hand to Many." *New York Times,* January 8, 1971.

· 7 ·

Banks, Dick. "Dance Theatre of Harlem Draws Bravos at Ovens." *Charlotte Observer,* March 10, 1973.

Calloway, Earl. "'Rhythmetron,' a Witty, Moving Work of Art." *Daily Defender,* May 22, 1973.

Croce, Arlene. "Forces of Harlem." *New Yorker,* May 13, 1974.

Dunning, Jennifer. "Dancing Her Way Up." *New York Times,* August 25, 1974.

Ford, Tanisha C. "Zelda Wynn Valdes: A Fashion Designer Who Outfitted the Glittery Stars of Screen and Stage." *New York Times,* January 31, 2019.

Hemeter, Mark. "Harlem Dancers Astonish, Excite." *States-Item,* February 26, 1973.

Kisselgoff, Anna. "Harlem Company to Share Stage with City Ballet." *New York Times,* May 3, 1971.

Syse, Glenna. "Harlem Dancers Strike the Spark." *Chicago Sun-Times,* May 19, 1973.

· 8 ·

"Changing the Face of Ballet: Original Dance Theatre of Harlem Member Reflects on the Company's Wide-Ranging Impact." *Day,* October 21, 2018.

Dunning, Jennifer. "Louis Johnson: 'I Love Dance—Any Kind of Dance.'" *New York Times,* September 28, 1975.

Kriegsman, Alan M. "Ballet's Great Scott." *Washington Post,* May 9, 1981.

Obituary for Richard A. Gonsalves. Chapman Funeral Home. https://www.chapmanfuneral.com/obituaries/Richard-A-Gonsalves?obId=20627796.

· 9 ·

Barnes, Clive. "Harlem Dance Theater Scores London Triumph." *New York Times,* August 7, 1974.

"The Black Model Breakthrough: Black Is Busting Out All Over." *Life,* October 17, 1969.

Croce, Arlene. "What You See Is What You Get." *New Yorker,* April 5, 1976.

"Dance Theatre of Harlem: Where Talent Abounds." *Ebony,* June 1974.

Jacobson, Robert. "Dance Theatre—The Pride of Harlem." *Cue,* February 20, 1976.

Kling, Ruth. "A Beautiful Dancer Leads Three Lives." *Daily News,* July 18, 1974.

Percival, John. "Arthur Mitchell: Dance Theatre of Harlem." *Times* (London), August 3, 1974.

· 10 ·

Barnes, Clive. "The Extraordinary Achievement of Arthur Mitchell." *New York Times,* May 11, 1975.

Floyd, Karen. "Debra Austin—Breaking Barriers in Ballet Shoes." *Elysian Magazine,* April 22, 2021. https://readelysian.com/debra-austin-breaking-barriers-in-ballet-shoes/.

Hodgson, Moira. *Quintet: Five American Dance Companies.* New York: William Morrow, 1976.

Maynard, Olga. "Dance Theatre of Harlem: Arthur Mitchell's 'Dark and Brilliant Splendor.'" *Dance Magazine,* May 1975.

Tomlinson, Mel A., as told to Claudia Folts. *Beyond My Dreams: A Biographical Memoir,* Turning Point Press, 2018.

· 11 ·

Barnes, Clive. "Ballet for Blacks?" *New York Times,* December 26, 1971.

———. "Black Ballet—A Good Idea?" *New York Times,* November 26, 1972.

Kriegsman, Alan M. "Gordon Parks's Noble Bow to 'Martin.'" *Washington Post,* January 15, 1990.

SHEILA

Christa, Gabri, dir. *Sheila*. A Gabri Christa Production, 2021. https://www
.gabrichrista.com/work/sheila.

· 12 ·

Brockway, Merrill, dir. *The Dance Theatre of Harlem*. Dance in America series.
WNET/13, Turner Classic Movies, March 23, 1977.
"Dance Theater of Harlem Cancels Season at Uris." *New York Times*, April 4,
1977.
Goodman, George, Jr. "George Benson is a One-Man Festival." *New York Times*,
May 6, 1977.
Haacke, Lorraine. "Dance Theatre Opens Dallas Visit." *Dallas Times Herald*,
March 25, 1977.
Light, Janet. "Cincinnati Dancer Joins Harlem Company." *Cincinnati Enquirer*,
January 11, 1977.
Moore, Patty. "Dance." *Dallas Morning News*, March 25, 1977.

· 13 ·

Dunning, Jennifer. "A Fling with Harlem Dancers." *New York Times*, February 17,
1978.
Howard, Adam. "How Lumet's 'The Wiz' Became a Black Cult Classic." *Grio*,
April 11, 2001.
Kennedy, Gerrick D. "On its 40th Anniversary, a Look at How 'The Wiz' Forever
Changed Black Culture." *Los Angeles Times*, October 24, 2018.
Kisselgoff, Anna. "A Rare Appearance for Harlem Dancers." *New York Times*,
August 5, 1977.
Kriegsman, Alan M. "Louis Johnson: High Stepping in the Land of OZ." *The
Washington Post*, October 21, 1978.
Steinbrink, Mark. "Dream Factory: Dance Theatre of Harlem, the Inspiration of
Arthur Mitchell, is Changing the Life of the Black Dancer in America." *Ballet
News*, February 1981.
Stuever, Hank. "Michael Jackson on Film: No Fizz After 'The Wiz.'" *Washington
Post*, January 30, 2005.

GAYLE

Wilson, Alexis. *Not So Black and White*. Tree Spirit, 2012.

· 14 ·

Stevens, Ronald Smokey. *I Just Want to Tell Somebody: The Autobiography of Ronald Smokey Stevens*. Publish America, 2008.

Tyrus, Judy, and Novosel, Paul. *Dance Theatre of Harlem: A History, A Movement, A Celebration.* Kensington Books, 2021.

MARCIA

Backlund, Ralph. " 'Structure and Discipline' Through Dance." *Smithsonian,* July 1988.

· 15 ·

Anderson, Jack. " 'The Time Was Right to Try the Classics.' " *New York Times,* January 6, 1980.

Browning, Kirk, dir. *Stravinsky's 'Firebird' by Dance Theatre of Harlem.* PBS, May 5, 1982.

Darling, Lynn. "Harlem's Prima Ballerina Abarca: On the Brink of Stardom." *Washington Post,* October 4, 1979.

Deitch, Mark. "Return of the Dance Theatre of Harlem." *New York Times,* February 18, 1979.

Goldner, Nancy. "Making the Past Fresh." *Christian Science Monitor,* January 17, 1980.

Kisselgoff, Anna. "Dance: A Season Opens with Joy at City Center." *New York Times,* January 11, 1980.

———. "Dance: Harlem Troupe." *New York Times,* March 1, 1979.

———. "Dance: Harlem Troupe in a 'Paquita' Premiere." *New York Times,* January 13, 1980.

Norton, Leslie. *Frederic Franklin: A Biography of the Ballet Star.* McFarland & Co., 2007.

Rowes, Barbara. "It's No Stretch to Call Lydia Abarca One of Ballet's Most Under-Recognized Stars." *People,* October 8, 1979.

Simpson, Coreen. "Ballerinas: Their World, Their Beauty." *Flair,* August 1980.

LYDIA

Dunning, Jennifer. "Dance: Lydia Abarca is Back." *New York Times,* March 1, 1983.

· 16 ·

Fraser, C. Gerald. "Dance Theater of Harlem Cuts Back." *New York Times,* November 22, 1981.

Grant, Dell Omega. "Karel Shook, Dancer, Is Dead; Co-Founder Harlem Troupe." *New York Times,* July 27, 1985.

Gruen, John. "Dance Theater of Harlem, Feeling Accepted, Sets Sights on Artistry." *New York Times,* January 10, 1982.

Hall, Carla. "Home, Home on the Stage." *Washington Post,* February 11, 1981.

Welles, Merida. "Harlem Dancers Open in London Amid Pomp." *New York Times,* July 29, 1981.

"William Griffith Dies; Ballet Teacher Was 60." *New York Times,* December 7, 1988.

Willinger, Edward. "Dance Theatre of Harlem." *Dance Magazine,* May 1983.

· 17 ·

Bauer, Claudia. "Stephanie Dabney, Electrifying Prima Ballerina, Dies at 64." *New York Times,* October 8, 2022.

Beam, Joseph. *In the Life: A Black Gay Anthology.* Alyson Publications, 1986.

Dunning, Jennifer. "Paul Russell, 43, Leading Dancer for the Dance Theatre of Harlem." *New York Times,* February 19, 1991.

———. "Walter Raines, 54, Dancer and Choreographer." *New York Times,* August 31, 1994.

Kourlas, Gia. "Mel A. Tomlinson, 65, Ballet Star and 'Agon' Interpreter, Dies." *New York Times,* February 13, 2019.

Lee, Trymaine. "A Firebird No Longer in Toe Shoes." *New York Times,* October 5, 2010.

Wignot, Jamila, dir. *Ailey.* PBS, American Masters, 2021.

· 18 ·

Feuer, Alan. "Out of Money, Harlem Ballet School Closes." *New York Times,* October 17, 2004.

Howard, Theresa Ruth. "The Misty-Rious Case of the Vanishing Ballerinas of Color: Where Have All the Others Gone?" April 3, 2015. https://mybodymy image.org/the-misty-rious-case-of-the-vanishing-ballerinas-of-color-where -have-all-the-others-gone/.

Isherwood, Charles. "St. Louis Woman: A Blues Ballet." *Variety,* July 17, 2003.

Kaufman, Sarah. "Harlem's Flashy 'Woman': A High Stakes Gamble." *Washington Post,* June 12, 2004.

Kourlas, Gia. "A Phoenix Is Rising on Point." *New York Times,* April 5, 2013.

———. "Where Are All the Black Swans?" *New York Times,* May 6, 2007.

Nolan, Clancy. "Dance Theatre of Harlem Closes for Remainder of Season." *Playbill,* September 21, 2004.

Pogrebin, Robin. "Deficit Threatens Dance Troupe in Harlem." *New York Times,* May 26, 2004.

Shapiro, Laura. "Lovable Mess." *New York Magazine,* July 17, 2003.

Wakin, Daniel J. "Dance School in Harlem to Reopen." *New York Times,* December 1, 2004.

· 19 ·

Allen, Zita. "Honoring the Legacy of an Icon: Dance Theatre of Harlem's Arthur Mitchell." *Amsterdam News,* December 27, 2018.

Dunning, Jennifer. "Arthur Mitchell is Dead at 84; Showed the Way for Black Dancers." *New York Times,* September 19, 2018.

Katz, Brigit. "Remembering Arthur Mitchell, the Barrier-Breaking Black Ballet Dancer." *Smithsonian,* September 21, 2018.

Kourlas, Gia. "Columbia Acquires Archives of Arthur Mitchell, Dance Pioneer." *New York Times,* May 15, 2015.

Perron, Wendy. "Arthur Mitchell Obituary." *Guardian,* September 21, 2018.

· 20 ·

Copeland, Misty. *Black Ballerinas: My Journey to Our Legacy.* Aladdin, 2021.

"Misty Copeland and the Ballerinas of the 152nd Street Black Ballet Legacy." WBUR's Tell Me More! December 1, 2021. https://www.wbur.org/events/732427 /tell-me-more-misty-copeland-and-the-ballerinas-of-the-152nd-street-black -ballet-legacy.

RÉVÉRENCE

Manning, Mary Scott. "The Black Ballet Celeb Taking on Racism in Dance." *Washingtonian,* June 21, 2021.

Simor, George. "Cleo Quitman: Girl on Her Toes." *Sepia,* August 1968.

Woods, Kathia. "Dance Theatre of Harlem Founders to Help Usher in Philly's Next Generation." *Philadelphia Tribune,* March 12, 2022.

Index